T0320888

# Accomplishing Change in Teaching and Learning Regimes

# Accomplishing Change in Teaching and Learning Regimes

*Higher Education and the Practice Sensibility*

PAUL TROWLER

OXFORD

UNIVERSITY PRESS

# OXFORD
UNIVERSITY PRESS

Great Clarendon Street, Oxford, OX2 6DP,
United Kingdom

Oxford University Press is a department of the University of Oxford.
It furthers the University's objective of excellence in research, scholarship,
and education by publishing worldwide. Oxford is a registered trade mark of
Oxford University Press in the UK and in certain other countries

© Paul Trowler 2020

The moral rights of the author have been asserted

First Edition published in 2020

Impression: 1

Published in the United States of America by Oxford University Press
198 Madison Avenue, New York, NY 10016, United States of America

British Library Cataloguing in Publication Data

Data available

Library of Congress Control Number: 2019945450

ISBN 978-0-19-885171-4

DOI: 10.1093/oso/9780198851714.001.0001

Printed and bound in Great Britain by
Clays Ltd, Elcograf S.p.A.

# Preface: The Book's Backstory

This book brings together the different threads of my work in higher education research, writing, consultancy, and evaluation. This work has addressed a variety of topics, among them policy and change processes, leadership in university departments, accreditation of prior learning, student engagement, disciplinary differences, student voice, insider research, social practice theory, the teaching–research nexus, methodological issues, and evaluative practices (please see Trowler, 2019 for a list of my publications in these areas). Quite often a new direction was stimulated by winning a research grant; more often I was fortunate enough to be able to follow the path of my own inquisitiveness and my desire to 'sort things out' intellectually.

Until this book project began to form in my mind I had seen these as relatively separate areas of enquiry, a kind of intellectual 'hopping about'. But as I began to shape the form of the book, I saw that what they had in common was more obvious than their differences. Underneath them all was a path which led to the work you have in your hands. This book is the cloth woven from these threads.

Had I reflected more deeply on an insight I had in 1998, it is possible that I could have written this book in the first rather than the second decade of the twenty-first century. That insight was related to the work I did for my PhD, completed in 1996 and subsequently published as *Academics Responding to Change* (Trowler, 1998). That research was a five-year ethnographic observant participation study of a university, 'NewU'. During the first year or two of the research I was thoroughly engaged at NewU as an employee, spending many hours teaching, observing teaching practice, and, especially, being involved in committee work; at the time the whole curriculum was being revalidated along credit-bearing lines something like the American model. My doctoral research went along in parallel with this.

At some point, however, I underwent a perceptual shift. The professional work and the research work began to merge. My daily life as a lecturer became infused with the concepts, theories, and explanations I had been engaging with for my PhD. I began to see everyday behaviours and speech acts by my colleagues and students as specific examples of more general phenomena: broader educational ideologies; structured practices with historical antecedents; discursive repertoires rooted in tacit assumptions; agentic acts shaped and constrained by larger forces; examples of structured dispositions. I could see ideas developed by Bourdieu, Giddens, Fairclough, and other social scientists being enacted in my daily professional life. They were, literally, 'realized'.

A happy spin-off of this was that I found that this new, analytical perspective reduced the stresses and strains of professional life. Analytical detachment offered both stress-relieving distance and the effect of decentring my own self. The latter was the result of seeing more clearly the ways in which social practices are accomplished (and changed) through the continuing assemblage, enactment, and re-assemblage in daily professional life of materials, forces, and agency.

In short, I had walked through a conceptual portal which, once crossed, did not permit return to a previous way of seeing. Understanding and applying a set of interlinked 'threshold concepts' (Meyer and Land, 2003) had made me see in new ways.

This perceptual shift is what C Wright Mills (1959) famously described as 'the sociological imagination', although I didn't recognize this at the time. Mills described this way of seeing as involving a perspective outside of daily routines, viewing one's own actions and those of others from an analytical, distanced perspective. It is a viewpoint that is infused with concepts and theory. These help one to see the general within the particular, a world in a grain of sand (Blake, 1863). Patterns, the effects of broader structures on local circumstances, the influence of the past, and hints of the future become foregrounded. The 'dazzle' of everyday conflicts, irritations, and pressures recedes into the background.

In discussing the sociological imagination, Mills was primarily talking to sociologists and researchers. Most other authors who introduced similar ideas about perspective-change were also offering them to researchers and academics in cognate disciplines to their own. Examples are Berger's 'sociological perspective' (1963), 'sensitizing concepts' (Blumer, 1954; Charmaz, 2003), and 'sensitizing theory' (Sibeon, 2007). But for me, in writing this book, it is important that professionals, educational practitioners, should also take advantage of the insights such a perspective can bring.

In other professions, using this kind of research-based way of seeing to address problems and make improvements is far from unusual. The 'medical imagination' is an obvious example. With the specialist knowledge, the range of medical concepts, and the associated research-based understanding that they have, doctors see medical cases in a special way, and they act on the basis of that perspective. Research has uncovered the threshold concepts that are significant in that field, for example in clinical reasoning (Randall et al., 2018).

My particular flavour of 'sociological imagination' helped me see the world of higher education very differently thanks to the substrate of knowledge, concepts, theories, and explanations to which I had been exposed and with which I had engaged in my doctoral research. The shorthand for it is 'a practice sensibility'. This later served me well when I was a head of department. It helped me act with greater confidence about the likely outcomes of my actions and responses. This was not just to do with rational calculation; it was founded on research-based intuition: what in Dutch and Afrikaans is called *voorgevoel*—literally 'forward sensing'. *Voorgevoel* is different from 'foresight', which is conscious and explicit. Gevoel points to 'feeling', not thinking; it is tacit, a kind of gut instinct about dangers and opportunities. *Voorgevoel* is presentiment, with teeth.

With a good understanding of the nature of the context, both institutional and more locally, in which management, leadership, and change agency takes place, the practice sensibility is a powerful tool to have. Combined with an understanding of how to conduct ethnographic-influenced approaches to develop a good knowledge of context, it can at the very least help to avoid making counter-productive mistakes.

So, when you sit in yet another meeting, attentive to a heated discussion about (for example) whether and how to respond to student views on assessment, feedback, and students' level of satisfaction, this practice sensibility may provide the missing insight to unlock a way through arguments, power-plays, and the clash of competing positions founded on different ideologies and discourses. Rather than merely providing different theories of organizational change, ways of depicting organizations, or tips and tricks for making change come about, this book offers insights and prompts to spark a change in the way you view the world, your workplace, and the practices you see around you.

# Acknowledgements

I would like to thank the three reviewers of the original proposal for this book for their supportive and very insightful comments. The book is better than it would have been because of them. My particular thanks go to friends and colleagues who commented on the near-final version of the manuscript. Their detailed and constructive feedback also improved the book immeasurably. They are Paul Ashwin, Roni Bamber, Bernard Lisewski, and Torgny Roxå. Finally, thanks and love to my wonderful wife, Vicki, whose creativity and intelligence in discussing topics with which I was grappling shaped my thinking about important ideas in these pages. Her imaginative similes and metaphors were always illuminating, including the cocktail bar simile in Chapter 5.

The finished product is, of course, my own responsibility, as are any deficiencies in it.

# Contents

# List of Figure and Tables

## Figure

## Tables

# 1

# Acquiring the Practice Sensibility

Why should you read this book? Because it offers an important new way of seeing the professional world in higher education through conceptually informed lenses. The concepts and theory which constitute these lenses have been fully developed for the first time in this book, rebuilding and adding detail to earlier models and more general theory. Seeing the world in a new way both improves understanding and makes actions more effective, avoiding mistakes and smoothing the path to improved practices. The book also offers insights into appropriate ways to gain more information on which to base decisions, and ideas about doing light-touch research in specific contexts to better understand those contexts. Because the discussion is infused with real-life examples from higher education across the world, the book should also be an interesting read. I hope to inspire ideas and comparisons in your mind as you read the examples given.

An underlying principle of the book is that research, theories, and concepts should be deployed to make a difference for the better in the real world. What constitutes changing 'for the better', or enhancement, will vary from context to context and will hardly ever be without dispute and contest. Political processes are almost always intertwined with change processes. However, that is not a reason to avoid trying to develop a richer, more conceptually informed understanding of and approach to change. It benefits no one for there to be ignorance about how to implement policies, to have misplaced assumptions about the context of change, to lack sensitivity to the dangers of some courses of action, to cherish unrealistic aspirations, and to engage in fuzzy thinking. As Boughey (2018) notes from her own experience as a university deputy vice chancellor in South Africa, without a conceptually informed understanding of what is going on, her peers in senior management across the country resort to 'common sense' in developing policy—a very dangerous thing to do. Boughey cites the example of the 'psychologizing' of some black students' difficulties in progressing, resulting in the futile appointment of more and more university counsellors. For most of those students the issues are structural in nature, including the multiple demands of family, community, and conflicts of subjectivities, as well as lack of resources.

*Accomplishing Change in Teaching and Learning Regimes: Higher Education and the Practice Sensibility.*
Paul Trowler, Oxford University Press (2020). © Paul Trowler. DOI: 10.1093/oso/9780198851714.001.0001

The purpose of developing a practice sensibility, an acute sensitivity to the operation of social practices without consciously looking for it, is to enhance the ability to see bear traps, identify ways of 'going with the grain', and avoid blind alleys. It also helps to see beyond the 'dazzle' of personality clashes, individual choices, and simplistic ideas of 'what works'. It develops an appreciation of the particulars of context and the need to understand particular contexts in an anthropological way before trying to change them. Bowden and Marton (1998, p. 29) say this:

> People develop ways of experiencing [and] of seeing different levels of their domain expertise. A chess player develops a chess player's way (perhaps one of the different ways) of seeing board positions; a physician develops a physician's way of seeing medical situations, hearing the heart's sound using a stethoscope, seeing an x-ray or feeling the irregularities under the skin. A forestry officer, an artist, a photographer, a landscape architect, a biologist, a child from Abu Dhabi, each of these sees a particular forest in different ways, they see different things. To a great extent they have learned (or they have not learned) to see the forest in their own way.

When someone acquires a new way of seeing, their perception and experience of a phenomenon changes fundamentally, and the nature of those changes is multiple. One characteristic that shifts is the ability to 'sort things out' (Bowker and Star, 2000); to distinguish an object of interest from its surroundings and to appreciate its particular characteristics, seeing different facets of the same thing within different contexts, while recognizing 'sameness'. This ability comes from reflecting on multiple examples and learning about what is fundamental and what are simply epiphenomenal differences. Recognition rules are learned through inference, and these give the ability to distinguish 'this' from 'that', and to be able to recognize 'this' even in totally unfamiliar cases. Such rules are part of a new way of seeing, in whatever context.

The process of learning a way of seeing is what Turner (2001) calls a 'connectionist' account of learning. In this account we learn the nature of the concept inferentially through a process of receiving feedback on behaviour which concerns that concept. A good example is a baby practising saying a word until a positive response is achieved. Behaviours and responses that are successful are arrived at incrementally, and during this process concepts firm up cognitively because they are no longer receiving negative feedback, or no response, when applied. Social scientists describe this process as involving incremental teleo-affective responses. It results in what Bourdieu (1990) calls a 'sense for the game' and Giddens (1984) calls 'practical consciousness', aspects of which cannot be articulated because they are inchoate, impalpable, tacit. The much derided phrase 'I know it when I see it' (for example, a student's assignment that is worth 65 per cent) refers to this kind of knowing (Bloxham, Boyd, and Orr, 2011). The person who consistently and accurately knows it when they see it has learned to distinguish 'this grade' from 'that grade' through experience, reflection, and feedback.

A second aspect of developing a practice sensibility is to understand the meaning of the phenomenon of interest in specific ways, as illustrated in the example of the perception of a forest given in the quotation above. Powers of discernment and perception become honed so that limited data can offer much more information and understanding to the viewer. If the ability to distinguish an object of interest is concerned with identifying structure, then this aspect of ways of seeing is concerned with what those structures *mean*, with significance. The naïve chess player looks at the structure of a game in progress and sees very little. The grand master will perceive the structure of the board in a very different way and will attach meanings to it. Very importantly for our purposes, that grand master will be able to make fairly accurate near-term and longer-term predictions about moves, the changing structure of the board, and probable outcomes. He or she will also be able to identify potential bear traps for one or both players. The processes involved are both rational–cognitive and intuitive, based on experience and knowledge.

One implication of this discussion is that there are no tips or tricks that can be offered to the reader in a book like this. There is no external, learned rulebook to follow other than the inferential recognition rules developed by individuals through experience and reflection over time. As Smolensky, Legendre, and Miyata say:

> The richness of human behaviour, both in everyday environments and in the controlled environments of the psychological laboratory, seems to defy rule-based description, displaying strong sensitivity to subtle...factors in experience. (1993, p. 382)

However, simply setting out sensitizing concepts such as the 'moments' of teaching and learning regimes (TLRs) discussed in the following chapters is not enough to develop a deep sensitivity for practices. It is also necessary to see and reflect on different examples of those regimes both in the real world and through reading about them. Comparing different articulations of them in different cases, preferably talking with people who are experiencing different kinds of regimes, lends deeper insight and sensitivity. This becomes pressing in an HE system with a 'burgeoning number of part-time and sessional staff' (Tight, 2019, p. 175) who are likely to bring significant backstories to TLRs. Comparative analysis of them strengthens the ability to distinguish structures and deepens the level of understanding of the significance of the different moments and how they operate together in different ways. Professional knowledge and understanding, the development of a new way of seeing, occurs within a social context. Leaders and change agents are involved, with others, in a *situated* activity which involves assembling and reassembling a range of specific resources and interactional forms. Facilitating change is always a sophisticated, situated accomplishment (Gherardi, 2014, p. 46). This is why several vignettes and case studies are offered throughout these pages: they offer multiple instantiations of different aspects of a practice sensibility. All are based on observations of real contexts or on research accounts.

Let me offer here a first vignette to illustrate some of these comments:

In a review of a postgraduate programme at a university, the secondary data provided to the reviewers showed that there were wide disparities in the marking practices across the programme team. The external examiner, in his report, had noted this, saying: 'it's almost impossible not to get a distinction [in some modules].' Interviews with the team by the reviewers addressed this, as well as some other issues. At first it seemed that the solution would be simple: a team moderation exercise and subsequent discussion about how different markers were applying the marking criteria, and how to unify their approach. This solution was based on the tacit assumption that the very large differences in marks awarded were due to some staff misinterpreting, not understanding, or simply not using the marking criteria.

However, the interviews with programme staff demonstrated that everyone was aware of the different standards being deployed and that the underlying issue lay in the different 'backstories' of the academic staff. Some had been educated in a North American environment and had taught in universities there. This experience had led them to see anything less than a high mark as a failure. These staff, a minority within the programme team, began the marking process at 100 per cent and reluctantly worked downwards as they assessed students' assignments, only rarely going below 70 per cent.

It became clear that the differences in marking among the staff on the programme were due not to a misapplication of the marking criteria but to a fundamental philosophical difference. The imagined moderation exercise would be fruitless: the wrong prescription for the wrong diagnosis. A very different approach was required, perhaps simply involving surfacing to students the different philosophies among the team. So, the concepts of 'backstory', of tacit assumptions, and of the significance of different ideological positions were very important in understanding the situation.

This vignette demonstrates the more general significance of concepts such as backstory, codes of signification, conventions of appropriateness, tacit assumptions, and implicit theories of teaching and learning—the 'moments' described and discussed in this book. In the vignette these moments were differently encoded in, for example, a mark of 65 per cent for different groups of staff. For all staff on the team, 'knowing it when they saw it' still applied— but the significance of 'it' was very different for the different groupings. The vignette also provides an example of connectionist learning, discussed previously. It illustrates how the different staff members had been learning grade distinctions in very different contexts, and so had experienced very different sets of incremental teleo-affective responses. They carried these over to the new context: they were displaced practices (Diamond, 2013).

To achieve its purposes the book uses the chapter structure set out presently. This structure also reflects my personal academic journey, which began with research around the recording and accreditation of prior (experiential) learning and continued with my PhD research on how academics responded to and influenced changes in higher education. That led to my work on operationalizing concepts around 'culture', including the cultures of 'academic tribes', and associated factors around discursive production. Those issues involved me in ethnographic, insider, and qualitative research, which I subsequently researched and wrote about as topics in themselves. Policy-making and implementation, leadership, and change processes generally then became my main focus for some years, and I was involved in advising university decision-makers around the world at that time, as well as continuing to research the central issues involved in such issues. That experience culminates in this book.

Chapter 2, which follows, has a central purpose. It is to refresh, finesse, and make more sophisticated the idea of TLRs which I first developed in 2002, and which was subsequently deployed globally by higher education researchers and practitioners. Underneath the development of understanding TLRs in universities is social practice theory, which concentrates on recurrent behaviours in group contexts and the ways in which these are underpinned by tacit theories and sets of assumptions, meanings, and emotional responses. This is also elaborated in Chapter 2 with a particular focus on issues around change processes.

Chapter 3 discusses the ways in which TLRs can be investigated. An approach rooted in classical anthropology, the ethnographic approach, is outlined and different flavours of it explored through critical engagement with examples of their application. The limits of ethnography are discussed and a case is made for a practice-focused, multi-method research methodology to inform change initiatives.

Chapter 4 unpicks the different moments of TLRs, illustrating them through two case studies. One concerns a merged university in South Africa dealing with difficult issues around merging disciplines and curricula in a context of continuing structured disadvantage. The second centres on a Danish university in which discourses were shifting in line with an increasingly dominant neoliberal ideology permeating national policy-making. As well as illustrating the different moments of TLRs in transition, these case studies are used to enrich the depiction of social practices as both bundled and nested. This is very significant both conceptually and for understanding and enacting change processes.

Chapter 5 develops a theoretical understanding of how teaching and learning regimes come about—their genesis. It begins with a discussion of the power of disciplines in conditioning practices in university departments, a strong theme in the literature. While disciplinary differences are often important in conditioning local cultures, other factors are also at play. The genesis of TLRs is multi-causal, dynamic, contextually contingent and conditioned by history and its selective deployment. These characteristics are illustrated through vignettes and case studies. This chapter, and those before it, sets the scene for the one which follows: Chapter 6 addresses the most significant professional dimension of the book—changing teaching and learning practices in higher education.

Chapter 6 focuses on change processes in these areas and how they have been addressed. Drawing on vignettes and on well-documented case studies of organizational change, the chapter considers the forces of stasis and dynamism of the various elements which constitute TLRs. The implications for change agents are unpicked and the notion of a practice-focused way of seeing is further elaborated.

The concluding Chapter 7 sets out synoptically the conceptual, analytical, and theoretical contributions of the book. Readers who want a concise summary of the theoretical position set out here can turn to the first few pages of this chapter. The contribution for researchers and for professional action is summarized, and some suggestions for research with a practice sensibility are offered. The chapter shows how the characteristics and functions of theory in general are specifically addressed in the approach taken here. It summarizes what this approach offers and outlines the areas that need supplementary theories and designs—those less amenable to the social practice approach.

# 2

# Teaching and Learning Regimes

## From Framework to Theory

### The Nature of Teaching and Learning Regimes

I first developed the idea of teaching and learning regimes (TLRs) in 2002. I asked an educational developer, Alison Cooper, to work with academic staff undertaking a programme for those new to teaching in order to consider the nature and effects of TLRs in their departments. An initial article resulting from the collaboration (Trowler and Cooper, 2002) mixed theoretical development with grounded instances of the concepts involved. The argument was that training academic teachers in 'good practice' is of limited value because teaching is a collective endeavour and the TLRs they encounter back at their departmental base constrain and shape practices—and not always for the good. It was not an argument that educational developers always wanted to hear.

Since then the TLR framework has been applied by researchers, change agents, and others in higher education throughout the world. The TLR conceptual framework is usually applied to in some way improve the teaching and learning cultures in different contexts, helping to understand the current cultural context and to discern fruitful routes to enhancement.

This chapter elaborates, refines, and augments the TLR notion, using findings from some of the work in which it has been applied to increase its analytical and practical power and to give it more traction. The chapter moves from explaining the original concept, through using a real example where it offers insight, to showing how it has been used in the literature, and some of the suggestions for improvement found there. The chapter then interrogates the theoretical and ontological underpinnings of the conceptual framework. In doing this it moves the TLR idea from framework to full-blown theory. The newly developed concept of TLRs is then deployed in the rest of the book.

Rather than elaborating the notion of TLRs from the start, which could be over-abstract and unappealing, I will begin by offering an example taken from a well-researched case study account of a situation of changing educational

*Accomplishing Change in Teaching and Learning Regimes: Higher Education and the Practice Sensibility.*
Paul Trowler, Oxford University Press (2020). © Paul Trowler. DOI: 10.1093/oso/9780198851714.001.0001

circumstances. From that I will draw out conceptual points, thus grounding them within an example. From this case study I will unfurl the original eight 'moments' (interconnected dynamic elements) of a TLR, showing how there were two TLRs bumping up against each other in the case used. One of these was located in a higher education context, a fact that was significant in shaping its character. The other lay outside the HE environment and so was more school-centric.

Tara Fenwick (2004) gives an account of a university laboratory centre that delivered accredited instruction to 350 children in classes from pre-kindergarten to grade 5. This centre had been operating since 1996 and was directed by a university professor. The centre was situated within a large Canadian university and was partially supported by the university for its service as a research site as well as a school. Graduate students and academic staff visited classes to conduct research, experiment with pedagogical methods, and offer demonstrations. The centre employed a unique pedagogical approach, with project-based integrated methods. Compared to state schools, class sizes were small. Each class had a second teacher, designated a 'teaching partner', who assisted the main teacher and liaised with researchers.

After four years of operation the school had outgrown the space available for it and its director approached the local city school district about the possibility of a partnership. The city school district was proud of its diversified educational system and was happy to be involved in a partnership. The agreement was that the university laboratory centre school would be moved to the site of a city district-operated elementary school near to the university. There were extensive negotiations between the principal of the entry school, the director of the university laboratory centre, teachers, parents, and the city district:

> All parties pledged commitment to the partnership itself, as well as to mutual understanding and dialogue as a process for attaining it. Eventually a partnership agreement was created and implemented, but not without stormy meetings, polarised positions, misunderstandings and the departure of the public school principal on stress-related disability leave.
>
> (Fenwick, 2004, p. 175)

Fenwick's research showed that the university side and the city district side had very different understandings, language, and underpinning ideas about the partnership. For the city district, partners were described as 'stakeholders' and the university laboratory centre was seen as only one of '30 alternative programmes' that were viewed as large blocks to be incorporated within the school system. The situation was essentially a challenge which could be managed appropriately in a rational way so that the university centre could be smoothly integrated and aligned with current systems of operation, using well-understood policies and procedures.

This contrasted quite strongly with the meanings and approach from the university laboratory centre side. Rather than systems, policies, and processes, the approach was a more organic one. As the laboratory centre director said:

> There was never a formal framework under which the centre operated, which made it easy to understand your role—it was always evolving and changing. Often we were self-defined, sometimes it was defined for us and as it grew, of course it changed.   (Fenwick, 2004, p. 177)

Teachers, parents, and the centre were described as 'like a family'. There were personal relationships based on trust and concern about well-being. Parents were closely involved with classrooms and often dropped in. Decision-making was loose and informal with considerable consultation. The management structure was democratic and roles were fluid. Because of its unique pedagogy and the connections with the university and with research, the university culture pervaded both the practices in the laboratory centre school and the resources available to teachers and students.

In the negotiations, it sometimes appeared that there was commonality between the city district and the university centre. Both, for example, used the language of 'integrity' and 'core values'. But in reality they were often talking past each other. For the city district 'integrity' meant commitment to the whole system and integration with it, whereas for the university centre integrity 'was about preserving a small, special...community and its freedom-in-enquiry teaching and learning approaches' (p. 178). Similarly, the university centre's teaching partners were seen by the city district as 'teachers' aides', a lower paid, lower status, and inferior role.

Each side stereotyped the other—a characteristic feature of TLRs that we will see again in Chapter 4 ('Codes of Signification'). City district schools were described as 'hierarchical', 'prison-like', 'lacking creativity and spontaneity'. Conversely, the university centre was seen as myopic, undisciplined, emotional, unmethodical, self-centred, unaccountable, and unstructured.

The story becomes a more complicated at this point in Fenwick's account, and this is a good place at which to deconstruct the situation from a social practice perspective. Although Fenwick's account is entirely situated in a discourse analysis perspective, concentrating on the discourses used by the two sides and the contrast between them, I want to look more broadly at the two very different TLRs being described in her case study.

Teaching and learning regimes are expressed in and arise from a constellation of practices. In the situation just described we see multiple practices being performed. They involve holding meetings, teaching, engaging with parents, and so on. While the case study is pitched at a very general level, comparing and contrasting the city school district's teaching and learning regime with that of the university centre school, one could also drill down to these constitutive individual practices. There is a 'family of social practices' (Minick, 1996, p. 346) encountered in each regime in which motivations, participants' respective social positions, their relationships and ideological orientations, the technologies deployed, and the customs of language use are assembled in the constitution of each practice. In each case the practices draw on common strands from proto-practice reservoirs of ideologies, assumptions, discourses, and theories (see 'Proto-Practice Reservoirs, Practices, and Changes' in this chapter). There are very different currents flowing from these reservoirs into these two different teaching and learning regimes.

One very clear difference is the nature of the power relations in operation within the city district compared to those within the university centre. The first could be described as managerial, hierarchical, and rigid, and the second as democratic, fluid, and having changing structures and roles. These differences became significant in the process of negotiating a partnership, particularly in terms of who should be included in the negotiating space, how decisions are reached, and who is invested with significant power to decide.

A second difference involves the implicit (and sometimes explicit) theories of learning and teaching which existed in the two environments. In line with its more managerialist and hierarchical approach to management, members of the city district tended to default to a transmissive, didactic, and traditional approach to school education. The contrast in this was quite marked with the more constructivist, almost 'free school' approach (in the sense of student-led curriculum, methods, and timetable) of the university centre. Clearly, in negotiating a partnership and envisaging the future, this issue would become significant in relation to the nature of the newly located university school. This tension was played out at a personal level, and for the head of the university centre it became too much as she felt her teaching values were being threatened. She resigned from that role. Meanwhile, the newly appointed head of the city district school professed to agree with much of the teaching philosophy of the university centre and to be interested in a project-based pedagogy.

However, she could not sustain this in the face of dealing with her complex job and the responsibility she felt within the hierarchy, as well as her anxiety about approval within that hierarchy. She suppressed her own ideas, although this caused her stress also.

Very much tied to the implicit theories of teaching and learning are differences in conventions of appropriate behaviour and actions within the two environments. In the university centre parents would informally drop into classrooms, chatting to teachers about their child's needs and progress without an appointment. There were many informal conversations and impromptu staff meetings, often also involving parents and others. Very little was written down. The roles of teachers, parents, and administrators were fluid: 'we kind of slipped in and out of everyone's shoes at different times' (Fenwick, 2004, p. 177). As can be imagined, conventions of appropriateness in a more traditional city district environment were quite different: scheduled, formalized, recorded, and with clearly delineated (and hierarchical) roles. Again, in negotiating a partnership there needed to be some changes on one or both sides in terms of the understanding and practice of what would be considered 'appropriate' behaviour.

Intimately linked to conventions of appropriate behaviour is a fourth factor, the recurrent practices found in the two contexts. For long-term participants within any context these are usually normalized, in the sense that they go unquestioned and are in a sense 'invisible' to them. One example of difference in recurrent practices within the two contexts is the ways in which decisions were made, and the degree of formality in relation to this. For the city district, as noted above, formal meetings, with agendas and minutes and clearly defined roles and conventions of procedure, were normal. In the other context, however, decisions were made very differently and in a much more informal way. Underlying these behavioural practices were the conventions of appropriateness described above, as well as other elements of the contexts being elaborated here.

Two further elements which underlie recurrent behavioural practices are tacit assumptions concerning, for example, how decisions are best made or what the ultimate objective of education is, and, related to those, the 'meanings' that signs and symbols carry and the evaluative and flashes of emotional response that go with them. Words such as 'integrity' and 'core values' carried very different meanings in the two contexts, as noted above. As well as words, behaviours carry meanings and evaluative significance. In one context a formal meeting might signal efficiency and focus, whereas in the other it might signal the imposition of power and the exclusion of some voices. Such codes of signification are very important when it comes to change processes because initiatives and innovations will always carry these codes and so their reception on the ground will be strongly influenced by actors' understandings and responses (including evoked emotions) to such initiatives.

An additional element, which again is separable from each of the above only analytically, is the different nature of the discursive repertoires in use. It is evident that different discourses were deployed in the larger discursive communities of the university and the school district, and it is these on which Fenwick's article focuses. For her, discursive differences are a very significant element. She notes how there was shared language and discursive practices within each of the two groups she describes, and they became very important as they tried to reach agreement about the future. Participants did not identify the fact that they were deploying different discursive practices; they remained tacit. However the differences led to tensions, arguments, and anger about what were seen as differences in positions or interests. In Chapter 4 we will again see the significance of such planning meetings in exposing (if only to the analytical eye) discursive and other cultural differences.

Perhaps Fenwick overemphasizes the significance of discourse and does not give sufficient weight to the other elements described above: power relations; implicit theories of teaching and learning; conventions of appropriateness; recurrent practices; tacit assumptions; codes of signification. In any specific change process one or more of these will become of primary significance, but in almost all cases they will all play a role in shaping processes and outcomes because they are intimately interlinked.

One final element evidently significant in the university centre and city district situation is the personalities involved. On the city district side there were outgoing and incoming school principals, while the university centre had its own director who, initially, was an education professor working at the centre only 25 per cent of the time. She was not a good administrator, by her own admission. Again there was a change of role-holder as that person retired. The new acting director, by contrast, was a former professor and then senior administrator in the education ministry of the province. This person, everyone agreed, had better leadership and negotiation skills than the previous incumbent. Parents felt she carefully listened to and thoroughly understood their views. Even the city district school principals trusted her to competently steer a way through the negotiations.

In much of the literature on social practice theory, individual identities are considered relatively insignificant. There is what is sometimes called an 'inseparability thesis' which claims that individual identities, or better 'subjectivities', are essentially products of their context and will change as individuals move between different contexts. There is, in other words, an inseparability between social context, with its particular social practices, on the one hand, and individual subjectivities on the other. The former conditions, or even determines, the nature of the latter. Schatzki, for example, argues that the idea of 'a personality' is overwrought, that I-ness is 'not an inherent property of a thing or substance called the subject. It is instead a social construction, an achievement realized only through the incorporation of human beings into the institutions and structures of social life' (1996, p. 7). Specifically, 'subject positions are constituted within particular practices and so have a specificity germane to the practices involved' (p. 8).

Fenwick's account and the vignettes and case studies which will follow in this book demonstrate, however, that individual subjectivities are very significant in change processes, even though contexts can position and reposition them to some extent. Understanding the nature of the subjectivities in interaction and the likely patterns of how they will play out is a really important element in the change process, and it is dangerous to dismiss this through an overly strong adherence to the inseparability thesis.

## Eight Moments of Teaching and Learning Regimes

The analysis of the case study above, then, has drawn out eight elements of significance. Elsewhere I have referred to these as 'moments' drawing on Harvey (1996). That word indicates dynamism rather than stasis and gets away from the individualistic implications of words such as 'elements' or 'components'. The word refers to moments as in momentum, not as in moments in time. Moments are associated with movement. Moments have force: given certain conditions, they shape the direction of the objects they are acting on. In this case the objects are the social practices involved in teaching and learning.

Although I have disaggregated them, these moments are in fact entangled with each other, only separable in the analytical hand. They represent, in other words, a model of reality and a way of simplifying and illuminating it with the purposes of understanding it better and smoothing the flow of purposive change. The eight moments which I have exemplified above are:

1. Power relations.
2. Implicit theories of learning and teaching.

3. Conventions of appropriateness.
4. Recurrent practices.
5. Tacit assumptions.
6. Codes of signification.
7. Discursive repertoires.
8. Subjectivities in interaction.

Together they comprise a teaching and learning regime, and in this case study there were two very different TLRs with very different sets of moments: the city district and the university centre. Any group of people in an educational context who are engaged in a common project over an extended period of time can also be depicted in this way, in what might be called a 'workgroup'. Identifying the nature of the moments in a workgroup in an educational context offers a picture of the TLR there. The purpose of depicting such workgroups in this way is to better describe the workgroup's important features as well as the potential issues which may arise in changing, or attempting to change, the nature of the TLR. This can help one understand how initiatives for change, wherever they come from, meet practices on the ground, and can offer change agents ways of seeing how that understanding can make their task easier.

It would however be a mistake to assume that there is uniformity and consistency in relation to the moments of TLRs even within a single workgroup. This 'assumed consensus' mistake is made in most depictions of communities of practice (Lave and Wenger, 1991, with subsequent multiple publications by Wenger and the Wenger-Trayners). The Wenger-Trayners say this:

> members [of a community of practice] engage in joint activities and discussions, help each other, and share information. They build relationships that enable them to learn from each other; they care about their standing with each other . . . members engage in joint activities and discussions, help each other, and share information. They build relationships that enable them to learn from each other; they care about their standing with each other.
>
> (Wenger-Trayner and Wenger-Trayner, 2015).

From this perspective, communities of practice are distinguished from other forms of social groups in that they have mutual engagement, a shared understanding of the joint enterprise, and a shared repertoire of skills (Wenger, 1998, pp. 72–3). The teaching and learning regimes model does not assume consensus, shared information, and so on. The contrast between the two concepts is illustrated in Fenwick's case study to which I now return, picking up at the point at which I left the discussion of the case study earlier.

Fenwick discusses what she calls 'resistant discourses', and it is here that her story becomes more complex. Within both the city district and the university centre these were evident, and they became very significant in the negotiations. Parents, for example, gradually shifted from being marginal and relatively benign to becoming confrontational and oppositional. They resisted discourses of assimilation and began to oppose both the university centre and the city district. Some of them withdrew entirely and others researched possible alternative structures to those on offer, including the previous university centre programme. Individuals too adopted alternative positions to the dominant one in relation to one or more the eight moments of the regime in which they operated. Fenwick offers the example of a university centre senior teacher who found the teaching and learning practices there increasingly problematic: 'Teachers were getting away with anything' (Fenwick, 2004, p. 180). After directly but unsuccessfully challenging some of the practices and power relations within the university centre, this person resigned. On the other side, as briefly noted above, the new principal of the city district school contrasted her own 'emotional' approach with the former principal's 'methodical' approach and appeared more comfortable with at least some of the moments of the university centre regime than with the city district's. Nonetheless, she suppressed her preferred ways of working and understanding because of her job role, and 'found herself taking up dominant practices and suppressing her own language' (Fenwick, 2004, p. 181). There are, in short, some evident dominant practices within a teaching and learning regime but there will also almost always be conflict and dispute, at least under the surface, involving usually more than just one of the moments.

This might raise the question: What is it that makes a teaching and learning regime a distinguishable unit? In other words, what allows the analyst to identify a group in such a way and to use them as a unit of analysis? In what way is there, and is there not, a 'regime'? There are several responses to this. Firstly, a teaching and learning regime is distinguished by a common set of contextual concerns (Archer, 2007). To put it colloquially, what keeps members awake at night is the same thing, although they might have very different aspects of it to worry about, and they might be perceiving the nature of that 'thing' in very different ways from other sleepless members. A second response is that not everything is contested in terms of the moments in a particular regime, and so commonalities help to distinguish it. Contestation tends to centre on one or a small number of the moments, and the character of that contestation, both in terms of orientation and strength, will vary over time. There is consensus too, and often on the big issues. The presence of consensus is sometimes invisible to members whose thoughts and stresses tend to focus on the conflictual elements. Conflict tends to be at the centre of attention and to dazzle the eye, while consensus and calmly getting on with the job remain invisible in the background. Writing from a position not far from social practice theory—critical realism—Roy Bhaskar writes:

> Ontologically, the social world is an emergent, concept- and activity-dependent, value-drenched, and politically-contested part of the natural world. In it, social structures pre-exist and enable or constrain human activities.  (Bhaskar, 2014, p. ix)

The characterization of both consensus and conflict in teaching and learning regimes is one of the reasons for the use of the word 'regime' in describing them. Political regimes too incorporate both consensus and conflict, although important elements of them are often sustained by force or ideological hegemony. It is also true of a medical treatment regimen, in which compliance is gained by patients' trust in doctors, in their superior understanding and their power over resources and decisions. However, there may be resistance and conflict over its nature and application. An equally important reason for the use of the word is that it implies an underpinning set of rules and relationships that are not visible—a significance that is most apparent in the French use of the term, as in for example *le regime d'un moteur de voiture*.

A further, and very significant, point about distinguishing teaching and learning regimes is that they are permeable natural systems rather than closed and clearly bounded entities. They involve a set of social practices performed by a workgroup in a particular context, which are related to learning and teaching issues. But members of workgroups in universities also operate within other sets of social practices, for example to do with research, administration, the internal operating processes of the university, and so on. So rather than focusing just on the workgroup and its particular set of contextual concerns, the analytical eye needs to accommodate the fact that social practices are always bundled and nested within a larger system of practices.

The fact that social practices are *bundled* indicates that there is horizontal overlap; that different sets of social practices rub up against each other at the same time and in close proximity, spatially, and that individuals will find themselves shifting, sometimes within a short space of time, between different sets of practices. In Fenwick's case study it would be possible to see this operating around the university centre: its emphasis on pedagogic research and the collegial relationships within the centre would be influenced by the university context in which it is embedded and the other sets of social practices operating there. For the director of the university centre, a professor, the centre itself would be only part of the practice frameworks in which she was engaged, and she would move between them. Different priorities and concerns, different sets of assumptions and implicit theories, operate in such multiple contexts, but within an institutional setting there may be commonalities also.

The fact that social practices are *nested* indicates that there is vertical overlap, that practices at ground level, for example in a classroom situation, are intimately linked to more structural factors and their associated practices, such as those to do with teaching evaluation at the university and national levels. The actors involved in these nested practices will usually be very different, but that is not to say that the influence on one on the other is small; it is often very significant. In Fenwick's case study the nested nature of practices is most obvious in the city district setting, where larger practices relating to a whole geographical area and multiple schools impinged strongly on both the city district school and the negotiations to include the university centre school.

For change initiatives this bundled and nested character means that the reception on the ground of enhancement proposals will be influenced not only by the local teaching and learning regime, but also by other social practices with which it is enmeshed, both horizontally and vertically. Consequently, it is not only the analytical focus that needs to broaden beyond the regime itself; change agents need to consider the implications of the interactions of surrounding social practices for any change initiatives. I return to the significance and implications of the bundled and nested nature of TLRs later in the book.

Very often the organizational structures of universities, their decision-making architectures, mitigate against this broader perspective: teaching committees make decisions about teaching; research committees make decisions about research; but rarely does either consider the implications of decisions they make for practices which are outside the remit of their responsibility (Dill, 1999). Nor do they usually consider the experience at the ground level, where the multiple disparate decisions have disconnected and even contradictory implications and consequences. This can lead to at least the perception among ground-level actors of unnecessarily increased workloads, contradictory role expectations, and confused priorities. As the metaphor has it: groups of decision-makers at the top of the building each throw the beautifully formed pottery jugs they have created to the workers on the ground. But down there they look like a jumbled collection of unusable shards.

## How Regimes Have Been Researched and Understood in the Literature

In this section I look at some examples of how the concept of teaching and learning regimes has been applied in research into higher education contexts. Rather than trying to summarize such research, the interest here is in evaluating the application of the concept to issues around change processes in higher education, asking the question: What value does it add?

Bager-Elsborg (2018) examines the contextual influences on teaching, and particularly on lecturers' willingness to make changes to their teaching for enhancement purposes. She notes how the articulation of disciplinary practices is fundamentally shaped by the teaching and learning regime context in which it operates:

> Compared to deterministic explanations where certain types of knowledge lead to certain types of teaching, the practice view shows how the knowledge of the discipline can be interpreted differently when it interacts with other aspects.   (Bager-Elsborg, 2018, p. 198)

So TLR moments have a significant effect on classroom practices, and these may differ even within the same discipline, according to her study. She discusses in detail the tacit assumptions about students and student behaviour (the 'implied student' of a teaching programme: Ulriksen, 2009) as well as conventions of appropriateness related to the usually implicit notions of the purposes of teaching. This leads her to reject both a 'generic' approach to academic development ('good practice in teaching is the same whatever the discipline or context and so enhancement initiatives should be based simply on understandings of good practice') as well as the strong disciplinary essentialist approach ('disciplines have certain constant characteristics and distinctive teaching practices—attempts to change those practices need to take into account what works in each discipline').

Two disciplines, law and business administration, within two departments in a large research-intensive Danish university were selected as case studies.

Nine interviews with lecturers from law and eight interviews with lecturers from business administration were conducted.

Bager-Elsborg found that there was greater hesitation towards changing practices in law than there was in business administration, where the logic of private enterprise, responsiveness to the market, and students as consumers was more prevalent. But the author avoids the epistemological essentialism of much of the literature (see Chapter 5), arguing that there is a process of ongoing negotiation of meaning and appropriate behaviour—micro-social negotiated practices which result in habits and routines which are contextually specific. The teaching and learning regime is in a dynamic process of continual construction, while at the same time the constructive process is conditioned by the nature of the regime currently in place. A process of accomplishment is occurring, the sort referred to in the title of this book.

In terms of what this means for initiatives designed to improve teaching, such as those deployed by academic developers, Bager-Elsborg argues the following. First, understanding teaching as an embedded practice shows why change is usually slow: 'teaching is not an isolated, individual act but embedded in values, power relations, habits and routines, identities and feelings' (Bager-Elsborg, 2018, p. 209). Second, initiatives need to be aimed primarily at the departmental level and at the work group within it, because this is where reality-construction occurs. Third, negotiated disciplinary values and meanings are important and so initiatives also need to take into account the negotiated *disciplinary* values within a workgroup: legitimate and acceptable change proposals need be rooted in a good understanding of those values, but these will be specific to the locality:

> In conclusion, the academic developer needs to take on the role as an allied or a critical friend in the work with groups of lecturers ... It is very important that the developer brings in the expertise of the development practice combined with a sensitivity and curiosity towards the discipline in question to be able to act as a legitimate intruder.   (Bager-Elsborg, 2018, p. 210)

Bager-Elsborg's conclusions align very closely to those of Roxå and Mårtensson (2013), who apply the results of empirical studies they conducted previously (2009a; 2009b; 2011) to the question of the impact of academics' teacher training. They too note the significance of negotiation with a network of colleagues and of the creation at the workgroup level of ways of going about things, and of understanding what is happening. They conclude that a key factor is whether networks and workgroups have established their own agenda for teaching development:

> This key factor appears as the most important one for managers to focus upon once they overlook an organisational landscape of networks and work-groups from the macro level. The effects of training are likely to propagate on the meso level and even beyond depending on whether or not the networks or workgroups have developmental agendas of their own. If they have, insights made by individuals or groups during training can fuel further advancement of those meso-level agendas.
>
> (Roxå and Mårtensson, 2013, p. 228)

In their 2009b study the authors note how faculty members at their university (Lund in Sweden) can relate to the TLR concept regardless of which discipline they come from. These authors run pedagogical programmes for about one hundred academics per year. They introduce the TLR model to them and ask them to apply it to their own workgroups, discussing the responses afterwards. Roxå and Mårtensson say that the participants 'easily identify the different "moments" in their own departmental or disciplinary context' (2009b, p. 212). In their interviews with faculty members they found that there was a correl-ation between those that operated in TLRs that supported considerations of good quality teaching and learning, on the one hand, and a higher number of conversational partners that they had within their context, on the other. The practice generally was for these conversations to take place in private rather than in formal meetings, and they usually happened in places where those not invited to the conversation could not overhear them. There seems to be a 'backstage' nature to such discussions about teaching and learning and to the significant networks which participate in them.

For Roxå and Mårtensson, the problem with these significant networks and conversations is that they focus on particular aspects of teaching and learning in an ad hoc manner and do not draw on the pedagogic research literature and recognized wisdom of practice. They tend to have a transient and ephemeral nature. So:

> If academics within significant networks are introduced to the scholarship of teaching and learning...they might be better positioned to construct an informed understanding...Adopting a scholarly perspective on teaching, then, may offer them the tools to influence the TLR that rules their depart-ment.   (2009b, p. 217)

Boag (2010) used the TLR model in an insider case study of a single, multi-site university to investigate the cultural characteristics of a single programme team delivering an undergraduate degree and their responses to teaching and learning policy. He used documentary evidence and interviews as well as his insider knowledge and observations. One way in which he analysed the data was by offering multiple examples of the eight moments from that data, with his results confirming Roxå and Mårtensson's observation that insiders have no difficulty relating to them.

Boag concludes that the eight moments provide a useful analytical device without which it would have been exceptionally difficult to make sense of a considerable volume of data, and a feasible device for comparative analysis across different teams (though he did not do this). However, his analysis does not really go beyond depiction, using TLRs as a 'workable and useful way of defining the cultural characteristics of the team' (Boag, 2010, p. 239). As applied here, the conceptual framework does not help to explain change; nor does it give much in the way of pointers for change.

As in Boag's study, it is a common characteristic of much of the research that uses a social practice approach that the application of the model does not go far beyond using it as a descriptive categorical device. Mathieson (2012) is another example of this. Her research employed interviews with thirty academics across four merging disciplinary workgroups in a newly merged South African university. She proposes a framework for exploring teaching–learning and assessment workgroup cultures rather than focusing on using a social practice approach to explore and explain change processes. A further example is Powell (2013), who suggests that the TLR framework provides a useful analytical tool and is valuable in stressing the particular cultural characteristics of sub-groups within a university. It also helps understand the relationship between proposed enhancement initiatives and the TLR characteristics of those sub-groups. Once again, however, the heuristic value of the TLR idea does not go far beyond its descriptive power.

Lisewski (2018) uses social practice theory in general and the teaching and learning regimes framework in particular to study tutor-practitioners in a private higher education fashion school (tutor-practitioners operate in both academia and the fashion industry). In many ways his results align with those of Bager-Elsborg, though the implications of his study for directing change are deliberately left at an early stage: this was not one of his research questions. Lisewski's interest is in testing the value of social practice theory in relation to how the tutor-practitioners enact practice-based knowing in higher education. He critiques some of the more over-socialized versions of social practice theory which see individuals as merely 'carriers' of practices, doing what people did before them automatically and in an unreflective way. The tutor-practitioners were not 'cultural dopes' who merely act out a shared set of behaviours, motivations, feelings, and meanings. Instead, acting out practice-based knowing involved agency, negotiation, interpretation, and the active formation of meaning and identities. This involved the tutor-practitioners and their students as they went about their business, and talked about their business.

Although Lisewski does not focus his study on the implications for enhancement of practices, one can infer the significance of his findings in that respect. Seeing TLRs as dynamic, volatile, and highly porous suggests that the potential for change is greater than social practice theorists usually recognize. Indeed, they are often seen as quite conservative, able to explain stasis but not the process of change. The question, however, is how one can harness the volatility that Lisewski's study unmasks in deliberative ways—in ways which are beneficial rather than deleterious to all concerned. This is a question addressed in Chapter 6, 'Accomplishing Change in Teaching and Learning Regimes'.

## The Critique of Teaching and Learning Regimes

This section sets out and interrogates the main criticisms of the TLR concept, and of social practice theory generally, under three headings: the partiality of the theory; comprehensiveness; lack of theoretical purchase.

### Partiality

No social theory is 'correct'; none is an accurate representation of reality. Social life is too complex, too nuanced, and too dynamic for that to be the case. A theory that came close to describing reality would be too complex to be valuable to the analyst. The point of social theory is to simplify and, to some extent, to essentialize reality. It is to offer illumination, explanation, ways of describing, better foresight, improved descriptive language, and several other things. Theories can be useful in various ways, or their value can be limited. Theory offers a number of interlinked concepts which model social reality rather than describe it or 'capture' it. To confuse the model of reality with the reality of the model is, as Bourdieu said, a dangerous thing.

Because a theory is a purposive approach to modelling reality, adopting one theory for the purposes of illumination, explanation, or anything else inevitably simultaneously foregrounds and occludes. While the significance of some characteristics is highlighted, others fade into the background.

To view this in operation, Hannon et al. (2017) brought three theoretical frameworks to bear on a single set of interview data from a single workgroup. The frameworks were: teaching and learning regimes; Archer's social realism; and a socio-material approach from Fenwick, Edwards, and Sawchuk (2011). By deploying these three they hoped to surmount the limitations of taking a single position as well as avoiding the circularity pointed out by Ashwin (2012), which can mean that data merely offer support for the concepts upon which their collection was founded.

Hannon and colleagues collected data from a university department that specialized in teaching emergency health programmes at a South African university: Emergency Healthcare. The workgroup of six participants taught the department's clinical health care degree programme. It included a head of department and five early to mid-career academics; of these, two had recently completed a Graduate Certificate in Higher Education qualification and two had recently made the transition from practitioner to academic. There were six interview transcripts and one focus group transcript concerning the teaching and learning practices in their department. For the TLR part of their study, the authors asked: 'In what ways do local regimes (in this workgroup) accommodate, shift and change to account for the new scholarly expertise and institutional knowledge carried by a group of academics who have completed the Graduate Certificate in Higher Education?'

Hannon and colleagues describe the different moments in operation within the emergency healthcare department at the time of the research. They conclude that

> teaching and learning regimes can draw attention to how change emerges and is stabilised in collective academic contexts, they can also highlight the 'unchallenged orthodoxies'... that become embedded in schools and departments... Two 'moments' demonstrate the regimes: particular activities are collectively attributed with significance and meaning over others, in this case, moderation of assessment; and in the capability of participants to identify implicit theories of teaching that have hitherto framed their practices.   (Hannon et al., 2017, pp. 213, 220)

However, these authors note:

> the boundaries between these cultural moments are not always clear-cut, nor
> is there any underlying commitment to unearthing causal mechanism.
>
> (Hannon et al., 2017, p. 220)

They conclude that elements of TLRs can help depict some aspects of social processes, but in some cases the conceptual brush is too broad to helpfully illuminate reality, and the conceptual framework does a poor job of explaining why things are as they are or how they change. On its own, the TLR framework is inadequate to be of much help to the theorist or to the change agent.

Much the same conclusion was reached by Mårtensson et al. (2014), who also contrasted three perspectives to assess their heuristic power: the formal lens; the political lens; and the cultural lens. They were interested in establishing links between 'quality work' and concrete practices in academic micro-cultures reputed to have strong teaching and learning abilities. What they found was that a focus on teaching and learning regimes, on micro-cultures, was inadequate in itself to illuminate the organizational contradictions between the goals and practices of the formal organization on the one hand and the preoccupations with change and development within the micro-culture on the other. A full picture can only be obtained by using both the formal lens and the cultural lens, and understanding the interactions between them through the political lens.

A similar conclusion, though drawing on different theories and lenses, was drawn by Frølich et al. (2013). The analytical framework they found valuable in understanding how individual higher education institutions deal with institutional pluralism was itself pluralistic. Their framework was inspired by institutional theory, the sensemaking perspective in organization theory, and strategy-as-practice. By using these multiple theories they were able to connect macro-transformation processes with micro-processes of organizational strategising.

The significance of adopting different lenses with multiple theoretical perspectives has long been acknowledged in management studies. For example, in their book *Peak Performance for Deans and Chairs* (2010), Roper and Deal apply Bolman and Deal's (1991, further developed in Bolman and Deal, 2017) original four-frame model of understanding organizational change to university settings: the structural frame; the human resources frame; the political frame; and the symbolic frame. Table 2.1 shows how perspectives on organizations like these can shape the ways in which planning processes are also conceived.

**Table 2.1.** Four perspectives on universities as organizations

|  | Mechanistic | People-focused | Micro-political | Meaning-making |
|---|---|---|---|---|
| **Organizational perspective** | Like a machine in which the top team create a 'vision' and strategy | Development of capabilities of staff | Deal-making, conflict, and bargaining | Shared understandings of purposes and what counts as success |
| **Leadership role** | Direct, reward, sanction | Empowering others | To make deals which further the goals of the organization at minimal cost | To make the right appointments and to inspire others |
| **Leadership's challenge** | Ensuring organizational structures are appropriate to the goals set | Aligning the needs of the organization and those of its people | Acquiring and keeping resources and power to achieve goals | Maintaining coherence and unity of meanings and direction |
| **Central concepts** | Targets, responsibilities, hierarchy, formal accountability | Skills, ownership, relationships | Competing interests, operation of power, resource-maximization | History and the future, ceremonies, culture, rituals |

Abes (2009, 2012) sums up the benefits of combining multiple theoretical perspectives—of exploring the 'borderlands' around theories:

> [The] researchers should consider experimenting with the choice and application of theoretical perspectives, bringing together multiple...theoretical perspectives to uncover new ways of understanding the data. Rather than being paralysed by theoretical limitations...experimentation of this nature can lead to rich new research results and possibilities.   (2009, p. 141)

There is some consensus in the literature, then, that applying the TLR framework on its own offers only a partial account.

## Comprehensiveness

A number of authors have suggested that the moments which comprise a teaching and learning regime are not comprehensive, and that they miss some significant elements both in depicting stasis and for explaining change. Here

I will offer two examples, namely Boag and Lisewski, both discussed briefly earlier. For Boag (2010) in the study described previously, the eight moments are incomplete. Missing moments are 'biographical histories', 'personal values', and 'membership of other TLRs'. He also considers that Fanghanel's (2007) concept of 'positioning' would be a useful additional feature because it recognizes that academic staff position themselves differently according to issue and time.

Lisewski (2018) concurs that there is a missing moment in the depiction of TLRs previously set out, and that, just as Boag argues, it relates to personal biographical histories. He contends that in his study of tutor-practitioners in a higher education fashion school, 'the heuristic power of SPT can be enhanced by the addition of [their] practice biographies as a TLR moment' (p. 1). These personal 'backstories' play an important role in influencing the practices as they were enacted in the fashion school that he studied. Moreover, he proposes the analytical application of the recursive relationship between practice as a connected entity and practice as performance as a further TLR moment. In other words, the 'templates' of practice and their specific and unique articulation in particular contexts interact with each other in ways which should be considered as an additional moment in the TLR.

Reflecting on the TLR idea many years after its first development, I would add that it is also missing one significant aspect of social practice theory: the socio-material dimension. As I indicate presently, the interaction between artefacts through which practices are mediated and within the context of which they are performed has significant influences on the practices themselves. This influence is two-way: the nature of the practices shapes how the artefacts are deployed, utilized, ignored, or reshaped. So in critiquing the original notion of teaching and learning regimes, I would emphasize the omission of any reference to the mediating artefacts within a particular regime. This omission has serious implications in particular for the management of change and for the illumination, for change agents, of any particular context. It is also important because any change initiative will almost always involve new or re-shaped artefact or artefacts.

## Lack of theoretical purchase

Like Boag (2010), Fanghanel (2009, p. 205) also suggests that the TLR framework is 'a useful analytical tool in theorising the relationship between macro and local contexts, and the dynamics within academic teams'. However, she considers individual agency to be conceptualized at a relatively abstract level of analysis, and so this limits the theoretical purchase on the ways in which individual participants interact with microstructures. Similarly, power relations are recognized but underplayed with regard to marginalized voices such as contract researchers, fixed-term teaching staff, and part-time teaching staff. For her there is no discussion as to how consensus might be reached within an academic grouping; conflictual relations usually seem to be fixed in time in the TLR account. Fanghanel questions how the moments relate to each other within a specific practice context and, like others, asks where the boundaries of TLR are. Relatedly, she suggests that TLRs in universities will probably become 'hazier' as professional roles and identities within universities become mixed and merged, as Whitchurch (2009) argues is happening.

A further issue relates to how the TLR framework accounts for the ways in which regimes move from one state to a different state. If, as I have claimed (Trowler, 2009, p. 187), TLRs are in a 'state of provisional stability—any description of them is true only for now', then why has there been silence, so far, on how this process could be examined and accounted for? In other words, what is the theory of change and how does the TLR notion explain the relationships between TLRs themselves and the forces acting on them, given that they are open, permeable natural systems?

For Ashwin too (2009), a practice approach in general tends to focus on the stability of practices rather than the distinctive ways they play out in particular teaching–learning interactions. These intimately linked interactions are of central significance in his thinking. Moreover, while the notion of TLRs gives a sense of how processes are shaped by the characteristics of a particular locale, it does not give insight into institutional cultures at a more macro level, nor does it give a sense of where institutional cultures and differences between them originate from. There is no explanation of how their dynamic and shifting aspects of teaching–learning interactions on the ground can be characterized or explained:

> In summary, although the TLR gives a good sense of the processes that situate institutional cultures in relation to particular teaching-learning interactions, it does not help to conceptualise what those institutional processes might be or how teaching-learning interactions might be characterised in terms of institutional cultures.   (Ashwin, 2009, p. 49)

For Ashwin, Bourdeusian concepts are more effective at achieving this. The linked notions of field, capital, and habitus (Bourdieu, 1990) give a more developed sense of these issues. At the same time, Bernstein's concept of the pedagogical device can offer an explanation of how curricula are produced (Bernstein, 1990; 2001). While the idea of TLR emphasizes local factors in this process, a Bernsteinian approach shows how causality involves 'the interweaving of local, national and global processes which together give apparently the same disciplinary knowledge practices different structures and different institutions' (Ashwin, 2009, p. 103). In general Ashwin considers that adopting social practices as the research object (as against, for example, perceptions) is not helpful in thinking about the interactive aspects of teaching–learning processes. He considers this not only a conceptual problem but also a methodological one; it is a problem with the tools that the concepts make available to generate data about teaching–learning interactions.

So the challenge for this book is to build on the strengths of the TLR conceptual scheme and address the areas where it has been questioned. The TLR account has recognizability for those who work in higher education: they can easily see it in their everyday life. It, and its different moments, have the power to operationalize otherwise jelly-like concepts such as 'culture'. There are real improvements in the way we depict change processes, and the forces for stasis, in universities through applying the concepts. Yet there are some areas where conceptual development and greater theoretical traction is required. This book takes up that challenge.

## The Underpinning Social Practice Theoretical Concepts behind SPT

The theory of teaching–learning regimes is firmly situated in a social practice perspective. This has a number of unique features and I will deal with them under a series of headings.

### The unit of analysis

A practice perspective refocuses analytical attention away from the individual actor, the acting agent who is driven by self-interest, ideology, or something else. In higher education it takes the focus off the individual academic teacher and places it on his or her workgroup (D'Eon et al., 2000). Instead of a focus on individual actions, behaviours, and choices, the focus is on situated *practices,* on recurrent behaviours in which groups of people regularly engage. This also takes the attention away from structural determination of behaviour: for example, the idea that people are simply 'social dopes', as Lisewski put it, who unthinkingly act out pre-programmed patterns of behaviour determined from above.

Schatzki's early (and problematic) description of social practices points very clearly towards the kinds of moments disaggregated within the concept of a teaching and learning regime. He says that a practice is 'a set of considerations that governs how people act. It rules action not by specifying particular actions to perform, but by offering matters to be taken account of when acting and choosing' (1996, p. 96). The following sorts of things are taken into account, he argues: 'manners, uses, observances, customs, standards...maxims, principles, rules, and offices specifying useful procedures or denoting obligations or duties which relate to human actions and utterances' (p. 96). This list brings us near to TLR moments such as conventions of appropriateness, implicit theories of teaching and learning, power relations, and so on. However, the language of 'considerations' and 'to be taken account of' suggests a conscious purposiveness that does not reflect the unconscious, unconsidered, automatic nature of practice performance. Schatzki's thinking on this matter changes in later work. For me, the language of 'structured dispositions' better captures the way practices are conditioned on the ground.

A further problem with that early depiction is its reference to 'how people act'. This focuses on individual actions, but social practices are extra-individual in at least three senses. The first is that a practice is an organized constellation of multiple people's activities: it is social in nature, although different people may be doing different things, albeit to the same end (Schatzki, 2012). A second sense is that the co-constitution of meaning happens as people work together; they are developing a mutually constructed (but circumscribed) reality, albeit with different 'takes'. A third is that practice is inevitably relational, involving social interactions that form fairly consistent patterns (Kemmis, 2009). Schatzki (2005, p. 481) writes:

> The organization of a practice is an array of understandings, rules, ends, projects, and even emotions. This organization can be described as a normativized array of mental states: a normativized array of understandings, desires, beliefs, expectations, emotions, and so on. As indicated, however, these organizational mental states are not the states of participants. They are features of the practice, expressed in the open-ended totality of actions that compose the practice.

Reckwitz's definition of a practice has almost become the standard one, but taken alone it misses this social, relational, aspect of practice:

> a routinized type of behaviour which consists of several elements, interconnected to one other: forms of bodily activities, forms of mental activities, 'things' and their use, a background knowledge in the form of understanding, know-how, states of emotion and motivational knowledge.
>
> (Reckwitz, 2002, p. 249)

An alternative definition is offered by Spaargaren, Lamers, and Weenink (2016, p. 8). This one tries to squeeze in a theoretical position regarding structure and agency and the power of materiality:

> social practices are shared, routinised, ordinary ways of doings and sayings, enacted by knowledgeable and capable human agents who—while interacting with the material elements that co-constitute the practice—know what to do next in a non-discursive, practical manner.

Schatzki (1996) goes too far, in my view, in distinguishing between 'integrated' and 'dispersed' practices. The definitions immediately above refer to the former. Schatzki argues that dispersed practices are not context-specific but can be recognised as practices. He offers the examples of describing, ordering, following rules, explaining, questioning, reporting, examining, and imagining (Schatzki, 1996, p. 91). Harries and Rettie (2016) offer the extended example of 'walking' as a dispersed practice, while Jarvis (2017) contends that 'exercising authority' is another. These are not location-specific and are abstracted from an orientation to specific goals.

In themselves and alone, verbs cannot be practices because verbs recentre the focus onto the performer and decontextualize individual activity from specific material and social contexts. This is not only analytically empty but also contradicts the ontological standpoint of social practice theory, which is (to repeat) *situated social* practices.

## Proto-Practice Reservoirs, Practices, and Changes

Because of the refocusing away from the individual, the practice perspective involves a shift from the 'ABC' theory of change (Shove, Pantzar, and Watson, 2012), that is, from a focus on individual Attitudes, Behaviours, and Choices.

Instead the focus is on the enactment of practices and the potentialities that these indicate. Because of the mutual construction of reality, each enactment is unique: even though people draw on and enact proto-practice *reservoirs* (sets of meanings, discourses, ideologies, assumptions), practice theory also stresses the importance of individual and group *repertoires* (Bernstein, 1999). These point to the unique ways of accomplishing different types of practice that are developed in a particular context, albeit within the general framework of the proto-practice reservoir of knowledge and understanding about the accomplishment of a particular practice.

Individuals remain important: the specifics of the backstory, background knowledge, and motivations of each person in the workgroup are significant in shaping the specific enactment of a practice and its potential outcomes, as are the resources to hand and the available affordances (Barnes, 2001; Shove, Pantzar, and Watson, 2012). This is one reason why practice theory stresses the significance of *context* for social science analysis.

Mikkelsen and Wåhlin (2019) illustrate how reservoirs of ideologies are drawn on and shaped in different ways on the ground through their empirical study of diversity management in an organization in Denmark. They note that at different levels in the organization they studied one can find people with different socio-economic backgrounds, including foreign-born minorities who tended to be located at the lowest levels. Interviews revealed how different ideologies were evoked by respondents at these different levels in the hierarchy. Sensemaking about diversity management involved mobilizing competing ideologies which prioritized and were constructed around, respectively, economic and business drivers; social justice; and social categorization, exclusion, and exploitation. The authors write:

> Top management articulated only positive ideologies of diversity management to strategically shape employee sensemaking towards noticing, interpreting and collectively enacting only the positive dynamics of diversity management. We, however, found that employees' hidden and forbidden sensemaking revealed meaning struggles over which and whose experiences of diversity management should gain privilege.
>
> (Mikkelsen and Wåhlin, 2019, p. 16)

Shove and colleagues distinguish between 'practice-as-entity' (generally understood models of practices) and 'practice-as-performance' (their situated enactment). Practice-as-performance always involves a unique configuration of knowledge, skills, resources, constraints, and possibilities. But at the same time, practice-as-entity offers a template within which the reconfiguration accomplished by the situated performance is achieved (Sustainable Practices Research Group, 2012; Shove, 2012). An analogy might be the difference between studio-recorded pieces of music available for download (the entity), and the live performance of the same pieces.

In considering changes in higher education, the rules and resources drawn on to create unique performances are of greatest significance. Partly for this reason, the term 'practice-as-entities' is not the right one in my view: it suggests something solid and concrete (like a music CD, to continue the analogy above). The rules and resources which structure practices locally consist of different strands, currents of influence, and types of influence, such as ideologies. They are not 'models' of practice.

A similar conceptualization of 'background' practices is found in the notion of institutional logics (Friedland and Alford, 1991; Thornton, Ocasio, and Lounsbury, 2012). As the term suggests, this limits its scope to institutions but still conveys the idea that broader constructions of practices, symbolic structures, and rules guide specific institutional behaviours. Thornton, Ocasio, and Lounsbury (2012, p. 2) use the first two authors' 2008 definition of institutional logics, itself an adaptation of one from 1999. The 2012 definition is:

> The socially constructed, historical patterns of cultural symbols and material practices, including assumptions, values, and beliefs, by which individuals and organisations provide meaning to their daily activity, organise time and space and reproduce their lives and experiences.

These logics delimit behavioural choices, shaping the categorization of reality and the beliefs, meanings, and motivational frameworks within institutions. Behind 'logics' lies another level of influence: 'institutional orders'—although the differences between 'orders' and 'logics' and the different roles they play are not well elaborated in the logics literature. On the ground, there is agency as these structured dispositions are enacted in specific 'performances' (my word, not theirs).

The institutional logics literature incorporates many theoretical similarities to my own. It is interested in the operation of power, in how the 'friction spheres' of competing frameworks of meaning and practices, horizontally and vertically, shape each other. It is interested in the ways different orders of practices work and what the limits of agency and of structure are. It views contemporary practices as historically contingent. However, despite being theoretically rich, there is a certain impoverishment to the perspective when applied to empirical studies in specific domains. The explanatory power behind local behaviour and outcomes tends to be tangential, the empirical purchase rather weak. The approach is organization-centric and business-centric too, and so is restrictive as a framework for a broader analysis.

For these reasons I prefer to take and adapt Bernstein's term 'reservoirs' of practice, referring to them as proto-practice reservoirs. They are the source of the elements of practices and from them the moments of teaching and learning regimes are drawn: meanings, theories, values, discourses, notions of appropriateness, and ideologies, as well as sensemaking. These structure the dispositions which infuse practices through the moments of a TLR. Recognizing and appreciating their instantiation on the ground is a very significant aspect of a sensibility for practices.

A practice-based theory of change can use ethnographies of situated practice performances to understand the proto-practice reservoirs which inform them, and to understand how they change. Warde (2005, p. 140) rightly argues that 'the source of changed behaviour lies in the development of practices'. But the word 'practices' here needs to be understood in a broader sense than just local, situated, and specific performances; it refers instead to the proto-practice reservoirs which condition them.

At the heart of this issue is the question of structure and agency. The local development of unique repertoires and their enactment in specific but repeated performances of practices in different locales is agentic. However, to repeat, each local enactment of practice draws on proto-practice reservoirs. These are structural in nature, that is, they impose regularities on social behaviour—dispositions to act in certain ways. They are reservoirs of ideologies, ideas about appropriateness, meanings and understandings, ways of categorizing the world, notions of morality, and so on. Giddens (1984) summarizes such lists as consisting of 'rules and resources' which together partly constitute social structures. Rules (or 'conventions', which is sometimes a more appropriate word) have normative and codifying dimensions, while resources have both authoritative and allocative ones. Resources include: symbolic structures which help categorize and explain the world; discourses which act as a resource for local repertoires of description and conceptualization; ideologies which structure what is valued and prioritized, triggering motivations and dispositions. Rules or conventions include understandings of what is, and is not, appropriate in different types of circumstances and role-behaviour dispositions.

In conditioning TLRs, the scope of performances, and the shape of repertoires, proto-practice reservoirs have a 'virtual' existence. They are not palpable; you cannot see them, and they are sometimes hard to describe. Yet they have a real influence on agency, while (according to Giddens at least) their performance also helps to shape and change them (in the longer term) in the iterative process he calls 'structuration'. Meanwhile, there is a 'real' and palpable dimension to other aspects of structures: *resources* can include physical things, such as buildings, money, media. *Rules* may be enforced in very physical ways, such as by law enforcement systems.

## Practices as emergent, and the related problem of scaling up

Geels illustrates the emergent and historically contingent nature of social practices with the example of the transition from horse and carriage to automobiles during the period 1860–1930 (Geels, 2003). In the early days, 'society cars' were exclusive and designed to show off wealth by 'promenading' in parks, exactly as had happened for decades with horse-drawn carriages. The practice was simply carried over using the new technology rather than taking advantage of that technology's broader potential. Geels traces the influence of many other previous practices on the deployment, discourse, and routines around the newly available automobile, some of which are still in place. He notes that 'radical innovations do not break through in one step, but through a sequence of small steps' (Geels, 2003, p. 22). Add-ons and hybridizations frequently occur, with innovations gradually developing their own trajectory out of previous practices. The early stages of innovations in particular are tightly tied to past practices and previous technologies, conditioning the present and the immediate future very strongly. Niche practices gradually transform into a stronger and wider patchwork of regimes until eventually they form part of the natural practice landscape (Geels, 2003, p. 4).

However, Geels' reassuring model of gradual scaling up only happens given certain preconditions, which is why scaled-up 'pilot projects' rarely translate into system-wide results in the longer term. Because the backstories behind, and current conditions around, different contexts differ so widely, the chances of pilot projects being applicable more broadly are small. Moreover, as scale increases, the significant factors at work change: the processes involved are not linear.

The literature review conducted by Paul Ashwin into the effects of enhancement initiatives in England, including the institution-based Centres for Excellence in Teaching and Learning, concluded:

The central issue . . . seems to be that rather than focusing on how to enhance teaching quality across the sector as whole, the different enhancement initiatives focused on single issues and sought to engage individual institutions or departments in relation to these issues. These individuals were then expected to lead to changes across the sector. All of the available evidence suggests that while this approach has had benefits in particular enclaves, there is no evidence that HEFCE's enhancement initiatives have led to sustained sector-wide cultural changes in teaching and learning in universities.    (Trowler, Ashwin, and Saunders, 2014, p. 17)

So, changing practices in specific locales, even if multiplied many times, does not necessarily lead to systemic-level changes.

## The normalized character of practices

For individuals involved in complex practices it is often difficult to express what they are doing and why they are doing it. This is partly because the practices have become 'just normal' and therefore invisible and obvious. It is also partly because practices are embodied; they involve emotions and tacit assumptions and theories as well as observable behaviour. Participants are making use of what Giddens (1984) calls 'practical consciousness', knowing how to 'go on' in daily life without conscious attention to how the performance is accomplished. Doing so actually involves acquiring and deploying a set of dispositions, perceptions, and behaviours which give participants a tacit 'feel for the game', an intuitive understanding of what is 'right' (in those circumstances). This is very close to the Bourdieusian (1990) notion of 'habitus', a set of structured dispositions to behave in particular ways. Individuals develop a 'practical sense' which they deploy through the 'practical skills' they acquire.

## The socio-material dimension

A practice perspective gives considerable significance to the role of artefacts in practice performance, to the mediation of human behaviour by tools, architecture, designed contexts, and other material arrangements and artefacts (Fenwick and Nerland, 2014; Schatzki, 2015). As noted above, this is missing in the original formulation of the TLR framework. While humans inscribe function and utility on such artefacts, the artefacts themselves also inscribe, constrain, and condition human behaviour. Shor (1996) offers the example of classroom layout:

> Like plants growing toward sunlight, students are expected to sit in rows facing the lecturing teacher as the front, the unilateral authority who tells them what things mean, what to do, and how to become people who fit into society as it is.  (pp. 11–12)

There is, therefore, a mutual entanglement of artefact use and practice accomplishment: as artefacts change, so do practices, but practices are also inscribed on artefact use. In media-rich contexts this insight gives great significance to virtual worlds and their permeability with practices in the physical world. To understand how observable practices are shaped and reshaped in such contexts involves looking into the artefacts which mediate the virtual as well as the 'real'.

## Situated cognition

Practice theory emphasizes the context-specific nature of knowing, saying, doing, and relating. Understanding and explaining the social world has significant limits because of contextual contingencies: what is known and practised in one context does not always apply in another. This renders simplistic notions of 'what works' and of 'evidence-based practice' rather dangerous in social science and in planning change processes. Social practice theorists tend to talk about adaptation rather than adoption of practices, policies, solutions, and answers. From a practice perspective, innovations are almost always domesticated, that is, adapted and reworked into a shape that fits and is suitable for the sets of social practices already in place. In addition, as noted above, practices are always historically contingent and emergent; they come from a past which has led to, and to some extent is still evident in, the present, and they will lead to a future where echoes of current practices will be found (Boud, 2012).

So social practice theory looks at the social world as ensembles of practices; regular sets of behaviours, ways of understanding and know-how, and states of emotion that are enacted by groups configured to achieve specific outcomes through their activities. These are reproduced and to some extent transformed by social agents. However, the social realism of practice theory generally stems from an insistence that there is more to social reality than a relativist social constructionism; that social structures exist and have significant effects on practices, even though social agents may not be aware of them or their power. Practices always have a material dimension, and one which periodically involves an uneven struggle for control of resources, power, and discursive and knowledge practices. The works of Archer (1995), Bourdieu (1990), Giddens (1984), Schatzki (2002), Warde (2005), and others illustrate these points, with different emphases in each.

Both consensus and dispute (or at least unspoken difference) characterize these different dimensions of motivation, emotion, understanding, knowledge, and appropriate bodily practices in most contexts. Yet as Archer (2007) points out, there is a usually a common set of contextual concerns which shapes agendas and priorities for everyone involved in mutual activity.

## Practice Architectures

Kemmis and Mahon (2017) have offered some tools to understand the significance of institutional location in their discussion of practice architectures. Their deployment in conceptualizing the genesis and trajectories of TLRs can help addresses the valid criticism made by Ashwin (2009) that the original TLR account did not adequately conceptualize how institutional location constrains TLR moments.

The set of concepts involved in the depiction of practice architectures shows how the institutional location shapes local 'site ontologies' (Schatzki, 2003; 2005)—practices on the ground there, the specific ways of *going on*. They offer an account

> of what practices are composed of, and how practices are shaped by, and shape, the cultural-discursive, material-economic, and social-political arrangements (practice architectures) with which they are enmeshed in sites...of practice.   (Kemmis and Mahon, 2017, p. 109)

The first of the three types of arrangements described in the quote above highlights the significance of discourses in conditioning what one can talk about and what is difficult to talk about, what is acceptable and what is not. The second refers to the arrangements in physical spaces that constrain and shape the ways that practices can be done within an institution, especially the nature of the physical environment, the material and financial resources, and the division of labour. Finally, the social–political arrangements limit and direct the way that relations can occur—the hierarchies, the groupings, the distribution of power. These three arrangements mediate the conditions of practice and the way that they are enmeshed in specific institutional settings:

> For example, in a university setting, the leading practices of a faculty executive team can produce policies that enable and constrain, and thus prefigure, the teaching practice of university academics. Such relationships of enablement and constraint between practices become more complicated and more indeterminate in highly complex practice landscapes...like universities.   (Kemmis and Mahon, 2017, p. 112)

This description of practice architectures resonates very strongly with the moments of TLRs. In the language I use to describe those, Kemmis and Mahon are primarily talking about discursive repertoires, materiality in interaction, and power relations. The moments in operation in TLRs on the ground in a university may be in harmony with those found in the wider institution, or they may be in tension, involving the friction spheres previously mentioned. However, the Kemmis and Mahon argument is that institutional practice architectures make practices on the ground within them easier to sustain if they are congruent with the wider formation.

The arrangements also shape the ways in which individual learning journeys and professional journeys are made by students and staff respectively. They offer some accessible routes, but close off others. They condition the number and location of points at which decisions can be made, where movement can progress or change direction (Penuel et al., 2016). So, practice landscapes with their specific practice architectures are very significant. Within a higher education institution there are multiple and overlapping sets of practices interacting in complex ways. The way they mesh, and their broad constraints and opportunities are framed by the practice architecture of the institution within which they take place.

It is worth elaborating on how this happens through a case study. Vicki Trowler, Murray Saunders, and I conducted a research project in 2018 for the Quality Assurance Agency Scotland (Trowler, Trowler, and Saunders, 2018). The project brief was to explore the different ways in which higher education institutions around the world told their students about how they had used student feedback to improve things; how they 'closed the loop' through communicating their actions back to students. Out of this information QAA Scotland wanted us to develop a set of principles about effective communication concerning the use of feedback that student associations and HE institutions could use, following effective examples we had found in universities internationally.

Using interviews, a survey, and observant participation we discerned three distinct institutional practice architecture types which were significant in affecting this issue: atomistic, multiple, and integrated architectures. In institutions with atomistic architectures ('atomistic institutions') ad hoc practices took place in isolated locations with no strong organizing framework institutionally. At best there was only a student appeals procedure rather than a fully integrated accountability system. There was no perception of an overarching system or unifying principle at these sites. As one respondent said:

> The individual professors can decide what they want, then students can ask for a commission if they are not happy. It is a very formal process and there are no dialogic systems in place.

By contrast, in institutions with integrated architectures ('integrated institutions') there was a well-defined set of institutional procedures and structures through which student voice is articulated and discussed, with actions being taken and clear lines of reporting. In each case we found that these integrated architectures were strongly influenced by government policy agendas such as, in the UK, the Teaching Excellence Framework (TEF) or the National Student Survey (NSS), and were oriented towards them. So, for example, in one 'integrated' institution there was an annual strategic planning process oriented around the NSS and resulting in a strategy document which incorporated the student voice and responses to it. By contrast, 'atomistic' institutions tended to exist in less regulated national or regional contexts where institutions were more autonomous and less accountable.

A respondent in an 'integrated' institution said this:

> Particularly impressive is the way LetUsKnow [an online student feedback system] is integrated in a systematized way into a well-ordered system. It would be easy to rely on the collegiality of [our institution] and the positive attitudes of the top team and staff towards learning and teaching, student engagement etc. But the structures mean that there is resilience in what the student union does, which doesn't rely on personalities.

Some integrated institutional formations could be described as 'values-based', with staff appointment procedures very strongly focused on ensuring that institutional values such as student focus and prioritizing high-quality teaching were not diluted. Other integrated formations were more bureaucratic in character, with a heavy stress on well-understood policies and procedures which could offer longevity and robustness to the integrated system of student voice-related practices. In both cases, but especially in the former type, there tended to be a harmonious relationship between TLRs on the ground and the practice architecture of the institution.

Between these two contrasting architectures, atomistic and integrated, were institutions with 'multiple' architectures. These were universities with a range of practices in different sites. Some demonstrated systematization, consistency, and longevity, much like integrated institutions. Other sites tended to be idiosyncratic and lacking robustness in relation to hearing the student voice, responding to it, and giving an account of responses to it. Here, architectural influences appeared to be operating at a sub-institutional level.

In terms of Kemmis and Mahon's three aspects of institutional architectures, cultural–discursive, material–economic, and social–political arrangements, these had very different features in each institutional type, and were oriented in very different directions, according to priorities which contrasted quite sharply. The empirical details of the study indicated that the Kemmis and Mahon model needs further elaboration, however. It takes little account of what Dill (1999) refers to (rather inappropriately perhaps) as the 'learning architectures' of institutions. By this he means the organizational frameworks, committee structures, and lines and modes of communication internally. Our study revealed that these were very important in creating and sustaining institutions with integrated architectures, but had a very different character in atomistic and multiple architectures. They are the arterial system of the institution, and may be sophisticated and well functioning, or poorly implemented and sclerotic.

We were interested in how these three architectures shaped the communication with students and the nature of the student–institution relationships. Figure 2.1 situates the different ways in which students and institutions are reciprocally positioned in roles which shape the type of response to student voice arising from, and appropriate to, that context and those roles. We found that the different practice architectures strongly influenced the relationship possibilities that institutions could have with their students.

The continuum maps the different relationships between students and institutions and the related ways in which each is positioned. Student representatives and the student body may be seen as consumers, representatives, partners, or agents in articulating the student voice, taking actions, and communicating those actions to others (the *students* line). The institution

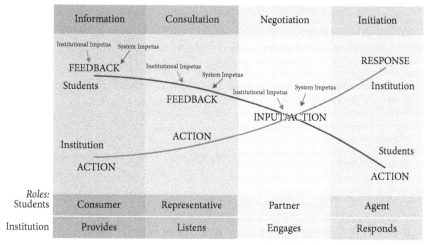

**Figure 2.1.** The student voice continuum
(Trowler, V. et al., 2018, p. 15)

(the *institution* line) may be situated as providing, listening, engaging, or responding.

The integrated, multiple, and atomistic formations illustrate quite starkly the concept of practice architectures (Kemmis and Mahon, 2017; Mahon et al., 2016)—how practices are shaped not only by proto-practice reservoirs but by features of institutional context. Evident also, beyond individual institutional practice architectures, is the nested character of practices, with national-level political cultures, policies, and forces operating, as Figure 2.1 shows. In the UK, the National Student Survey and the Teaching Excellence Framework are significant in shaping practices, at least in some institutions. Within institutions with an integrated formation the committee and reporting structures are deliberately aligned with such policies where they offer advantage. In turn, these policies are driven by dominant forces in the political culture, particularly neo-liberal ideology which stresses target-driven practices, student choice, and creating an information-rich environment in which rational choices can be made. At the level of individual teaching and learning regimes in 'integrated institutions', the locus of generative forces shaping them lies outside them to a much greater extent than is the case in institutions with an atomistic formation. In the latter there is much greater latitude for internal forces (such as the discipline, backstories, and others dealt with in Chapter 5) to shape the moments of the TLRs locally.

Like institutional architectures, these system-level conditioning forces also have cultural–discursive, material–economic, and social–political arrangements which can (but sometimes don't) shape institutional practice architectures and condition local practices on the ground. In the clearest example of an integrated formation in our sample, there was a high level of congruence in this set of nested practices.

## Theory and Practice Implications from the Chapter

The discussion in this chapter has shown that there are limits to the heuristic power of the TLR framework of concepts as originally developed, both in terms of its theoretical purchase and as far as its value in undertaking change initiatives is concerned. While that early formulation could greatly increase the granularity and precision of depictions of local practices and could offer a framework for understanding workgroups' current states of consensus, disagreement, conflict, shared understandings, and problematic misunderstandings, it lacked ability to go much beyond this. A more powerful, fully theoretical perspective needed to build on this descriptive power. It needed to develop in such a way that, theoretically, explanatory ability is enhanced for the theorist and its predictive and indicative qualities are made available to the change agent. This became the task of this book.

In terms of change processes, the eight moments can be augmented by significant features which are of value in enhancing change initiatives. Built into the model of teaching and learning regimes developed here is an appreciation of the socio-material within the contexts of operation of any regime: the significance of the artefacts in use, the built environment and physical layouts in which practices are performed, and the way these conditions practice and could be summarized as 'materiality in interaction'.

Built into it also is the ability to appreciate, depict, and extrapolate from the historical and emergent properties which form the basis for contemporary practices and shape individual subjectivities within regimes. This enhances explanatory and, to some extent, predictive power and could be summarized as 'backstories in process'.

Broadening the analytical lens to include features of the context which go beyond the boundaries of the regime or regimes of interest also enhances explanatory power and offers a more comprehensive picture for those interested in practice and enhancement. While theoretically social practice theory understands practices as bundled and nested, this feature has not been present in most studies and uses of the TLR theory to date. Neither has a fully theorized appreciation of the significance of institutional context. This addition could be summarized as 'regimes in interaction'.

So, it is necessary to augment the original concept of TLRs with these three 'missing' moments:

- materiality in interaction;
- backstories in process;
- regimes in interaction.

These additions offer an account that is more holistic, dynamic, and encompassing. Beyond that, the rest of the book attends to a wider landscape than the original theory of TLRs did, elaborating on the roots of TLRs and their moments—their genesis. With this augmented perspective at the forefront, Chapter 3 considers how the researcher and the change agent can best gain an appreciation of teaching and learning regimes of interest to them, with 'appreciation' meaning different things for their different purposes. Subsequent chapters of the book go on to develop an enhanced theoretical perspective on the TLR framework, bringing out in more detail the proto-practice reservoirs from which the TLR moments flow and the implications of the augmented TLR theory for both researchers and those concerned with the enhancement of practices.

# 3

# Practice-Focused Strategic Ethnography

## Introduction

This chapter proposes fruitful ways in which TLRs can be apprehended in particular contexts, how we can fill out the details of 'context' in full colour and high definition, and how we can see the dynamic flow of TLR moments as they shape and are shaped by elements of the context. Chapter 2 concluded that the significant moments of teaching and learning regimes in university work-groups are:

1. power relations;
2. implicit theories of teaching and learning;
3. conventions of appropriateness;
4. recurrent practices;
5. tacit assumptions;
6. codes of signification;
7. discursive repertoires;
8. subjectivities in interaction *with the addition of:*
9. materiality in interaction;
10. backstories in process;
11. regimes in interaction.

Because the topic of the book concerns accomplishing change in teaching and learning regimes, and its theoretical disposition is a social practice approach, this chapter on methods and methodology is a very focused one: it is primarily about the ethnographic research design. This is because social practice theory is 'ethnographic in its sensibility' (Miettinen, Samya-Fredericks, and Yanow, 2009, p. 1312). This means that there is congruence between the methodological strengths of ethnography and the characteristics which are significant in a social practice approach: behavioural dispositions, ways of thinking, discourses, subjectivities, power relations, interaction with artefacts, emotional responses, and motivations. The ethnographic style can unpick the assemblage of moments in the context under study. So much is this the case that there is a

*Accomplishing Change in Teaching and Learning Regimes: Higher Education and the Practice Sensibility.*
Paul Trowler, Oxford University Press (2020). © Paul Trowler. DOI: 10.1093/oso/9780198851714.001.0001

special term (a rather ugly one) for the approach: praxiography—literally the depiction of practices. Moreover, as one of the founders of interpretive anthropology, Clifford Geertz, says: 'to know a city is to know its streets' (1983, p. 167). A practice approach is focused on the street level, with, if done well, an intense appreciation of the power of the city, the state, and the world beyond them.

Sadly, most attempts to provide general guidelines, toolkits, or advice for the deployment of a practice-focused ethnographic approach have limited value. SPT insists that contextual contingencies condition appropriateness, including appropriateness of choices of research design and data collection methods. The issues being addressed in the specifics of the context of research, the nature of 'the problem', and the backstories all condition what is appropriate. What *is* possible is to set out some examples from the literature, some concepts, some alternative approaches, and leave it to the reader to determine what is appropriate and what not for their own context and purposes. My intent, therefore, is to evoke ideas and plans informed by a practice sensibility, to stimulate thought on the basis of the material in the chapter.

The flavour of practice-focused ethnography of interest here adopts a strategic approach, one that is concerned with change initiatives and with real-world issues and 'problems' in universities. This is not ethnography for its own sake but ethnography for a purpose: that of the accomplishment of change in TLRs and the development of research-based understandings and possible solutions to pressing issues in universities.

The strategic character of this research design is shaped by what social practice theorists know about enhancement initiatives. These issues will be addressed in more detail in Chapter 6, but here I want to draw out six key axioms which are rooted in the research and evaluation studies I have conducted over the years, the relevant literature, and my observations in professional life in higher education:

1. New practices, like present-day ones, are emergent and historically contingent; they don't come out of nowhere.
2. When initiatives are deliberately introduced into a context, the way they are received and understood is shaped by the practice characteristics already in place.
3. The characteristics of any initiative may be more or less congruent with the nexus of practices already found in the locale.
4. Where there is congruence between an initiative and current practices, the likelihood of successful and sustained implementation is higher.

5. The outcomes of initiatives will be different in different locales, and the imagined nature of their outcomes is rarely realized in full: initiatives are usually 'domesticated' for a better fit to specific contexts.
6. 'Problems' faced by universities are perceived as such from a specific standpoint, rooted in current practices, assumptions, and priorities that are prevalent in a given locale. Actions taken to address them affect other locales with different practices, assumptions, and priorities.

These axioms indicate where the chief focus of practice-focused strategic research needs to lie. It prioritizes the past and present nexus of practices in the location of interest and on the characteristics of proposed initiatives or perceived issues that need resolution. Importantly, it attends to the degree of fit between enhancement initiatives and current practices and the likely reception and implementation of change initiatives as they are shaped by practices-in-place.

For example, a national higher education quality assurance body might ask, as the Quality Assurance Agency Scotland did, 'how can our universities better communicate to students what actions they have taken as a result of student input' (QAA Scotland, 2018). Practice-focused research into the topic needs to illuminate the nexus of practices around student feedback and the nature of relationships within *particular* universities and their students and student representatives in order to understand what kinds of enhancement might have a chance of succeeding. Or again, when a university asks 'how can we make our curriculum more relevant to the needs of industry and the employment prospects of our students?', research should uncover (among other things) the current shape of the assumptions, priorities, and subjectivities which shape curricular foci. That example is expanded in Case Study 1 in Chapter 6.

Researchers and change agents who are 'insiders' in the context of interest are those most likely to deploy such an ethnographic approach. Naturally, the term 'insider' is a relative one (Trowler, 2011a; 2012a), but minimally it is used here in the sense of the researcher being in the same institution as the work-group or department of interest. The challenge of this chapter is to provide resources for these researchers and change agents which will enable them to apply the idea of teaching and learning regimes in a way which smooths the change process for all those involved, improves outcomes, and reduces the gap between original intentions and actual outcomes. Ideally, the aim is to conduct ethnographic research which employs a fine-grained, immersive approach which develops 'thick description' (Geertz, 1983) of the structured behavioural dispositions, social relations, sets of discourses, ways of thinking, procedures, emotional responses, material relations and motivations in play. Beyond that agenda such an approach should uncover the historical antecedents to current practices and the broader context in which they operate.   (Adapted from Trowler, 2013a)

The rest of the chapter addresses issues of practice-focused research design and then data collection methods. What texts there are addressing methodological issues from a social practice perspective tend to be quite disappointing (Schatzki, 2012; Gherardi, 2012; Higgs et al., 2012; Miettinen et al., 2009; Spaargaren et al., 2016; Jonas et al., 2017; Nicolini, 2017). They are often pitched at a high level of generality and do not offer much in the way of practical inspiration. One reason is that they often attempt to identify designs and methods that are specific to a social practice approach, different from the 'run-of-the-mill' designs and methods of social science. In a few cases there may be such unique approaches, and in some cases traditional research methods may be less appropriate for a social practice approach. However, generic designs and methods can also be valuable when underpinned by SPT. The difference is that the researcher or change agent is using them to interrogate social practices. They approach the tasks of research design and data collection methods with a key criterion in mind: 'How well will this design and these methods allow me to access the different moments of the teaching and learning regime/s I am interested in?' As well as practice-focused research design, data capture and analysis needs to be done with a 'sensibility for practice' (Sedlačko, 2017). Nicolini (2012, p. 8) elaborates on what such a sensibility seeks from research:

> Practice theories conceive social investigation as the patient, evidence-based, bottom-up effort of understanding practices and untangling their relationships. They question how such practices are performed, and how connected practices make a difference; they ask why it is that the world that results from the coming together of several practices is the way it is, and how and why it is not different.

More than this, however, a practice sensibility requires the analyst to think beyond individuals, beyond their personal attitudes, behaviours, and choices, and instead to see behaviours as enmeshed in a nexus of practices which shapes and constrains but does not determine what they do. For example, in looking at cases of plagiarism by some overseas students in a UK context, a practice perspective appreciates that there may be displaced practices at play. In their home context, collaborative learning and writing practices and the unacknowledged use of other authors' work may be entirely consistent with prevalent conventions of appropriateness and tacit assumptions about learning and teaching. In the UK, however, these moments, these practices, constitute an academic crime.

Practice-focused research design and working with data become much easier when armed with a disaggregated conceptualization of a situated bundle of social practices provided by the concept of teaching and learning regimes, together with a sensibility for practices.

## Practice-Focused Research Design: Classic Approaches to Organizational Ethnography

The use of ethnography in organizational research is not new and it is worth looking at some different approaches that have been tried, to assess their value to the objectives set out above. The section which follows interrogates various approaches to data collection which could be described, at least in part, as 'practice-focused ethnography'—that is to say, that they have at least a partial ability to apprehend, within a workgroup context, structured behavioural dispositions, social relations, sets of discourses, ways of thinking, procedures, emotional responses, material relations, and motivations in play, as well as to uncover the historical antecedents to current practices and the broader context in which they operate. In short, when applied to higher education contexts they are able to access the different moments of teaching and learning regimes, the way they interrelate, and their possible consequences for the outcomes of enhancement initiatives.

## Ethnography in the commercial world

The annual Ethnographic Praxis in Industry Conference (https://www.epicpeople.org/) brings together researchers who apply ethnography 'to create business value'. Conference proceedings contain many reports of this approach in practice. One example relates to the invigoration of the Tesco brand. In 2011 a team of academics trained nine managers to become in-house ethnographers at fifty-two Tesco stores (Brannen, Moore, and Mughan, 2013).

Their study lasted for three months and had the aims of understanding and evaluating the core practices that comprised the essence of Tesco's advantage and identifying sources of learning from Tesco's foreign subsidiaries to assist it in an increasingly competitive environment.

Another example comes from Intel, a company which has found ethnography so valuable that it employed twelve anthropologists and other trained ethnographers (Anderson, 2009). Their task was initially focused on particular innovations, especially their likely reception when moving into potential new markets. Ethnographers would attempt to understand how people live their lives in these potential markets, visiting consumers in their homes or offices to observe and listen, seeing people's behaviour in their own terms. The ultimate question was: 'Is this a potential market for our (new) products?' This focus broadened in later years to informing strategic, long-range planning. Anderson argues that 'by understanding how people live, researchers discover otherwise elusive trends that inform the company's future strategies'. With this broader focus, Intel ethnographers attempted to answer such questions as 'are baby boomers retaining their PC and TV habits as they age, or are they comfortable shifting to new media' and 'what differences are there between...the technology perspectives of teenagers, who have used cell phones since they were in elementary school, and those of older generations, who came to them only after becoming proficient with PCs?' (Anderson, 2009).

Such questions are, of course, about social practices in different groups. However, that concept and its many associated insights were not deployed by Intel. It is a characteristic of most of the corporate ethnographic studies that they lack an underpinning social theory: their purposes are instrumental and their approach pragmatic, even when it is concerned with long-term planning. Without an explicit social theory underneath a research design, the researcher lacks both map and compass; criteria of significance are absent and there is no apparent pattern to the web of connections between the phenomena observed through data collection.

Lack of appropriate theory can also mean that potentially valuable directions for the ethnographic gaze are missed. In the examples immediately above, that gaze is directed at the present and future. But social practice theory also highlights the significance of the past, where current practices have come from, and what the trajectory into the future may be.

Perhaps one of the most sophisticated examples of organizational ethnography, and probably one of the best in the commercial field, is the study of ICI by Pettigrew (1985). Although the details are now outdated, the way in which Pettigrew collected and collated ethnographic data about the organization and used it to tell a story in an engaging way is a valuable model for ethnographic organizational research. Pettigrew argued for a political and cultural perspective on organizations, one that is attentive to their backstories and the social context in which they operate and aware of the processual nature of organizational change. Based on eight years of research, the intricate detail which Pettigrew reported is hard to emulate but, happily, is unnecessary for the purposes addressed in this book. One great strength of his approach, and a very unusual one, is that it is based on explicit and detailed theory, although this shifts: Pettigrew moves from a classic Organizational Development perspective to something closer to a practice perspective, although the 'practice turn' in wider social science had not yet occurred at that time.

## Biography of artefacts

In their 2010 article, Pollock and Williams seek to address the theoretical and methodological weaknesses of many studies of technology and work organization, particularly the fact that they are usually short-term and single-site studies of the implementation and/or impact of technologies in organizational settings. They advocate a Biography of Artefacts perspective which emphasizes the value of an ethnography which is longitudinal and involves a multi-site research design underpinned by explicit theory. Pollock and Williams write:

> Research needs to be extended spatially to see how technological fields and markets are constituted and organised as well as temporally to address the longer term evolution of the technology and its associated organisational practices (e.g. including further implementations and feedback into future technology supply and the extension of a product into other markets). This is no small feat.    (Pollock and Williams, 2010, p. 10)

They advocate choosing both research settings and the scope of studies in a way which is informed by *provisional* understandings, both theoretical and empirical, of the contexts in which technologies are being shaped. This in addition to the research questions and issues being studied. A Biography of Artefacts approach is a considered one, carefully planned and goal-oriented. The words 'provisional understandings' are very significant here: research design choices are not made at random; rather, they are based on sets of explicit theoretical assumptions (such as the provisional understanding of the nature of the teaching and learning regimes in place) as well as on educated guesses, one might say, of significant points in the processes being undertaken in research contexts.

The problem with the 'Biography of Artefacts' approach for the purposes addressed here is that the artefacts need to be considered in relation to, and as part of, an interaction with the nexus of social practices of interest, and not just other artefacts and processes (Pollock and Williams, 2013). Moreover, it is not enough to simply research the changing ways in which an artefact is conceptualized over time; rather, it is necessary to research how it influences and is influenced by the practices in the context of interest. Therefore, rather than only a biography of artefacts, a biography of *practices* is required. This involves exploring how practice bundles develop over time, with practices being substituted or transformed, reconfigured or realigned. The trajectory of change in practice bundles may be small; the same practices may be augmented but remain fundamentally the same, or, more rarely, may be entirely replaced by completely new ways of using artefacts, applying competences, and experiencing different ways of understanding, feeling, and valuing.

From a social practice perspective this can be reframed as shifting, as one moves from the left to the right of Table 3.1, from 'recrafting practices' to 'substituting practices' (Spurling et al., 2013). Importantly, however, another possibility exists for changing practices—shifting the way sets of practices interlock. The notion of bundling highlights how practices are enmeshed in other practices: the lecture with the seminar, with virtual learning environments, with assessment practices, and so on. Focusing only on changing the character of 'the lecture' as a technology misses its situatedness in these other practices and so the mutual effects that are occurring on the different practices. Indeed, there may be deleterious unintended consequences in other, linked, areas of practice, resulting from a change in one practice element. So, instead of focusing just on one area of practice, an intervention can aim to shift the ways in which the different but interconnected practices relate to each other. When this is taken into account it is more likely that interrelationships

**Table 3.1.** Changing practices

| Incrementalism (Enhancement) → | | Innovative incrementalism (Reform) | → | Transformation (Reinvention) |
|---|---|---|---|---|
| Recrafting practices | | → | | Substituting practices |
| Do the same in the old way but better | Add new things to old things and do them in the old way | Do completely different things in the old way | Do completely different things in some new ways | Do completely different things completely differently |

between the different practices will move in desirable rather than undesirable ways (Spurling et al., 2013). Where this happens the effects will also be temporal: the practice trajectory will change as the patterns of practice inter-actions are changed.

## Strategic ethnography

Strategic ethnographic research design usually takes the form of ethnographies in multiple locales and different methods in one institution and at different stages of innovation and implementation. In the literature on policy imple-mentation, such research designs are usually referred to as 'trajectory studies'. They aim to demonstrate how the deployment and conceptualization of an innovation is shaped and changed during its trajectory, and how this occurs in different locations.

Vesa and Vaara (2014) elaborate on the idea of strategic ethnography, evolving it into what they call the '2.0' version. This involves deploying four methods within ethnographic research: autoethnography, video ethnography, comparative ethnography, and virtual ethnography. The first 'can provide a better understanding of the lived experiences of different types of strategists in different settings'; the second 'allows detailed analysis of strategic practices in their sociomaterial context'; the third 'enables comparison of processes and practices in different settings'; and the last, virtual ethnography, 'will further our understanding of the virtual aspects of organisational strategy work' (p. 288).

They refer to 'strategic ethnography 2.0' because they claim that their fourfold approach can 'take advantage of new technologies and/or more creative and more complex forms of engagement with research sites' (p. 289). However, in truth this approach is largely impractical. Autoethno-graphy too often dissolves into bad autobiography. To be done well it requires the ability to dispassionately reflect on one's life and experiences, to appreciate the precursors to one's current frameworks of meaning, and to situate oneself within a context in a neutral, analytical way. These are rare qualities indeed, and the ethical issues associated with autoethnography are huge because accounts will inevitably be entangled with real people in potentially identifi-able situations. One of the few examples of autoethnography done well is Struthers (2012). Most importantly, autoethnography would only be of value in a practice-focused strategic ethnography if the researcher or change agent has been a long-term member at the site of interest.

Although it is true that mobile phone technologies make video ethnography a more practical proposition than it used to be, significant ethical issues are involved. It does indeed give access to displays of emotions and multimodal analysis, offering exceptional detail on the 'nano' episodes of daily professional life which, though small, can often have intense significance. An interesting example is Martens and Scott's study (2017) which demonstrates how the analyst can deploy different ways of 'looking' at different aspects of performance using video data. However, collecting this kind of data is fraught with ethical issues, perhaps especially for insider researchers.

Comparative ethnography is also a challenge to researchers who have limited resources and who lack a research team. Like video ethnography, it holds the promise of granular-level insights, for example in comparing the different articulations of the same discipline or sub- discipline in different university contexts, but practicalities limit its value for in-depth understanding.

Finally, virtual ethnography is more practicable, particularly when accessing publicly available online textual material. The distinctions between the physical world and the virtual one are becoming less significant, and the porosity between the two and their mutual interactions mean that any ethnography must include a significant element of researching the online world.

Perhaps the most significant point made by Vesa and Vaara (2014) is the value of deploying imaginative and integrated multiple methods, aligned to the strategic purpose of the ethnography. A similar point is made by Georgiou and Carspecken (2002), who attempt to synthesize critical ethnography (itself involving a dual approach) and ecological psychology. Likewise, Nicolini (2017, p. 19) describes four linked methods for 'capturing' social practices:

> the analysis of the concerted accomplishment of orderly scenes of action; the examination of how scenes of action have been historically constituted; the study of the development and disappearance of individual practices; and the inquiry into the co-evolution, conflict and interference of two or more practices.

For Nicolini these strategies offer a richer, thicker, and more persuasive depiction of social practices than any alternatives. They involve following the genealogy of practices, their roots in earlier practices, and their trajectories into the future: in short, a biography of practices. But this needs to be supplemented by a configurational strategy, one which looks at the ways in which bundles of practices interact and interrelate in the present. It also needs to be sensitive to conflict, rather than slipping into a functionalist orientation which simply assumes 'fit' and concerted action in a clear direction.

Sedláčko (2017) also proposes a fourfold approach to research methods, with different 'sensibilities': a focus on recurrent behaviours and the artefacts with which they interact ('converse'); a focus on everydayness; a focus on the work of assembling, structuring, and ordering; and a focus on reflexivity. So, a practice-focused method should attend to doing, interacting, and the artefacts in use. For Sedláčko the mundane, the ordinary, and the taken-for-granted are important in this, but the analyst needs to question participants' accounts and explanations, asking (with Geertz): 'What is going on here (apart from the obvious)?' With Nicolini, he argues that there needs to be attention to possible conflicts and disruptions, with attention to:

- the ongoing achievement of assembling (stabilizing, structuring, and ordering);
- the multiplicities, resistances, conflicts, breakdowns, and ruptures emerging and being overcome throughout assembling;
- the historical and situational productivity of such assemblages, that is, the means through which they achieve particular (strategic) effects including, for example, shaping the fields of the possible for future practices (pp. 55–6).

In all this the researcher needs to be reflexive and sensitive to the significance of the assemblages and relationships into which s/he is woven and the implications of these for the truth claims of his or her accounts.

## Practice-Focused Institutional Ethnography

Institutional ethnography is an approach described by its founder, Dorothy Smith, as the study of 'textually mediated social organization' (Smith, 2005; 2006). The use of verbal and written language, textual material, and sources which contain language is particularly significant in institutional ethnography. For Smith, language serves to co-ordinate subjectivities. The research approach begins by identifying a guiding perspective within a particular institutional order, and uses that to work outwards to other perspectives. Smith calls these perspectives 'standpoints'.

Working outwards in this way identifies a series of issues or problems which are relevant to the people occupying that standpoint. These local issues are only the beginning, however. They are the starting point from which research into institutional processes proper is begun, and this includes the structural forces which impinge on the everyday world of actors within the organization.

Smith says that this unfolding research design means it is not always possible to specify the design in advance. But for her, the design of an institutional ethnography is highly structured: 'Each next step builds from what has been discovered and invades more extended dimensions of the institutional regime' (2005, p. 35).

Devault (2006, p. 294) summarizes the institutional ethnography approach as follows:

> Institutional ethnographies are built from the examination of work processes and study of how they are coordinated, typically through texts and discourses of various sorts. Work activities are taken as the fundamental grounding of social life, and an institutional ethnography generally takes some particular experience (and associated work processes) as a 'point of entry.' The work involved could be part of a paid job; it might fall into the broader field of unpaid or invisible work, as so much of women's work does; or it might comprise the activities of some 'client' group.

The standard mix of ethnographic approaches is usually deployed (interviews, focus groups, observation), but with an emphasis on documentary analysis. The discursive repertoires employed in textual artefacts are given special attention, as is the effect of these on the organization of social relations within the institution.

Smith's original approach was not neutral: she was interested in investigating and uncovering structured inequalities within institutions, and in particular how women are subjugated through daily processes, texts, and discursive repertoires. One example of this is 'academic housework', the phenomenon of women academics more frequently finding themselves doing a kind of work which is time-consuming but does not result in promotion or recognition, such as counselling students in difficulty (Macfarlane and Burg, 2018). A further example of inequalities structured by gender is the low status and pay of administrative staff in universities—a category of staff that is disproportionately female.

The ways in which these phenomena have come about, and how they are made to continue, are, for Smith, ideal candidates for research through institutional ethnography. They are issues that are always central concerns for SPT (although Smith is not a practice theorist). For Smith such research should result in changes that matter: they should benefit people rather than just being about them, uncovering the ways in which subjugation and disadvantage work, explaining causal mechanisms and so suggesting ways of tackling them.

Institutional ethnography both recognizes and takes into account macro structural forces which condition continuing relations of advantage and disadvantage. In this way it addresses one of the criticisms of more traditional ethnographic research: that it is short-sighted and cannot see beyond the local to larger, macro, structures which are conditioning behaviours, lived experiences, and outcomes at the micro level (Hammersley, 1993; Porter, 1993). There is an obvious path towards shifting institutional ethnography in a practice-focused direction, by turning the attention from individuals and their roles to recurrent social behaviours and ways of seeing which are linked to broader social patterns.

It remains unclear how to get started when beginning a traditional institutional ethnography, and what the limits of any investigation are. The researcher is left asking two questions: 'How do I know where to start?' and 'How do I know when to stop?' There is also a further question about the level of analysis taken in determining a standpoint. Again, the researcher should ask: 'Can I talk about the standpoint of *students*, or is that too broad a category?' and 'If I talk about the standpoint of mature, distance learning students, am I in danger of occluding significant differences within that category?' and 'Am I privileging one standpoint over another in the research design decisions I am making?' A practice-focused approach can instead concentrate on the sets of practices of interest (especially in relation to Smith's concern with structured inequalities) and ask questions about the different standpoints found within them.

## Affective Organizational Ethnography

For Silvia Gherardi (2018), previous approaches to institutional/organizational ethnography have lacked a sensitivity to issues of affect. She wants to 'trouble the narrative of a linear methodology for doing [ethnography] with insights from feminist studies and in relation to the turn to affect and the debate on post-qualitative methodologies in general' (p. 2). The turn to affect occurred in the mid-1990s and Gherardi's take on it proposes that the researcher should ask what affect does in relation to practices and organizational life. More than that, she wants the researcher to be attuned, affectively, emotionally, to the subjects of the research. This involves an appreciation of the entanglement of text, actors, materialities, language, and agencies. It also involves an appreciation of 'flow', of process, and its importance to placeness, to context. Finally, it involves the researcher and fieldwork actually having an effect, either intentionally or unintentionally, because of their embodied interaction with the site of research. The researcher offers an interpretive analysis which changes, in some way, the thing being interpreted. Gherardi writes:

> Affective ethnography may be conceived as a way to move away from 'matters of fact' to 'matters of concern'. Matters of concern have to be liked, appreciated, tasted, put to the test. Matters of concern are disputable, they move, they carry one away, they *matter* ... The so-called 'turn to affect' may have an impact on ethnographic practice as an invitation to pay attention to embodied knowledge and to all the small things that happen, as the surging capacities to affect and to be affected. Affective ethnography relies on the capacity to enact embodied knowing, while attending to data in motion ... and producing experiments and texts troubling with elusive and vulnerable knowledges they claim to represent.   (Gherardi, 2018, p. 13)

This ambitious agenda has moved some distance from Smith's institutional ethnography, and places considerable demands on the researcher. It also raises important ethical concerns, which apparently did not trouble Gherardi herself, and so it needs to be approached with considerable caution ethically. The next section considers the factors to be borne in mind in determining an appropriate approach to ethnographic research with teaching and learning enhancement in mind.

## Designing an Appropriate Model of Ethnographic Research

For the change agent wanting to utilize the idea of teaching and learning regimes in order to better plan and implement the change process in their institution, this discussion raises a number of design challenges related to attempts to improve understanding of the current context.

Ethnographic approaches are longitudinal in nature, and from a social practice and TLR approach this is preferable: practices are dynamic and emergent; the past conditions the present and the future emerges from that combination, as Smith recognized. To understand possible futures requires an understanding of backstories and the way they play upon the present context. Questions remain, however:

- Does the researcher always need to design the research in a longitudinal way?
- How far back does one need to go, and how extended does the research need to be, if the design is longitudinal? (The account above has examples ranging from three months to eight years.)
- How can one trace the many connections between the multiple and diverse elements linked in a relational network of practices? (Schäfer, 2017)

For any ethnography which describes itself as 'strategic' there needs to be a very specific goal, with design and activity decisions guided by that goal throughout the process. But the goal can be very general in nature, as in institutional ethnography, with its interest in uncovering structured disadvantage. Alternatively it can be very specific, as was the case in the Tesco example. Broad goals allow for an 'unfolding research design', which happens in institutional ethnography. Strategic ethnography is much closer to hypothesis-testing, with its underlying idea of 'provisional understandings' to be tested. But there is an underlying tension in contrasting strategic ethnography on the one hand and institutional ethnography on the other: the question is, whose goals does the research serve? Change agents may be tasked with implementing what is very often situated as a 'reform', 'harmonization', or 'enhancement' initiative, but those on the ground may be sceptical, seeing these as discursive tricks. They may suspect hidden agendas and question the motives of those proposing change. This may well have deleterious implications for the data-gathering process.

Some dimensions of the different accounts of ethnography described above can be discounted. The positioning of comparative ethnographies as *always* beneficial is simply wrong: if the focus of interest or the change agenda does not require a comparative method, there is no point in using one. As already noted, autoethnographic skills are complex and difficult: training, careful attention, and a considerable amount of time are needed to do it well.

On the other hand, the inclusion of some version of virtual ethnography will in almost all cases be necessary in research into higher education contexts. Similarly, the injunction to use video recording or other data capture techniques which are appropriate for a better understanding of the relationship between artefacts and the physical environment on the one hand and social practices on the other will also likely be beneficial, if ethically challenging. The kinds of documentary analysis championed by institutional ethnography will be significant for research into teaching and learning regimes in university contexts.

## Data collection methods with a sensibility for practice

Traditionally, in anthropology, ethnography relied on participant observation. The process was time-consuming and involved full immersion by the researcher in the culture of interest. This approach certainly accessed the recurrent practices and the discourses and background of that culture. Where the researcher or change agent is and has for some years been a member of the workgroup or department of interest, this approach remains possible. In most cases, however, it is simply impracticable. In social science generally, 'ethnography' has come to mean a mixed-methods approach involving interviews, focus groups, documentary analysis, and other tried and tested methods. For most researchers and change agents, data collection needs to be 'smart': practicable, efficient, and productive of rich, valuable data. These characteristics are not always prioritized in the literature on methodology. Such an approach needs to be able to access the significant moments of a teaching and learning regime and illuminate the likely reactions to and potential 'domestication' of any innovation or enhancement initiative.

The detailed analysis of often mundane but illuminative incidents is one way in which these goals can be achieved. The characteristics of any TLR's moments are often occluded in its day-to-day processes. Neither the participants—for whom the moments have become naturalized and therefore mainly invisible—nor the researcher can easily apprehend them. However, from time to time an incident occurs which foregrounds aspects of the moments—areas of previously submerged conflict, division, and discursive differences.

This is probably best illustrated by an example. A UK university proposed introducing the accreditation of prior *experiential* learning and giving applicants advanced standing (in other words, exempting them from certain courses) when they could demonstrate appropriate experiential learning. While many academics had no problem with giving advanced standing for *certified* learning, their perspective on the nature of knowledge and learning, and on what they were doing as academic teachers, led them to object to this proposal. For others, however, this was a progressive move which would widen access to HE and recognize the importance of life experience. These different ideological currents had hitherto gone unnoticed: this proposal unearthed them and made them visible (Trowler and Hinett, 1994).

Hillyard (2012, p. 13) suggests the need to develop an 'inclusive ethnography' which is theoretically and methodologically innovative, which uses new technologies for data collection borrowed from other areas of social science. Hillyard suggests it is important to go beyond now mundane data collection strategies such as interviews and focus groups. While they have their uses, they rely on respondents' honesty, recall, and ability to see what, for them, has become naturalized. Interviews and focus groups can offer only a partial account of that which is difficult or impossible to describe: they draw on discursive consciousness to depict practices that rely in part on practical consciousness (Giddens, 1984). Importantly, interviews and focus groups do not directly access practices. They are *accounts* of practices, though analysts sometimes assume that the accounts *are* the practices—a very dangerous assumption, as Kane et al. (2002) indicate. Where such mundane approaches are deployed, there is a need for innovative ways of eliciting data which is rich and which covers the taken-for-granted. Additionally, there may be a need to supplement them with other approaches.

Although, as noted in Chapter 2, several researchers and educational developers report that respondents can recognize the moments of the TLR in their own contexts, gathering data in a way which asks them directly to describe one or more moments can result in rather superficial data. This is neither efficient nor valuable. Coming at the issue 'sideways' allows respondents to consider scenarios or other situations in ways which denaturalize their own contexts, and thus yield useful data. 'Useful' here means data which expose the background of meaning and emotions, theories and discourses which are embedded in recurrent practices and social processes. Research techniques need to be able to uncover the multiple dimensions of social practice: saying, doing, relating, feeling, valuing.

Offering respondents evocative materials such as fictional vignettes, a series of statements about their situation, or other artefacts can be illuminative (Spalding and Phillips, 2007). A variation on this is to ask respondents to produce their own artefacts, such as drawings, photographs, sociograms, or other written or graphic material, with a subsequent in-depth interview or focus group. A further action-oriented refinement is to use such materials in Alain Touraine's *l' intervention sociologique* method set out in 1981. Here a three-stage approach is adopted: focus groups discuss their group actions or shared social experience, then other actors involved in the situation of interest are interviewed. Finally, hypotheses developed are presented back to focus groups in order to construct an analysis and consider implications. This approach, though time-consuming, can uncover the different moments of practices in an effective way (McDonald, 2002).

Projective techniques such as asking respondents to imagine themselves as another person or in an alternative situation help to remove them from the taken-for-granted nature of everyday knowledge. Another projective technique recommended by Gherardi (2012, p. 162) and Nicolini (2009, p. 209) is 'interviews with the double'. This is a form of projective interviewing involving asking interviewees to imagine themselves as 'other' in some way. Both authors argue that this technique is useful in uncovering tacit knowledge but needs to be combined with other approaches to more fully elicit such knowledge. Lisewski (2018, p. 71) used this approach in his research. He presented interviewees with this challenge:

> Imagine that you have a double who will have to replace you for a 'typical' class that you have to deliver tomorrow. Describe how you would best prepare your double to ensure that s/he is not unmasked. Please focus on how your double should teach (the process of teaching) to ensure that your practice-based knowing is best articulated to your students to ensure that they do not discover the switch.

Oblique questions come at the issue of interest from an angle, and the analysis of subsequent responses is usually inferential rather than direct. Questions such as 'was there ever a golden age in higher education?' can reveal underlying assumptions and educational ideologies. Taking a discourse analytical approach to the data from this technique can offer greater depth.

Focus groups' retrospective discussions of critical incidents can be very valuable. An example is the incident concerning the virtual meeting in the section below entitled 'Observant Participation with a Sensibility for Practice'. The social nature of such techniques can reveal differences of viewpoint, assumptions, and priorities across the different moments of the TLR concerned.

Looking beyond innovative techniques for data collection, the analyst can also use concepts and theory to augment the value of more traditional techniques. Wendy Sims-Schouten and Sarah Riley (2014) draw on the tradition of 'synthesized' discourse analysis. They analyse the interactive accomplishments of talk, locating these accounts in the socio-historical context of the discussion and so locating the situated nature of meaning-making through discursive accomplishments. What this means in practice is a way of 'listening' to real discourse in particular contexts which is attentive to three key components of that discourse:

1. The rhetorical strategies employed by participants in order to achieve their interactional goals, such as establishing their authority.
2. The wider discourses drawn on by participants to make sense of themselves, the topic of discussion, and its context; for example, discourses of 'impact' of research or of student employability.
3. How the material, embodied, and socio-structural/institutional contexts of participants provides legitimacy to the utterances of the speaker and the understandings of listener/s. For example, the resources and practice architectures of the institution in which the talk is located condition what is and is not 'sensible' to say and to argue.

What these authors are suggesting is that it is not necessary to 'trick out' the methodological techniques in use with new and fancier ones. A fuller understanding of the data can instead be achieved through making even everyday techniques, used alone, work harder through a deep infusion of conceptual analysis.

## Viewing both critical and mundane incidents with the sensibility for practice

Understanding how departments and workgroups engage with contentious issues can be particularly valuable in exposing the different moments of teaching and learning regimes. Difficult meetings, difficult encounters, and ongoing heated discussions expose lines of fissure, contrasting ideological undercurrents, different priorities, the operation of power, and the significance of intersubjective relationships. As Spaargaren, Lamers and Weenink write (2016, p. 10):

When things move smoothly, when practices can be enacted on the automatic pilot, and when performances are successful the way they have been done in the recent past, there is no need to shift to the 'cognitive driving modality'. Only when special occasions occur, for example when new objects or ideas are brought into the practice, or when practices collapse, are disturbed or de-routinised in ways that courses of future action are no longer innate to the practice and no longer 'obvious' for the practitioners, only then a temporary switch is being made to the discursive, reflexive, cognitive, conflict or consensus generating mode of doing and saying. The fact that social life is taken for granted most of the times [sic], does not preclude creativity, reflexivity and social innovation to play an important role in the process of social (re)production.

Observing and perhaps participating in a situation of the temporary break-down of routines, 'de-routinization', can be very illuminative, as Goffman's (1967) work on breakdowns in the interaction order shows very clearly. Such breakdowns cause participants to reflect on previously taken-for-granted behaviours and understandings, and so can be very revealing for the researcher.

## Gaining an external view

Understanding the nature and sources of complaints and appeals can some-times be valuable, as they disrupt the taken-for-granted and sometimes ask actors to evaluate recurrent practices. Administrators, human resource prac-titioners, and educational developers often bring an external view to depart-ments and workgroups. They are sometimes able to adopt a comparative standpoint that is less possible for insiders to take. Students who are studying across departments on combined degree schemes can themselves offer valu-able insights because of their different experiences. This is also true of ex-students, who, with the benefit of hindsight and the experience of a different context, can often see more clearly what is invisible to those inside.

## Observant participation with a sensibility for practice

Insider researchers have the advantage of being party to events, both critical or mundane, which give insight into the moments of the teaching and learning regimes to which they belong. Approaching these as a novice, as a legitimate but new insider, can be particularly illuminative because practices are not yet normalized for novices. Observing such events with the sensibility for practice can be very revealing. This is best illustrated by a real-life vignette, derived from observant participation undertaken by Trowler, Trowler, and Saunders (2018).

A UK university used the traditional structure of departmental meetings, which included representatives from each of the department's programmes giving feedback, with programme leaders responding to it. The other business of the meeting included verbal programme reports (including communicating actions taken in response to previous student feedback), new module validations, revisions to practices, and so on. Generally, student participation here was extremely limited or non-existent: students frequently had nothing to say even though they had received the agenda and paperwork in advance, and in most cases were invited to talk to programme leaders if anything needed clarification. Their student cohort feedback to the meeting tended to be very brief, with a short reply and a statement of intended actions in response, if any response was provided, from programme leaders. There was no interaction between the different representatives, commenting on each other's reports or on the actions taken since the last meeting.

Because industrial action by the university lecturers' union was being taken on the date of one of these meetings (and intermittently on subsequent dates), a decision was taken to change the format of the meeting. It would be held virtually, opening in advance of the lecturers' strike and remaining open for written contributions to an online forum for a number of weeks. This allowed striking members of staff to participate in the meeting without disrupting its business and without having to break the strike.

The nature of the contributions from students and staff changed entirely in this extended online format. Because programme reports had to be written— including written statements of actions taken as a result of student feedback— often within the extended period of the meeting itself, much more detail was available to students and they had longer to consider it. Large face-to-face meetings can be intimidating for students, even mature postgraduate students, and this is at least a partial explanation for their reticence to contribute in previous meetings. The online mode was beneficial in this respect: student representatives contributed much more fully, making very long reports ('like an essay') with elaborated requests for action and sometimes criticisms.

Students made useful comments about the actions taken in response to previous feedback from their programme and (for the first time ever) made comments about each other's reports. In short, the online format shifted the dynamic from one-way communication to a much more engaging, consultative, and egalitarian format with considerably extended contributions from all participants when compared to the face-to-face format.

The minutes of this meeting included many pages of discussion between student representatives and programme leaders, compared with two or three on average for the previous format. There was much more detail in both feedback and communication of subsequent actions, much more criticality as well as helpful suggestions on the part of students, and more action taken in response.

At a subsequent staff meeting, departmental staff considered whether this model would be a good one to continue with, replacing the traditional format even without the imperative of the strike. There were some positive comments but on the whole there was concern about a number of issues:

- some student comments were felt by some members of staff to be 'not appropriate';
- the discussion was 'quite public' and should be contained within a programme group;
- some of the issues leading to critical comments 'should be dealt with in advance';
- some student representatives, it was felt, 'didn't understand the purpose of the meeting'—a clear rubric needed to be provided;
- this format 'doesn't allow for the previous practice where students send me [a member of staff] loads [of feedback] and I filter out what is not relevant';
- more positively, one contribution said that this format highlighted mis-understandings in a way the previous format did not, providing an opportunity to address them.

The consensus was that a virtual discussion area could be opened before the meeting, but that the meeting should continue to take place on a face-to-face basis and only that formal meeting should be minuted.

At the departmental meeting subsequent to the virtual extended one, the Chair (who had also chaired the staff meeting) said that while it was preferable to have a face-to-face meeting, it might be desirable to use the virtual learning environment as a pre-meeting 'to allow the discussions in the *real* [emphasis mine] meeting to take into account pre-meeting discussions'. One rep replied that she had no strong views: the face-to-face meeting was helpful, and extra space would be helpful too. A second thought it was a good option for those not able to attend the meetings. A third agreed that busy people would find it helpful to take part in the pre-meeting.

Viewed through a practice-sensitive lens, these reactions highlighted concerns about shifting power relations between students and staff as well as issues of subjectivity. The more open format challenged established power relations and discursive control. The space for the student voice increased, and what students' representatives had to say became more extended and articulate. They engaged in a conversation, not telegraphic statements. The effects of power differentials had been mitigated to some extent through the online format—a result of the introduction of new artefacts and materiality into social practices, which, as SPT suggests, reshapes those practices. However, in later discussions among staff, concerns about shifts in power and legitimacy meant that possibilities began to be closed down and the space for a range of voices using an extended repertoire was reduced.

An alternative discursive style had been introduced by the online format, another aspect of reshaping through artefact change. It had allowed a more conversational style, more interactional and less formal than was the case in the physical meetings. Voices became dialogical, interactive, stimulating further ideas and discussion. This contrasted quite markedly with the sequential declarative discursive style of formal physical meetings. Again, this had a significant effect on the tone, tempo, and rhythms of the expression of student voice. Instead of solo players performing in sequence, the extended virtual event became more orchestral in nature. However, these discursive shifts were situated by some staff as 'not understanding or misapprehending the nature of the meeting and its purposes'.

Conventions of appropriateness were also challenged by the shift in modality. How appropriate it is thought to be for students to give voice to particular sorts of concerns is usually implicit, but in this vignette it was brought out and made explicit. Tacit assumptions about who can speak, and what they can and cannot speak about, became surfaced to some extent.

The vignette also illustrates the conservatism of social practices, their tendency to 'snap back' to previous practices, how site ontologies have resilience. Deliberative and sustained change is frequently difficult because practices have their own momentum. The vignette also foregrounds the limits of rhetoric about student voice and inclusiveness. This department was known as a particularly inclusive one, friendly to students and concerned with engaging them in the research and cultural life of the department. Yet many of the comments about the online meeting show the limits of this: the need to defend reputation, power, and control by effectively censoring or silencing the student voice where it threatened to be disruptive. The Chair's decision at the subsequent meeting was a wise one: anything more than this compromise would have created problems. It at least created a platform for further changes when possible.

From a change agent's perspective, the vignette indicates areas of sensitivity in this department. Innovations which appear to threaten existing power relations, require a ceding of control, and challenge current subjectivities are likely to meet resistance and revisionism. Opportunities for successful adoption, and adaptation, will be increased where there is a sensitivity to the 'delicate' moments in this particular teaching and learning regime.

## TLRs in a Nexus of Practices: The Limits of Ethnography

One of the challenges for research design, data collection, and robust analysis is the fact that social practices always operate within a nexus of other practices, sometimes geographically removed and often involving different projects and people. Again, this is best illustrated by an example. An English university had concerns that one particular ethnic group, and especially males from that ethnic group, were not benefiting as much as others from a year zero programme designed to prepare them for higher education in science. The roots of this problem seemed to lie not only, or even primarily, in the teaching and learning practices within that university. Instead they were partly located in home backgrounds and expectations and demands of family and community. They also partly lay in allocation procedures within schools which tended to route the students into BTEC qualifications rather than more academic ones, with potentially deleterious consequences for their skills in an academic environment. Ethnographic research into teaching and learning regimes within the university alone would not yield a full picture of the roots of this disadvantage; nor could they be precise in determining likely ameliorative actions, which may anyway best be taken in other locations.

To conclude: different flavours of ethnography are available, and only the researcher or change agent wishing to deploy that approach can construct a version appropriate to the specifics of their context, the resources available, and their areas of concern. But ethnography alone is not enough—an awareness of the nested and bundled nature of the practices being illuminated and the significance of phenomena outside the university walls, as well as an appreciation of structural conditioning of practices, are all significant. These need to infuse the design of the research. Most importantly, data analysis needs to be undertaken with a sensibility for practices.

# 4

# Teaching and Learning Regimes

## Moments in Transition

A teaching and learning regime consists of a family of practices informed by a set of moments specific to each regime. These moments and the practices they constitute represent local instantiations, applied to teaching and learning, of proto-practice reservoirs which 'feed' them. Within a TLR there will be tension both between and within the different moments because the streams from the reservoirs are drawn upon in an agentic and dynamic way. Contest as well as some elements of consensus characterize TLRs.

Despite the dynamism incorporated in this depiction of social reality, for some writers social practice theory is not well suited to understanding and explaining change issues. Because it views the social world as involving the recurrent accomplishment of different practices in a highly routinized way, practice theory is sometimes seen as being a theory of stasis rather than of change. Its critics suggest that it has an in-depth, well-developed explanation of why things remain the same, but in effect can only describe rather than explain why practices change over time. Nicolini (2012, p. 2) says this:

> the social world appears as a vast array or assemblage of performances made durable by being inscribed in human bodies and minds, objects and texts, and knotted together in such a way that the results of one performance become the resource for another.

This durability and entanglement of practices might be seen to create a problem for those interested in researching and influencing the enhancement of learning and teaching from a social practice perspective. Diamond (2013) recounts numerous case studies in which the immense inertia of sets of practices led to the collapse of communities and even civilizations. This happens especially when practices are displaced: where practices which worked in one context and time period are transposed to another for which they are in fact very inappropriate. Diamond is describing a kind of

*Accomplishing Change in Teaching and Learning Regimes: Higher Education and the Practice Sensibility.*
Paul Trowler, Oxford University Press (2020). © Paul Trowler. DOI: 10.1093/oso/9780198851714.001.0001

Darwinism based on practices rather than genes: maladaptive practices have disastrous results.

It is evident that practices in schools and in higher education contain the legacy of those from the nineteenth century and beyond, and from other places such as the church. However, they are overlaid by new practices in a kind of sedimentary process: in education, revolutionary change does not appear to happen easily. Rather, there is an agglomerative process which can mean that sets of practices from earlier periods sit uneasily alongside new ones. There are instances, though, as Diamond also recounts, of practice adaptation in new contexts. Old practices are repurposed and become well adapted: church-based robes, processions, and titles on display in graduation ceremonies offer huge marketing value, for example. So the problems (where they are such) of inertia and 'snapping back' to previous practices are not inevitable or always negative.

The kinds of displaced practices narrated by Diamond are, however, often significant. Practices from other times and places represent 'social ghosts' (Silva, 2014) which affect very different times and places. For example, notions of plagiarism and collaboration (see Chapter 3, 'Introduction'), Western notions of 'knowledge' and 'quality', and so on all have significant effects. These apparitions from the past and other places are barely visible, but they haunt us—remnants of history disturbing the present, or completely disrupting it, as the 'decolonizing the curriculum' movement has it.

An additional issue affecting SPT's ability to explain social change is the fact that some varieties of the social practice lens involve seeing a 'flat ontology'. This means that practices everywhere are of the same ontological nature and significance. Other than in detail, there is no effective difference between practices at a restaurant and those in the boardroom of a multinational corporation. This ontological perspective would seem to rule out the power of structural forces in conditioning, even forcing, change. In critiquing this idea, Spaargaren, Lamers, and Weenink (2016, p. 14) write:

> How can social scientists be so naïve to think that the worlds of multinationals and the unemployed, of global superpowers and small-island states, of Nobel prize winners and the illiterate or of dictators and prisoners, can be regarded as made from the same ground materials and as essentially the same? Are there no institutions (e.g. the Roman Catholic Church, museums, capitalism, the Olympic Games) of hundreds of years old that play a dominant role in the development of society as a whole?

A connected problem is the issue of agency. Reckwitz (2002) sees individual people as 'carriers' of practices, which can be interpreted as reducing them to the status of *Homo Sociologicus*—a conception of men and women who act out scripts without personal agency. Some interpretations of practice theory do appear to adopt this model, although Reckwitz himself suggests that both structuralist ('carrier') and agentic ('carrying out', adapting, performing) forces are at play. We saw in Chapter 2 that the distinction between proto-practice reservoirs and practice repertoires is one way of capturing this integration of structure and agency. I stressed in that discussion that the interpretation of practice theory being offered here does *not* rest on a flat ontology and is acutely cognizant of structural forces. I return to this issue later in the chapter.

It is certainly true that there is no well-developed theory of change in the practice literature, particularly in relation to higher education contexts. What this chapter does is to address each of the moments of TLRs in turn, offering examples of how each moment has changed in order to analyse the different ways in which change processes occur in a cluster of practices. To repeat, the moments being addressed are:

- power relations;
- implicit theories of teaching and learning;
- conventions of appropriateness;
- recurrent practices;
- tacit assumptions;
- codes of signification;
- discursive repertoires;
- subjectivities in interaction;
- materiality in interaction;
- backstories in process;
- regimes in interaction.

The chapter holds the inherent danger that, by treating the moments separately, it could reinforce a view that they can and should be disaggregated. This is only being done for analytical and illuminative purposes. It is worth reinforcing here that the separation of the different moments *is* only an analytical one, and that in the real world they are inseparably entangled, mutually infused. Likewise, it is possible to distinguish different categories within these eleven moments, though to consistently do so would be to artificially divide them. Five of the moments flow from proto-practice reservoirs: implicit theories of teaching and learning; conventions of appropriateness; tacit assumptions; codes of signification; discursive repertoires. These are not invented de novo in every context, but are locally reshaped versions of wider understandings, discourses, and ideologies. Together they constitute a set of understandings and meanings. A further five of the eleven describe characteristics of the local context, the individuals involved, and the broader practice architecture of operation. They are: power relations; subjectivities in interaction; materiality in interaction; backstories in process; and regimes in interaction. These are intimately connected to the reservoirs, but not in a direct way. For example, materiality in the form of the design of lecture theatres and the layout of classrooms instantiates implicit theories of teaching and learning. How power relations are shaped and operate is closely and mutually connected to discourse production and deployment.

'Recurrent practices' refers to repeated behaviours and the specific mix of social practices found in any TLR—its 'practice family'. A TLR, then, consists of multiple practices around teaching and learning performed by a workgroup over an extended period of time. The moments infuse all the practices performed by that workgroup. They lend them a certain consistency and regularity. However, as already noted, different currents flow into the TLR and so contest, division, and power-plays are at work too.

## Moments in Transition in South Africa

In this section of the chapter I want to wrap the discussion of the eleven moments of TLRs within an extended case study, situating them (as practice theory recommends) within a specific context. I do however add flavour to this central ingredient by appending illuminative examples from elsewhere. The main case is based on research I conducted ten years after the formal transition to the post-apartheid government in South Africa. I spent some days at the site of the research talking to on-site change agents. I conducted eighteen formal interviews, with the choice of interviewees purposively sampled. This research was not ethnographic in nature, being much lighter-touch than that.

In the research location there had been four previously distinct institutions of higher education within the same geographical and administrative area. The government at the time was pursuing a policy of merging institutions, including these four. Driving this policy was the problem of the legacy of apartheid: historically black institutions, including some institutes of technology, had been under-resourced, with some students underachieving; meanwhile, historically white institutions were comparatively well-resourced and highly selective, with more students achieving well. Rates of retention were dramatically different in the different kinds of institutions. The four previously separate universities discussed here represent both historically white institutions and historically black ones. The merger policy, then, was an attempt to 'lift all boats', addressing the background differences by mixing and learning from the best.

These four institutions therefore became one. However, this meant that there were multiple departments with the same disciplinary focus: for example law, sociology and physics. These also had to be merged, and decisions made about the location of the merged department, its management, and so on. Most importantly for the purposes of this chapter, decisions needed to be taken about the syllabus and about approaches to teaching and learning. The different departments had different specialisms and pedagogical foci; they did things in different ways and in some cases had very different understandings of priorities, just as social practice theory and the idea of TLRs would predict.

The new vice chancellor determined that in those cases where there were multiple departments there should be a period of discussion among them. A 'common curriculum' had to be agreed. Where teaching continued on more than one campus, the content must be the same and completely synchronized across the locations so that the student experience was the same regardless of location. This, of course, led to a difficult period of staff meetings, communication, and decision-making. Issues of power, subjectivities, underlying assumptions, and recurrent practices were foregrounded and exposed in this change process. The presence of different teaching and learning regimes in the same discipline moved from the tacitly understood to the explicit.

This was the point at which my research began. It was not concerned with the merger or its success, although those are interesting questions in themselves. For me the main interest was in seeing what happens when the different moments of teaching and learning regimes are exposed in this way. As Chapter 3 made clear, such disruptive times can be valuable: they can reveal a lot more than is evident from the routine enactment of practices. In South Africa, at that moment, elements of the proto-practice reservoirs were very distinctive and apparent. The 'transformation' agenda infused higher education, as elsewhere, in this case in the removal of the structural barriers for some ethnic groups that had been imposed by apartheid. The proto-practice values, ideologies, and discourses associated with this agenda were seen to be instantiated almost everywhere in the site of this research.

Below I recount short vignettes derived from the interviews I conducted, selected because they each illustrate one of the different moments in transition at the research site.

## Codes of signification

The first vignette concerns the codes of signification informing the views of a chemistry lecturer. It illustrates rather succinctly the codes concept: the nexus of denotative codes, associated connotations, evaluative responses, and flashes of emotion evoked by thinking about the different campuses, which were previously different institutions. The lecturer still refers to them, and thinks of them, as separate institutions in this interview, although by now they had been merged into one. For him, one of the other institutions in particular ('UniY') had much lower academic standards and a disregard for teaching. For him, thinking of that institution evoked images of a rather slapdash and careless approach to students and teaching issues. In the discussions about achieving a common curriculum in chemistry he had noticed that all the institutions were culturally very different, with UniY being 'miles behind us'. Codes of signification were also attached to this respondent's own institution, with its reported 'strong culture of teaching and learning', as opposed to UniY, which was seen to have 'no culture at all'.

For this chemistry lecturer the outcome of the common curriculum negotiations was a good one, with UniY adopting his campus's courses and the pedagogy being 'very very learner based'. He described setting up and delivering, with the help of postgraduate students, Saturday morning tutorials for his undergraduate students at which he gave extra help to 'the kids' who work through workbooks which he had developed. He contrasted this positivity with his own image of staff in UniY who would react negatively and pessimistically to such a proposal. He imagines their response: 'If we did that our students wouldn't come because our students are different from your students.'

The point here is not whether one institution was *actually* better than the other, or whether one really did have 'no culture at all'. Rather, it concerns the images, emotions, and other responses evoked by the image or concept of the previously different institutions and of the nature and character of their staff. Where change issues are concerned, these codes are important, even though they are 'only' perceptions, stereotypes, images. The Thomas theorem (Thomas and Thomas, 1928, pp. 571–2) states that 'if men [sic] define situations as real, they are real in their consequences'. Berger and Luckmann, in their classic 1967 work, make a much stronger argument: that reality is socially constructed from the hardened bricks of shared assumptions, beliefs, and symbolic structures sustained over generations. These are instantiated in stereotypes and prejudices in specific times and places. The apartheid regime itself, of course, offers a particularly stark example of this.

In one sense the Thomas theorem is obviously right. The history of humanity is littered with the effects of beliefs, particularly with the effects of strong beliefs that tolerated no opposition, or even minor variation or doubt. In another sense it is obviously wrong: it is not an aircraft passenger's belief in the laws of physics that keeps it aloft. The Thomas theorem clearly needs to be surrounded by caveats, but in the social world in general, and regarding change issues in particular, it does have some value.

From a practice perspective, where the focus is not on individual 'men' but on a set of practices of which codes of signification form an element with greater substance and wider spread than simply personal opinion, this theorem becomes more pertinent. It reads something like: 'Evoked responses are real in their effects.' The responses take the form of evaluative emotions: immediate judgements of value and status, of repulsion or attraction, of derision or admiration. To give an example from the UK context: I was involved in the quinquennial review of a department of English literature some years ago. There was a discussion about student involvement in assessment, student-to-student peer assessment in particular. The suggestion was immediately met with mirth, even derision. The very idea of using marking criteria to assess students' essays also evoked an immediate emotional response. One staff member said that marking criteria are to an English literature essay as an OXO cube is to a cow: reductive, desiccated, dead. But as Haidt (2012) argues, judgements hit us first in the form of gut reactions. Only later, given time and the need to do so, do we rationalize them into a developed argument, as that staff member did.

The Thomas theorem is significant in another way: in relation to what it is that evokes codes of signification. While change agents and leaders characterize the rationale for changes in one way, the interpretation of the 'real' motivations may be quite different, and codes of signification may be evoked in relation to that interpretation. For example, in an English university a compulsory '9 to 5 office hours' policy for academics was introduced, requiring them to be on the premises during these times. The rationale given by senior management was that staff's work–life balance was being eroded by the felt need to be available by email at all times. Thus, work outside the period

9am–5pm was discouraged by the policy. However, many academic staff felt that there was a subterranean motivation: to monitor and control academic staff better. Whichever interpretation was 'correct', the amended Thomas theorem tells us that the staff's reading would have important consequences.

Lee's (2010) case study of a Hong Kong university offers another example of the significance of subterranean motivations, this time exposing the veracity of their perceived nature:

> The [university management board] claimed that its decision to recommend to the Council to phase out the [associate degree] programmes was based on the financial difficulty of offering the programmes in a self-financing mode. The [management board] argued that the decision was an inevitable conclusion since it had exhausted all possible means to reduce the speed and magnitude of the funding withdrawal with the [Hong Kong] Government who remained unsympathetic and unwilling to provide any further assistance. The decision was also claimed to have been reached by consensus within the [management board], but there was no consultation with the College staff.
>
> In contrast, the College staff perceived that the management used the funding withdrawal as an opportunity to remove the [associate degree] which they considered to be low level work not commensurate with the status of a university. This view coincided with the responses given by members of the management interviewed in this study, who concurred that the subterranean reason for the decision was to shed the [associate degree] work to focus on degree, postgraduate and research work to better place the University in its objective of improving its international ranking. The management tried, through redefining the University's educational mission, to establish its goals as the organisational goals, which were in contradiction to the College staff's goals.   (Lee, 2010, p. 138)

So, codes of signification operate both in relation to 'front of stage' explanations and projected 'backstage' (Goffman, 1969), or subterranean, reasons and motivations. Once evoked, interpretations, reactions, and emotional responses among staff at the ground level are discussed, rehearsed, and often amplified 'under the stage': over coffee, in private, and in places where gossip is purveyed.

Outside of higher education, the way in which signs encapsulate and encode emotions, ideologies, and propaganda is particularly obvious. Politicians' names are reductive signs, evoking strong responses which are visceral in nature. The reasons for the reaction can be rationalized and explained, but the initial reaction is emotionally direct, more to do with feelings than with thought: 'Mrs Thatcher'; 'Donald Trump'; 'Che Guevara'—those signs with longevity becoming encoded, seemingly forever, on T-shirts and bumper stickers, in tattoos and internet memes, and in the 'linguistic landscape' generally (Caldwell, 2017). Advertising agencies no longer just try to make us buy products directly (they tend to use social media 'influencers' for this); instead, they want us to love brands through the codes of signification which encapsulate them: 'Vorsprung Durch Technik'; 'The Listening Bank'. Signifiers of aspirational lifestyles, with their associated products, are also heavily deployed, both in advertising and by some sponsored social influencers.

In recent years the 'fluent device', a character or slogan around which brands are built, has become heavily used. These are often animals which have associated catchphrases. In the UK currently, a nodding bulldog mascot called Churchill, who is 'dependable and very British', replies 'Oh yes' to questions about the quality of a company's insurance. Meanwhile a 'lovable and customer-focused' Eastern European meerkat called Aleksandr repeats the word 'simples' about comparing the market to make good choices. These are compressed signifiers with an important semiotic job to do for those that fund them.

Happily, the meerkat example brings this diversion from my core South African university case study back round to that country. The point has been to show how codes of signification permeate all aspects of our lives, including professional lives in higher education. For the 'common curriculum' policy being discussed here, they infused many aspects of the discussion. The illustrative vignette I chose for this section is just one of many available to illustrate the significance of these codes in the departmental discussions.

## Tacit assumptions

This vignette comes from a head of media studies. Part of what is interesting about it is how far this depiction is from a 'community of practice', with its shared assumptions and values, purposes, and discourse. Here, instead, we get the impression of multiple, often conflicting assumptions. Most of the time these are under the surface, tacit, but for the head of department with an overview they can be obvious because they are also real in their effects. He says, using a phrase that is probably true of most academic departments, 'there are more factions in my department than there are staff'. He notes how the factions shift dynamically according to the issue, but that underpinning this dynamism are very different, and usually tacit, assumptions about the nature of media studies, the purposes of higher education, and the priorities that academic staff and universities should have. He illustrates the point by talking about the links between his academic media studies department and the advertising industry. He quotes the Auden poem: 'Thou shalt not be on friendly terms/with guys in advertising firms.'

But he does not agree with Auden's sentiment. He has a friend in advertising, John, with whom he has a highly productive relationship in which they share ideas and offer constructive criticisms of each other's approaches to the media, sparking off each other. He contrasts that with academics in his department who 'can get so possessive and anal about ideas', and whose underpinning assumptions about the advertising industry and its relationship with academia are fundamentally different from his.

What is also apparent in this description are the linkages between different moments. To repeat the point made at the beginning of the chapter, they are being separated here only for analytical purposes. In a sense one could see 'industry', and in particular 'guys in advertising firms', as evoking flashes of emotional responses associated with the meaning such words carry, and so as representing codes of signification: signs in the semiotic sense. While that is true, there is something more going on here; these 'guys' are implicitly being held against a set of assumptions about the nature and purposes of higher education and are found wanting. Being on friendly terms with them is dangerous because it raises the spectre of an alternative vision of higher education, a pollution of its high purposes.

As with other moments of TLRs, tacit assumptions do not come from nowhere. They are tied to educational ideologies which condition the answers to key questions such as: 'What is higher education for?' 'Which is more important: research or teaching?' 'Are skills or propositional disciplinary knowledge more important?' 'Is talent distributed evenly across society?' 'What is meant by academic standards, and what is happening to them?' Individual backstories, institutional practice architectures, and other factors will also condition sets of assumptions in play and how they impact when changes are being considered.

## Conventions of appropriateness

This vignette is from a geography senior tutor talking about the use of tutorials led by graduate teaching assistants. It highlights very different conventions of appropriateness in the different campuses of the case study university concerning support for students and who should provide that support. In the rest of the interview with this respondent it was clear that the issue had simply not been on the agenda previously on his own campus: it hadn't needed to be because the convention was in place, invisible, uncontested. Yet the strength of feeling on the issue is evident in the interview: 'We believe *very* strongly in the tutorial.' This issue was a point of contention in the discussions about the common curriculum: his geography department was simply not willing to compromise on the issue. They felt that any attempt to remove the first year postgraduate-led tutorial would seriously undermine the quality of education because it was the only point at which first year undergraduate students got individual attention and support. The tutorial also had a diagnostic function, spotting weaknesses in individual students and helping to ameliorate them. On other campuses tutorials had been abolished 'as having only a nuisance value, being a luxury'.

Evident here again is the way in which the moments interweave in reality, as opposed to the analytical distinction drawn between them. The way in which this respondent positions the other campuses as signifying a lack of real concern with students and a greater concern for efficiency and an easy life is codified in the text; codes of signification are also in play.

This example shows how conventions of appropriateness are normalized within workgroups and simply become taken for granted, invisible. They illustrate how cultural characteristics are both constructed and enacted, involving both agency and structure. Though they had each previously existed as institutions within the relatively small South African higher education system, these different campuses had developed different conventions in their approach to teaching and learning, including within the same discipline. In Chapter 5 I discuss the genesis of teaching and learning regimes and whether, as much of the literature argues, disciplinary characteristics are especially significant in this. The different conventions of appropriateness which develop over time, such as the ones illustrated here, exemplify one way in which agency creates differences.

## Subjectivities in interaction

In this vignette from the interview with a chemistry lecturer in a department of physics and chemistry we see described the ways in which subjectivities 'hammer' each other (McDermott and Varenne, 1995, p. 326). A constant dynamic of self-positioning and attempting to position others occurs. In contrast to the so-called inseparability thesis (Sawyer, 2002) which argues that individual identities, subjectivities, are almost totally conditioned by the community of practice in which they operate, this vignette foregrounds the power of individual identity, an authoritarian personality seemingly immune to contextual shaping.

The interviewee describes how, in the discussions about the common curriculum, one individual dominated, and was determined to have his own way: 'He was a little Hitler.' He was also in a position of power because he was in charge of both physics and chemistry in a different department from the respondent, who describes him as 'obstructionist and political'. So much is this the case that the chemists in particular couldn't abide him and left for jobs elsewhere.

This difficult person's objectives were primarily to put a common curriculum into place that required complete uniformity across physics and chemistry. There had to be 'common tests, common curriculum, common everything'. In dealing with staff he displayed an authoritarian personality, immediately reporting upwards anyone who didn't agree with him and his philosophy of commonality. The staff in his department were in fear of him, and wouldn't discuss the common curriculum freely with other departments in the negotiations about it. The respondent expressed concern, both in the interview and to this 'little Hitler', that this attempt at complete standardization was logistically impossible and crushed lecturers' autonomy: from now on they would have to teach by the book in lock-step with other campuses. But the process and outcome of the discussions about the common curriculum in these disciplines was based on personality, 'the cut and thrust of personality', rather than logical analysis and reasonable discussion.

This respondent attributes the approach of the person discussed to their personality. We learn from this vignette that the person is obstructionist, 'political', an authoritarian manager, and an over-forceful advocate for a rigid interpretation of the common curriculum. There are, however, other explanations for these reported characteristics, including explanations concerning management practices, the importance of hierarchies, the perceived need for 'strong leadership' in a time of turbulence, and perhaps the pervasive influence of managerialist ideology. Again, that individual had become a signifier for a kind of intractable personality disorder in the mind of this respondent. Whether or not that was true is really only important when testing the inseparability thesis. As the Thomas theorem predicts, the perception of the person held by academic staff was real in its effects: several members of staff resigned.

## Recurrent practices

In this small vignette we hear from a physics lecturer and head of department (not the department referred to above) talking about her attempt to switch from a didactic to a more student-centred approach. Essentially, this person was trying to challenge and change the heavily teacher-centred, chalk-and-talk approach previously adopted in her department. The fact that she was doing so again demonstrates individual agency (in contrast to the *Homo Sociologicus* 'carrier' idea). However, a question asked by her colleagues—'why aren't you doing your work as a lecturer?'—suggests that the task would be an uphill one. Not only was she challenging entrenched recurrent practices, but she was trying to change associated conventions of appropriateness—in this case, what it means to be a physics lecturer.

In the interview she noted that the transformation agenda in South Africa, aimed at righting the wrongs of apartheid, meant there were now many more under-prepared African students entering higher education. Classes were much bigger and the students needed more support than had previously been the case. She saw it as part of her task to try to address this, by challenging the recurrent practices in teaching physics which had been developed at a time of smaller classes and highly qualified, well-prepared students. She had considered setting up a foundation year to help prepare the students better, but had rejected that in favour of something 'a bit more radical': transforming the way physics is taught. She worked to transform the pedagogical approach from a transmissive one, in which the students are passive and the lecturer delivers the material, to one where students engage with carefully structured tasks and discuss them with each other and with the tutor. This was a move to a student-centred approach, which she felt would help the less prepared students. She wanted them to emulate the thought processes that physicists go through in interacting with difficult concepts, to think like physicists from the beginning. She wasn't afraid of students 'getting things wrong or being stuck', because this would help them to see where the limits of their understanding lay, and they could get help to stretch them.

The innovation was successful: pass rates went up. But only some modules were taught in this new, innovative way. The old recurrent practices still remained there, 'and other physicists looked at you and said "why aren't you doing your work as a lecturer?"'

At work here, again, are contrasting educational ideologies, part of the structural proto-practice reservoirs from which local practices draw their choreography. In Trowler (1998) I reported my analysis of the literature on educational ideologies which had identified very common conclusions from research on ideologies that work in educational contexts (the literature mostly concerned schools) but which used very different names to describe them. Four 'currents' of ideology were identified by most authors and were also apparent in my ethnographic study. My terms for these were:

- 'enterprise', which prioritizes promoting employability in students, advocates resourcing STEM subjects at the expense of others, promotes a curriculum aimed at performativity and skills development, and sees education as concerned with improving national economic performance;
- 'traditionalism', which sees induction into the discipline and the development of the discipline as most important in higher education, with academics' roles primarily involving the creation of new disciplinary knowledge and nurturing the next generation of disciplinary specialists;
- 'progressivism', which focuses on the development of students' analytical and critical skills, their minds and their appreciation of culture, as well as their ability to cope with a changing world;
- 'social reconstructionism', rarely found in schools but prevalent in universities, and which focuses on critiquing the status quo and structural disadvantage and promoting alternative views of the world and ways of changing it.

Evident in the short vignette above about tensions around recurrent practices in teaching physics is the expression of contrasting ideological currents. The innovative head of department was expressing elements of progressivism, focusing on students' learning and the processes in which they engaged while tackling sometimes difficult material. Her colleagues, however, were expressing more traditionalist priorities, focusing less on the students and more on the transmission of disciplinary content from experts to novices. These ideological currents underpin and partly explain recurrent practices and the challenge to them from my interviewee. To repeat: they are structural in nature—'reservoirs' of values, concepts, priorities, and discourses which individuals draw on in their everyday interactions, creating 'repertoires' (Bernstein, 1999). Neither the head of department nor her colleagues should be described as 'progressivists' or 'traditionalists'. Rather, in this context and over this issue they were articulating elements of these different ideological currents which in a sense flowed through them. Fanghanel expresses this in terms of 'filtering' such currents: they '"colour" the way academics conceive of and approach teaching and learning in higher education' (Fanghanel, 2009b, p. 565).

## Implicit theories of teaching and learning

Here, another physics lecturer at a different campus reflects on the inappropriateness of the implicit theories of teaching and learning brought to a South African context by someone from another country. As noted above, South African lecturers are very aware of the significance of apartheid's legacy for disadvantaged students. The lecturers there were very knowledgeable about the ANC government's 'transformation' agenda which sought to address that legacy and saw that as part of their role, in addition to their educative function. In this context, notions of absolute standards, seen from a North American perspective, do not apply in the same way. This respondent also points out an example of the assumptions built into textbooks.

He recounts how a newly appointed theoretical physicist, who came from the USA, imported with him a belief in assiduously maintaining standards. His view was that the department should rigorously select only high quality students and then 'leave them to sink or swim'. He saw himself as the defender of standards, a solitary figure among staff who had little or no concern with maintaining the quality of work that students produced, with achieving 'excellence'.

It quickly became clear to the respondent that the North American situation from which this person came had left him ignorant of the difficulties faced by particular groups in South Africa and the structural legacies of the apartheid regime. Native South Africans tended to bring this understanding to the mix of any discussion about quality and standards, being acutely aware of how more limited understandings can result in exclusions and failures structured by ethnicity, class, and other intersectional factors.

With a little re-education, the American changed his position and developed a more nuanced understanding of the issues of standards and excellence. He also became aware, as the other lecturers also were, of the ethnocentric character of workbooks, and how, again, this worked against the disadvantaged. One instance was a workbook's example of the walls of an igloo to make points about the conduction of heat: 'Many of our black students didn't know what an igloo was!' So they eradicated such culturally based tasks and illustrations. Slowly the new lecturer divested himself of his implicit theories of teaching and learning and acquired new ones. His previously implicit theories had been exposed to the sharp South African light and been found wanting. He rose to the challenge.

Implicit theories of teaching and learning are occasionally made explicit, but are more often evident in comments and asides made by lecturers and by the flow of discussions in staff meetings. Very often, contention on a particular topic derives from contrasting theories, and again educational ideologies are frequently at the root of these differences. The didacticism of the traditionalist ideology contrasts strongly with the student-focused nature of progressivism. When the prioritization of skills, entrepreneurialism, and capabilities within enterprise ideology rubs up against expressions of social reconstructionism in the transformation agenda, or in the decolonialism movement, the arguments begin.

## Discursive repertoires

This vignette concerns a senior academic in a department of media studies at one of the merged university campuses talking about the common curriculum. The interesting aspect for our purposes here is the discursive repertoires used by this respondent, and the effect of some of her tacit assumptions and codes of signification on the change process. Even a brief account of some of these repertoires gives some indication of why 'they don't answer our letters'.

Like the earlier example (codes of signification), this respondent thought there were very poor academic standards at UniY. She considered that the staff there were competent in teaching media studies, but not much else. She describes how 'when we came to take over' there was the 'opportunity to re-write and regularise what they were doing', correcting what she described as 'a nightmare'. She recounts how 'we left the most difficult characters out of the negotiations' about the common curriculum. This was because 'I didn't have the time or patience or energy to take those people with me'.

She sadly recounts how the process on paper had been fairly straightforward, streamlining, regularizing, and revalidating courses which previously she described as a hodgepodge in terms of credit value and content. But on the ground, in reality, people continued to argue over everything and resist her rationalized scheme. She found that after her intervention there was a lack of communication with these recalcitrant lecturers: 'they don't answer our letters.' Even though in the planning document there are common outcomes and a high degree of systematization, there still was no common grading system in place. The effects of her approach and her deployment of discursive repertoires made it unlikely that one would easily be agreed.

It is interesting in the interview how the respondent switches between 'we' and 'I' when describing actions taken. It is also revealing that the tacit assumptions about other campuses and the staff on them become instantiated in the discursive repertoires used and in actions taken. The phrase 'when we came to take over' is indexical of a definition of the situation and of underlying values and assumptions. Discourse, assumptions, theories, and practices are intertwined in ways which can be invisible to the individual actor and the workgroups they inhabit but which have significant implications for processes and outcomes. They evoke responses in others which may be far from the intentions of the speaker or writer.

Discursive repertoires are intimately connected to ideologies. Neo-liberal ideology and its handmaiden, new managerialism, with their commodified view of knowledge and skills, are ideological currents that give rise to specific repertoires around teaching and learning. Using the 'delivery' metaphor (Reynolds and Saunders, 1987), for example, when discussing the curriculum or a course situates the acquisition of knowledge in the same category as online shopping. Talk of the higher education 'market', students as 'consumers', 'service standards', and the rest both reflect ideological assumptions and can reinforce a way of thinking about higher education. Just as important are the absences: what is *not* said and what alternative conceptualizations are marginalized and difficult or impossible to articulate.

While some theorists prioritize discourse in their studies and in their depiction of the nature of social reality, social practice theorists tend to see it as simply one of a number of characteristics of practices. For me, discourse refers to textual production as a social practice conditioned by social structures, including proto-practice reservoirs. This perspective places the emphasis on the structurally conditioned character of text. 'Structure' in this case means properties which lend coherence and relative permanence to social practices such as the production of text in different times and locales (Giddens, 1984). 'Text', by contrast, is the written, spoken, or visual product of communicative intent. Of course, there is no text without discourse and no discourse without text: discourse is articulated in text and text is structurally conditioned (Trowler, 2001; 2010). Any discourse has textual concomitants derived from relatively coherent 'discursive repertoires', the detailed characteristics of textual production, the denotative and connotative codes appealed to, and the specific systems of representation used. To repeat, in reality repertoires are entangled with codes of signification, implicit theories of teaching and learning, and other moments of TLRs.

In this interview the roots of the text clearly showed there is a rational–purposive, top-down, managerialist frame of reference at work, together with its associated values and priorities.

## Power relations

In this vignette the head of the law department at one of the campuses talks about the deployment of various forms of power as different aspects of the common curriculum were negotiated. There were three law-teaching campuses and he was very keen to ensure that any physical centralization of a unified law department should go to his location: this outcome 'would be best for us'. Meanwhile, law lecturers on the other two campuses wanted to stay where they were (the distances concerned were not inconsiderable). The head of department was successful in persuading the university to let his department become the location for law degrees; the other lecturers had to move to that campus.

He achieved this by arguing strongly that law in the newly merged institution should be associated with the tradition established in his department. They had established a 'brand', a market presence, and a strong reputation. In part this was based on their beautiful historical buildings as well as some which had recently been built, carefully designed by architectural consultants to retain the style of historical buildings. A new law library had been constructed. By contrast, on the other campuses, law had few resources and very limited library facilities. Staff on his campus had access to online databases and other valuable materials, while for others this access was patchy.

In addition, his department was able to persuade the university because it included persuasive personalities who were able to take the initiative. They pushed, quite aggressively, for the retention of their particular teaching and research interests in any agreed common curriculum. They had the power to achieve their desires because they had high status in the discipline and the profession. The respondent gave an example of a member of staff who was on the South African Human Rights Commission. As a result human rights was emphasized very strongly in their curriculum, and continued to appear in the common curriculum. It was hard for less prestigious academics to argue against such people, especially with sometimes domineering subjectivities. In the respondent's words, 'it was power plays, horse trading', with one dominant player taking the lead; these were strong personalities 'who feel they own their specialisms and tend to dominate'. Coming from a position of established authority, they were able to intimidate people and effectively say 'we've always done it like this, and we will continue to do so'. The respondent's department also had more students than the others, so they had weight of numbers. In negotiations they were able to use their substantial and high-quality first year intake as a negotiating tactic.

This account exposes numerous facets of power being played out. *Systemic* power is in play here (Haugaard, 2010, p. 425), the conferring of differential power at the disposal of agents which structures the possibilities for action. This includes Foucault's 'regime of truth' (1979, p. 47), the taken-for-granted order of things which 'naturally' confers relative advantage and disadvantage. There is also *constitutive* power—that aspect of power which shapes individuals, the way they relate, and the nature of the social world. Decisions are not made in the abstract but within systemic relations of power, and so individuals and groups are able to secure outcomes that operate in their interests more easily than others (Lukes, 2005, p. 19). This vignette also exposes various resources being mobilized in order to achieve this, including physical infrastructure, the ability to threaten and intimidate, and the use of relative success (itself founded on differential power and resources) to achieve the preferred outcome of one group. The systemic context has conditioned the relative constitutional power of the groups involved in the common curriculum discussions. In this instance the structures conditioning practices are not just virtual: they are palpable, concrete, material. It is probably not necessary to be explicit about how the legacy of apartheid had structured inequalities which led to the power differentials illustrated here, or about whether this respondent's previously separate institution was historically white or historically black, separated for different intakes of racial profiles under the apartheid regime. These are fairly obvious.

## Materiality in interaction

The respondents in this study did not explicitly address the significance of artefacts in the interaction between people, practices, and the physical world, though of course it is evident in the vignette immediately above. However, not only does this TLR moment underpin the practices recurrently performed but, and perhaps especially, they are significant as practices transitioned under the 'shove' they had received from the merger and the common curriculum initiative. Certainly, the significance of the socio-material had become more exposed in this transition period.

The campuses themselves remained as physical manifestations of apartheid: the quality of the buildings; the presence or absence of trees, grass, and open spaces; the facilities available to students and staff. These and many other factors in the physical world carried codes of signification about relative status, significance, and power, and they sometimes actually conferred power. These characteristics of the built environment, the internal architectural features, the quality of materials, and the level of maintenance set the stage for the performance of learning and teaching practices and conditioned the moments of the different teaching and learning regimes in significant ways.

These material contrasts were exposed very starkly by the merger, which meant that staff and students began to travel between the different campuses and could see, usually for the first time, the differences in the material worlds. The common curriculum initiative brought the issue right to the forefront of attention: decisions had to be made about where newly merged departments would be located, as well as about curricular issues. The vignette immediately above from the head of the law department captures this well. The 'lovely library', the well-loved historical buildings, the access to databases and 'online stuff' which was lacking in the other campus that taught law are all very significant. They condition the subjectivities of staff and students; they carry codes of signification; they shape assumptions about what it is to study law and what the future might hold as a result. They also embody theories about how teaching and learning happens, making it much easier to do it in one way rather than another: they scaffold and structure practice dispositions. Practices on the other campus, lacking all of these things and presumably the money to bring in 'architectural consultants', were also conditioned by materiality, but in a way which was not to the benefit of the humans studying, living, and working there.

Of course, these stark differences were legacies of the structured inequalities under apartheid, but an apartheid regime is not needed for this to happen; everywhere in the world materiality reflects and sustains structured inequality:

> Humans, and what they take to be their learning and social processes, do not float, distinct, in container-like contexts of education, such as classrooms or community sites, that can be conceptualised and dismissed as simply a wash of material stuff and spaces. The things that assemble these contexts, and incidentally the actions and bodies including human ones that are part of these assemblages, are continuously acting upon each other to bring forth and distribute, as well as to obscure and deny, knowledge.
>
> (Fenwick, Edwards, and Sawchuck, 2011, p. vii)

## Backstories in process

The vignette from the law academic and the discussion above also illustrate vividly the significance of backstories: the social ghosts from other times and places which haunt the present and help shape it. Interactions and negoti-ations about the merger and the common curriculum did not take place de novo, somehow emerging in a newly blown bubble. The participants brought with them not only their current practices embodying the different moments, but also their histories and their organizational sagas (Clark, 1972; 1973). Beyond that, all of the South African participants carried a very powerful *national* backstory. It is a story about the oppression of black people and others within the apartheid regime, the dominance then of the Afrikaner subgroup politically, the significance of different languages, the changes since the transition to an ANC government, the presidency of Nelson Man-dela, the transformation agenda in higher education, and the rest. Behind all that, of course, was the legacy of colonialism. It was evident in the languages spoken, the different traditions across types of university, and the curricula offered by each.

At the time there was a strange contradiction about South Africa. This was a country with eleven official languages, with multiple ethnicities varying in mix according to region, and with significant political differences which had almost resulted in violent civil war in the early 1990s. Yet at the same time there was a strong and shared national backstory, albeit with different 'takes'. 'The struggle' (against apartheid) still loomed large, and stories about individ-uals and institutions in that struggle affected discourses, subjectivities, and decisions in the present day in very important ways. In South Africa it was possible to see writ large what is true for other places writ small: the power of stories, perceptions, and emotions about the past to be centrally involved in shaping the present.

## Regimes in interaction

Clearly this merger situation created a forced encounter between different teaching and learning regimes. This is quite unusual, although so-called learning organizations sometimes look to situations analogous to their own in order to get a better perspective on what alternative practices are possible and perhaps preferable. What is evident from this case study is not only the significance of the interaction between different manifestations of the 'same' discipline on different campuses, but the broader sets of practices conditioned by national policy agendas. The transformation agenda had implications for practices around the recruitment and promotion of staff, for example. Affirmative action meant that where there were two equally qualified candi-dates, preference should be given to the candidate from a 'designated group':

women, people with disabilities, and people classed as black, coloured, or Indian under apartheid. For designated staff in particular, promotion decisions were affected by considering whether candidates should be allowed to 'grow into' their new position, having previously been held back by structural inequalities. Promoting diversity on committees and in staff profiles became highly significant. This was a radical change in practice from the situation of rigorously enforced separation leading to monochrome geographical areas, institutions, public bodies, committees, and marriages.

In this context, then, the 'regimes in interaction' moment is highly significant: it takes the focus beyond the TLRs involved, the curriculum-delivery workgroups in each of the campuses, and highlights the significance for the TLR of interactions at its borders and the infusion of priorities and issues from outside them. It helps the analyst understand the dynamism and turbulence, the conflicts and tensions around learning and teaching within a workgroup. These interactions shape the other moments in a TLR and enable and constrain what it does, how it does it, and how effective it is. They also condition the change process, delimiting what is possible, what might work, and what definitely will not.

Because of its significance for change processes and the enhancement of learning and teaching, the next sections discuss this moment further, examining in greater detail the interactions of practices within and by a TLR. Conceptually the ideas are elaborated and substantively they are illustrated by two more case studies, from Krejsler and Turner.

## TLRs as Open, Natural Systems: Nested Practices

The South African case study above is based on relatively limited data using a research design which does not, in fact, conform to the ideal of practice-sensitive ethnographic research. Because of its focus on merging departments in a merging institution and the imposition of the common curriculum, wider issues and influences can only be inferred, though naturally I talked at length with South Africans about these issues. It could also be argued that South Africa is a very special case. I would not agree. To repeat: the South African example merely shows more distinctly characteristics of the social world that exist everywhere.

In this section I want to zoom out from the detail of the moments in a particular context—the merging institution—and interrogate the significance of the nested practices in universities. As Chapter 2 discussed, practices are always bundled and nested within larger systems of practices. This means that horizontally different sets of practices rub up against each other at the same time and in the same place, influencing each other in sometimes unpredictable ways. This is bundling. Meanwhile there is vertical overlap, so that social practices at ground level are influenced by more structural factors, including static or dynamic proto-practice reservoirs. This is nesting, and it is the focus of the current section.

The next case study moves to a very different context and focuses on the national level more than the South African example. It helps to show how teaching and learning regimes constitute open, natural systems, which are permeable to these outside influences and are dynamic in nature. It demonstrates how there is conflict and tension within as well as openness to forces from without. The case study concerns 'reform' in the Danish university system and the transition of discourses within it. It is taken from Krejsler (2006).

Krejsler shows how, in Denmark, the meaning of 'university' and research agendas are increasingly situated in the discursive universe of the language of the knowledge economy. He tracks the transition from a vanishing Humboldtian university discourse towards a strengthening market and efficiency-oriented university discourse. As in the UK, universities in Denmark became self-owned, increasing their freedom, rhetorically at least, to operate in a research and education 'market'. This process, though, is not one-way: the title of Krejsler's article begins with the phrase 'discursive battles', and discursive repertoires and discourses are rarely hegemonic. Rather, they are the subject of contestation.

By 'Humboldtian' discourse, Krejsler broadly means textual production generated from a set of ideas including that academics should be free to research and teach truth and knowledge as they see fit. They do this within a collegial community of peers, with students free to learn independently and grow into autonomous, critical people. By contrast, a market and efficiency-oriented university discourse refers to textual production generated from a concern with rigorous leadership, efficient use of resources, the search for competitive advantage in an education market, and performativity-oriented research and teaching. Krejsler argues that 'this discourse seems to have fundamentally changed how one can think and talk about University, academics and research' (p. 215).

Krejsler does not illustrate with examples the discursive repertoires rooted in the two discourses that he identifies. Nor does he offer examples of the significance of the change from one discourse to another at the departmental or workgroup level, despite conducting interviews on this topic within two departments at each of three universities in Denmark. His article is pitched at a global and national level, where substantive details are given. However, the strength of his article lies in how he maps the foundations of the *discursive change* at those levels. This is of interest for the purposes of this book because it concerns how the moments of teaching and learning regimes shift and morph, and how the local is intimately connected to macro-level structural forces; how they are nested in other practices and structures.

Krejsler maps the generative forces behind discursive change towards a market and efficiency-oriented university discourse at the national and multi-national levels. The process of unifying strategies and harmonization within Europe (the Bologna process); the integration of universities into national knowledge economy strategies; and the guiding hand of the World Trade Organization, the Organisation for Economic Co-Operation and Development, and other global actors have combined to construct and propagate a discursive universe of knowledge economy language which permeates the university. Meanwhile, Danish legislative changes had their own effects. In 2003 the University Act was passed. The effect of this was to frame

> academic freedom/autonomy as an entity that university management announces within the framework of [a] university's strategic key areas and its development contract with the national ministry in order to come to grips with the demands of an increasingly competitive global market.
>
> (Krejsler, 2006, p. 211)

This was only one of a number of legislative acts described by Krejsler. Underpinning them was an ideology of neo-liberalism, with its new right emphasis on the hidden hand of the market, individualism, competitiveness, and free enterprise. Intimately linked to that ideology are axioms of New Public Management (NPM), a species of managerialism which emphasizes the need for professional managers to deploy the NPM toolbox of target-setting, contract-giving, evaluative monitoring, contract-limiting, results-measuring. These linked ideologies, sustained and propagated by global organizational structures together with their associated discourses can permeate all aspects of social life, service provision, and organizations.

In a decades-long career in higher education, I have been acutely aware of this permeation across different areas of my work contexts. Phrases such as 'line manager', 'curriculum delivery', and 'the higher education market', once unknown to academics, are now part of standard discourse and go largely unquestioned. Unknown too were annual performance reviews and the quantification and comparative analysis of nearly every aspect of academic practice. Metrics now permeate job applications and referees' letters as well as personal web pages. Dashboards and datasets are found everywhere. Altmetric, Academia.edu's analytics, Web of Science, and the H index are part of everyday academic conversation around the globe.

Health services, social work, and education are among those most clearly affected. While national and global in origin, neo-liberal ideology and discourse soaks into the fabric of daily professional life:

> This does not mean that there are not a host of other discourses that continually play roles in contesting what is currently dominant. It means, furthermore, that individuals become individuals by subjecting themselves to various discourses. And each such discourse allows individuals to fill out particular subject positions, which altogether gives different strategic scopes of action. In a simplified way the author of this article could be said to be defined as an individual and dispose of a particular strategic space as a result of the positions that he inhabits in a number of discourses: an urban mid-age late-modern man in a gender discourse, a middle-class ethnic majority Dane in a class discourse, a predominantly post-structuralist researcher in a university discourse, an activist for pluralism in a diversity discourse and so forth.    (Krejsler, 2006, p. 211)

What we can say about nested practices from this example is as follows. First, while 'nesting' refers to different levels of practices, it also points to structural forces which condition lower-level practices as well as permeating those at higher levels. In this case, the significant structural factor is neo-liberal ideology—now firmly part of proto-practice reservoirs globally. It shapes discourses, behaviours, priorities, understandings, and responses in different contexts and in relation to different issues. The example shows, I think, the impoverished nature of the idea of a 'flat ontology'.

Secondly, though, the example also demonstrates the continuation of dynamism and conflict. Despite the hierarchically nested nature of practices and the conditioning power of structural forces, this struggle continues and the hegemony of one set of practices or of one moment within a practice is never fully achieved (Trowler, 2001; 2010).

A third point to note is the significance of institutions in this case study. Social practice theory in general tends to occlude the importance of relatively permanent institutions such as legislative bodies, the OECD, the constitutive organizations of the European Union, the World Trade Organization, and so on. Its focus has tended to be on the dining table, the kitchen, energy consumption at the domestic level, and other 'zoomed in' contexts. Yet these organizations are very significant in shaping practices; they give arms and legs to ideologies, sustaining and nourishing them, weaponizing them. The end result is shifting practices as local contexts respond, often reluctantly and defiantly, to the changed circumstances imposed upon them and to reshaped proto-practice reservoirs. One might think of Greece struggling under the stringencies imposed upon it by European Union leaders, the European Central Bank, and the International Monetary Fund as it fell into economic crisis and debt. Again: so much for the flat ontology.

This Danish vignette vividly illustrates what Giddens was talking about when discussing social structures as involving rules and resources. These have both a virtual and a 'real' existence. The virtual involves ideologies and sets of understandings. The real includes powerful organizations which set rules and impose sanctions, while sometimes offering rewards. Practices on the ground are constrained both by the operation of power and of discourse. They are shaped and reshaped, constituted and reconstituted by forces flowing from proto-practice reservoirs. Performances are repeated, but re-enactments shift in response to the pressures and scaffolding generated by enmeshed practices, by materiality, and by forces from above.

The next section switches from a focus on vertical nesting to horizontal practice bundles.

## TLRs as Open, Natural Systems: Bundled Practices

There is always a temptation for the change agent or researcher to focus only on the practice or practices that they are interested in. How do graphic design teachers go about the business of teaching graphic design? How do educational developers go about their business of improving standards in teaching and learning in the university? This is entirely understandable, and in fact the concept of TLRs encourages it by foregrounding teaching and learning practices, occluding surrounding ones. However, practices and sets of practices are always enmeshed with other practices, usually in an interdependent way—in 'ecologies of practice' (Kemmis et al., 2013)—sometimes in tension or even in contradictory ways. They are bundled, interwoven, enmeshed, mutually permeating. Teaching graphic design or undertaking professional development will always happen alongside researching, committee work, seeking funding, leading, following, and a host of other situated practices. Some practice interactions are more generative of dynamism than others, more firmly interwoven, more productive of tensions and contradictions, or more integrative. Whatever the case, there will always be a complex of practices, a bundle. The precise nature of this bundle, the characteristics of the enmeshing, is one reason why context matters: how they work together affects in very specific ways how each of them operates.

This way of seeing is difficult to operationalize, to research, and to conceptualize. Understanding and describing the precise nature of a particular constellation of practices in any context represents quite a challenge. As noted in Chapter 2, Kemmis and Mahon (2017) have tried to offer some tools in this task in their discussion of practice architectures. Their account of organizational frameworks is operationalized in an insider ethnographically informed case study by Turner (2018). She gathered multiple types of data about teaching and learning practices and their development in three departments within a research-intensive institution. Turner was interested in understanding the practice landscapes in each of the three sites. She wanted to uncover their practice architectures in order to understand how the development of teaching and learning practice was affected by the bundling of other practices in each of the three. Behind this agenda lay the desire to improve the effectiveness of attempts to develop learning and teaching practice in higher education.

Turner offers a detailed depiction of each of the three departments. She uses the Kemmis and Mahon architecture framework, with their notion of the projects of practice (the multiple foci of workgroup efforts) as well as the moments of TLRs. The former was used to depict the enmeshed nature of the bundling, the latter to unpick the differences in the nature of the teaching and learning practices in each of the three departments. She shows how practices such as those associated with research, leading, and student learning enable and constrain aspects of the TLR in quite different ways in the different departments. In this way she paints detail into the Kemmis and Mahon theory in a full-colour, engaging way. Her depictions would resonate with anyone with experience in higher education virtually anywhere in the world, but they are accounts thoroughly infused with concepts and theory. For that reason, they are far more powerful than only simple depictions. She gives a vivid account and explanation of the complex interplay of practitioners, practices, architectures, and ecologies of practices and the way they create, sustain, or close off pathways of educational development.

It is worth quoting from Turner's conclusions about the enmeshed nature of practices and the significance of practice architectures for TLRs:

> Outside teaching and learning practice at these sites were other practices that shaped it in meaningful ways. Practices of influence across all three departments were those of student learning, research, departmental leadership, and disciplinary practice. Additionally, industry practice was seen to influence in department 3 [which was vocationally-oriented]. Consistent with findings from compulsory education, these practices gave and took energy, shaping teaching and learning practice in each department in unique ways... mediated often by the project of practice foregrounded at the site.
>
> (Turner, 2018, p. 153)

Both internal dynamics and external pressures greatly influenced how educational development could best proceed in each case. In the first department, practice traditions were just being formed as this new department came together, opening opportunities for a collective definition of the project of practice and the slowly solidifying recurrent practices around that. In the second department, change was characteristically slow, involving tensions and the need to resolve conflicts. Changes within the disciplinary practices were significant here as they took the digital turn, but progress verged on the glacial because of internal contradictions within the TLR. In the third department the enhancement of practice was an ongoing and iterative process arising from the traditions of learning and teaching development at the site, but was constantly under the influence of both student learning practices and industry practices in particular.

As well as the enabling and constraining features of the enmeshed bundles of practices, the enactment of practice itself within the departments influenced the architecture in an iterative way. The direction of influence was not just from the practice architecture to the teaching and learning practices: the internal dynamics of the latter also influenced the former. This occurred, for example, as a result of tensions or ideological conflicts which resulted in wider changes and through networked dialogue in a context of collaborative self-development (Turner, 2018, p. 155).

The conclusion is that for a change agent such as an educational developer, an anthropological awareness of the particular characteristics of a workgroup or other local site of practice is critical. Context is everything, and unpicking site ontologies helps to understand the internal dynamics of contexts, and so what may work and what may not in each case. However, local site ontologies need to be apprehended within a conceptually informed understanding of the broader institutional framework, and this is also an ontological issue. For Giddens the everyday concept of 'society' as a bounded and unified whole is inaccurate. Instead there are multiple sets of recurring behaviours, a mosaic of interlocking, mutually dependent, and dynamic practices. This chapter has demonstrated that the same is true of universities: they do not have a single 'organizational culture' but a *dynamic multiple cultural configuration* (Alvesson, 2002). This configuration involves sets of interdependent practices effected by workgroups which, in the process, contribute to their dynamic development. Nonetheless, this dynamic cultural configuration consisting of multiple sites of practice operates within a structured framework which both limits and scaffolds possibilities for change there.

In Chapter 6 I apply the ideas elaborated in this one to change processes more generally, setting out the implications for change agents. However, before that it is necessary to understand how teaching and learning regimes come about, and how they are maintained. Attempting to make changes for the future can only proceed effectively on the basis of a good understanding of the present, and so Chapter 5 is a necessary precondition for examining those change processes.

# 5

# Disciplines and the Generation of Teaching and Learning Regimes

In this chapter I review the prevalent idea that disciplines are the primary drivers of academic practices in universities. From this point of view, the teaching and learning regimes found in universities are primarily products of the disciplines within which they are located, and as a result share common characteristics in different universities around the world. The theory makes the same argument about research practices, but here the focus is upon teaching and learning. I critique the theory underlying this view, that of epistemological essentialism—the idea that it is the knowledge characteristics of disciplines that condition (or even determine) such academic cultures, including teaching and learning practices. In its place I offer an alternative account of how teaching and learning regimes are generated, one involving multiple factors operating together in dynamic, context-specific ways. Understanding this sets the ground for Chapter 6, which considers how TLRs change, and how they can be changed for the better.

## Epistemological Essentialism and Teaching and Learning Regimes

Both in the literature and in the everyday thinking of academics and others, disciplines have been considered a central force in generating practices in terms of both research and teaching. This is so much the case that Clark dismissed the significance of 'characteristics imported into the academic profession by individual members from their personal background and prior experiences . . . as the least important components of academic culture' (Clark, 1987, p. 107). For Clark, individuals' backstories are irrelevant to their present-day behaviours. This is some distance from a practice approach which sees practices as emergent in this sense as well as others.

This viewpoint is an essentialist one. *Strong* essentialism claims that the phenomenon in question, in this case a discipline, has definable and necessary

*Accomplishing Change in Teaching and Learning Regimes: Higher Education and the Practice Sensibility.*
Paul Trowler, Oxford University Press (2020). © Paul Trowler. DOI: 10.1093/oso/9780198851714.001.0001

characteristics, essential properties which distinguish it from other phenomena and make it 'itself'. It also proposes that these characteristics have generative power, which is to say that they significantly affect the world around them in specific and identifiable ways.

When applied to disciplines, strong essentialism claims that each discipline has clearly identifiable properties, including (usually): a body of knowledge; a specialized vocabulary; an accepted body of theory; systematic research strategies; well-understood ways of establishing robustness of theories and concepts; and identifiably different ways of teaching (Berger, 1970; Smeby, 1996; Donald, 2002; Krishnan, 2009). For each individual discipline, specific examples could be given of each of these general characteristics. As far as the generative power of disciplines is concerned, the argument has been that because each discipline has its own essential knowledge characteristics, these are generative in a very direct way (and in *every* case) of specific practice characteristics among disciplinary practitioners. The best-known proponent of this argument is Becher (1989). The title of his book, *Academic Tribes and Territories*, encapsulates the argument. Knowledge-based territories (with characteristics such as those listed above) create distinctive academic tribes. Burton Clark agrees:

> It is around disciplines that faculty subcultures increasingly form. As the work and the points of view grow more specialised, men [sic] in different disciplines have fewer things in common, in their background and in their daily problems. They have less impulse to interact with one another and less ability to do so...Men of the sociological tribe rarely visit the land of the physicists and have little idea what they do over there. If the sociologists were to step into the building occupied by the English department, they would encounter the cold stares if not the slingshots of the hostile natives...The disciplines exist as separate estates, with distinctive subcultures.
>
> (Clark, 1963, p. 63)

This specific form of strong essentialism, epistemological essentialism, is so termed because the generative property is epistemological: the distinctive knowledge characteristics of each discipline.

Although it is not the primary concern of this book, it was in the area of doing research that diversity across the disciplines and uniformity within them was first discussed by authors writing from this perspective. In 'hard pure' disciplines such as physics, research practices involve large numbers of people interacting and collaborating on mutually identified problems, often working together with equipment of high capital value, writing publications together and testing and building on the work of others. One could describe that situation as 'urban': highly populated, with considerable interpersonal interaction. Power lies in the hands of leading academics and gatekeepers of knowledge, but everyone in the field shares an approach to doing research and has common, usually tacit, ideas about the nature of knowledge and what is knowable. In 'soft pure' disciplines such as sociology, by contrast, the research landscape is rural and sparsely populated. Individual researchers plough their own furrow and take little regard of the work of others. Research practices do not usually involve laboratories or specially constructed experiments. Value is not placed upon building upon the already existing edifice of knowledge. Rather, the creation of completely new knowledge, ways of seeing and understandings is valued. So, from the epistemologically essentialist viewpoint, types of interactions, professional concerns, ethical codes, lifestyles, values, and beliefs are consistently found within research in the same discipline wherever it is practised, it is claimed. The same applies to 'hard applied' and 'soft applied' disciplines such as engineering and social work.

Looking at teaching and learning from this viewpoint, it seems possible to depict sets of social practices that are linked to disciplines and are found across the world wherever a particular discipline is practised. It is argued that there are always found within any specific discipline, for example, unique methods of teaching (signature pedagogies), similar amounts of time spent on teaching in preparation, commonalities in the distribution of time between different types of teaching, the same artefacts used in teaching and approaches to learning, and the same assessment tools. Relevant authors here are Clark (1987), Donald (1995), Smeby (1996), Neumann (1996), and Ylijoki (2000). What these authors are arguing is that disciplines condition, or even determine, the nature of teaching and learning regimes within them, though they do not use that language.

Some specific examples of the kinds of regime characteristics generated within disciplines as a result of their epistemological characteristics according to this tradition are as follows. In teaching, hard pure disciplines such as physics are claimed to have teacher-focused instructive methods, with large class lectures and an instructive or didactic approach delivering fixed content, backed up by laboratory sessions. The attention of students is focused on memorizing facts and applying problem-solving skills, and their achievements are measured by different forms of objective assessment, with model answers and guides indicating what is right and what is wrong. In such disciplines, according to this perspective, authority and power is vested in the teacher. The students aspire to acquiring the appropriate knowledge, discursive repertoires, and skills to enact the necessary recurrent physical practices. Meanwhile, in practice terms, things are very different in soft pure disciplines such as sociology, according to the disciplinary essentialist view. An observer interested in teaching and learning in higher education will see quite different recurrent practices and completely different underlying tacit theories, power relations, and so on. Assessment practices will focus on the development of critical thinking and argument; teaching practices will be more interactive and discursive. The development of skills will be cognitive and linguistic, with conceptual sophistication prioritized over the assimilation and retrieval of information. Ylonen et al. (2018, p. 1015) sum up this epistemologically driven view:

> The variations between the ways marks are awarded are complex and deeply rooted in subject pedagogy. The nature of subject teaching is highly varied in higher education, with arts and humanities subjects often having a greater focus on independent study and small group teaching through seminars, while the sciences have a focus on large group lectures and smaller group work is usually in, or related to, the laboratory.

The claims made in this tradition, based on research, relate to the following aspects of TLRs conditioned by disciplinary differences (Trowler, 2009, p. 184):

- academic teachers' interactions with students;
- teaching methods and artefacts employed;
- goals of education;
- theories of teaching and learning;
- orientations to students;
- conceptions of quality in teaching, learning, and assessment;
- moral orders of studying;
- academic teachers' approaches to assessment instruments;
- the place of student opinion in teaching and assessment;
- students' appreciation of lectures/formal tuition.

It is a characteristic of this essentialist literature, however, that the mechanism of the link between such characteristics and disciplinary features is only vaguely elaborated. Different terms are used to describe the linkage, ranging from quite soft terms such as 'preferences', 'styles', 'rituals', 'tendencies', and

**Table 5.1.** Linking epistemological characteristics and learning, teaching, assessment, and curriculum

| Teaching, learning, and assessment differences | Hard, pure, convergent, urban | Soft, applied, divergent, rural |
| --- | --- | --- |
| Common assessment instruments | Multiple-choice, closely focused exam | Open exam, coursework, continuous assessment |
| Marking practices | Assessment criteria strictly followed | Intuitive marking |
| Students' skills development | Skills and logical reasoning | Critical ability, fluency, creativity |
| Teaching approaches | Presentational techniques, didactic | Face-to-face settings, discursive |
| Use of ICT | ICT applications extensive | Limited ICT applications |
| Curricular structure | Linear progression in curriculum, agglomerative | Spiral curriculum |
| Student group work | Small groups work on predetermined problems | Small groups work discursively |

(Adapted from Trowler, 2009, p. 185)

'conceptions' to considerably harder ones such as 'approaches' or 'practices'. Table 5.1 sets out such claimed linkages.

## Relativistic, 'Voice' Approaches

This is a depiction of strong epistemological essentialism. However, other authors take a more moderate position, seeing disciplines as only one among many influences on practices in universities. Contextual factors related to the nature of the institution and national culture and policies tend to be important among these, making academic staff 'redefine discipline cultures to meet local needs' (Lattuca and Stark, 1995, p. 340). Significant authors here are Lindblom-Ylänne et al. (2006), Parpala et al. (2010), Virtanen and Nevgi (2010), Sampson and Komer (2010), and Barradell et al. (2017).

In addition to these supplementary 'real' influences there is the significant issue of *narratives* about disciplines. For some authors, the stories that academics tell each other about their disciplines are at least as important as any 'real' differences. *Beliefs* about research, teaching, the nature of the discipline, and what is important in higher education are very strongly generative of practices which are in a sense linked to disciplines, but only in a narrative fashion. Relevant authors here are Quinlan (1999), Brew (1999; 2001; 2003), Robertson and Bond (2001), Latour and Woolgar (1979). This 'voice' approach can be so agentic, or even relativistic, that it loses the characteristic of essentialism and cannot go beyond only contextual accounts. As such it has been heavily criticized from a social realist perspective by Young (2000; 2008), Maton (2013), and others.

The 'voice' approach tends to see disciplines as in decline as organizing structures, as do other commentators (Gibbons et al., 1994; Nowotny et al., 2001; Brew, 2002). The once clear boundaries have become unstable and highly permeable, and what were once clearly identifiable entities are now highly complex and dynamic. Parturition and growth in specialisms and numbers (Clark, 1996) mean that the space for uncertainty, narrativity, and relativism grows.

At the same time in higher education more generally, much has changed. New managerialism is in ascendency almost everywhere. There are reductions in state funding and a commensurate need for entrepreneurial activity to generate income. The rise of 'mass' higher education has happened around the globe. There is increasing state control and related predominance of vocational aims for higher education. For academics there have been the simultaneous processes of work intensification and work degradation. These pressures lead to changes in academic cultures which may be unconnected to, or only partially mediated by, disciplinary characteristics.

The 'voice' approach loses the analytical power to capture these trends: it depicts disciplinary characteristics and their links to social practices as locally specific and unpredictable. Essentially the argument is that practices are conditioned by the stories told by practitioners: this is a social constructionist, completely agentic perspective that lacks appreciation of structural conditioning.

## Moderate Essentialism

Sayer (1997) argues that despite their simplifying nature, essentialist approaches are necessary in social science for two very significant reasons. Essentialism offers conceptual clarity: it gives ways of categorizing and distinguishing between phenomena, identifying their nature and offering the ability to 'sort things out' (Bowker and Star, 2000). Social reality is just too complex to capture and understand without some degree of essentialism. Secondly, the power to explain, establishing the nature of the social world, showing how phenomena are linked, and unravelling the workings of multi-causality also requires essentialism. Without some kind of causal account there can be no explanatory purchase. Sayer therefore recommends the development of a moderate essentialism, arguing that this is a prerequisite for a *critical* social science. In order to uncover structural disadvantage and the operation of power it is first necessary to have conceptual purchase on the properties of phenomena and outcomes emergent from them. Sayer argues that, by contrast, a strong anti-essentialist or 'voice' position has no emancipatory possibilities because it depicts social reality as 'a turbulent system, where "order" and "consensus" emerge locally and for the time being, if at all' (Fuchs, 2001, p. 4).

In Trowler (2013b) I applied a moderate essentialist approach to understanding disciplines. Taking a view derived from Wittgenstein's (1953) notion of family resemblances, a moderate essentialist position maintains that the category 'discipline' (as distinct from, for example, a 'hobby') does not require a set of always present characteristics which constitutes its essence, such as those described above. Neither does any individual discipline consist of a single identifiable set of core characteristics. Just as family members share a cluster of features, not all of which are present in any one individual, individual disciplines consist of different characteristics which may or may not be present in any individual instance. In both cases we can still recognize family members and individual disciplines, and we can distinguish them from others. This is moderate essentialism because it recognizes that phenomena have objective defining features but does not require them all to be present in every instance.

In terms of the second characteristic of essentialism, its generative power (and here my focus is the power to generate the moments of TLRs), this is also recognized within a moderate essentialist position. However, the depiction of how it works is more complex than in strong essentialism. First, a moderate position argues that there is no necessary link between the set of distinguishing characteristics and their generative properties. Some or even all of the distinguishing features may be powerless or weak compared to 'accidental' properties existing in particular contexts; external factors which have nothing to do with disciplinary characteristics are also likely to generate effects. So the shape of a teaching and learning regime may have a lot, a little, or nothing to do with the discipline which is being taught. However, this is not fixed in time: the generative power of disciplines is more like a wind turbine than a power station; it varies according to a set of dynamic contextual factors:

> a moderate essentialist position argues that generative effects are contextually contingent and provisional upon other factors. Causality is multiple

and the interplay of factors influencing behaviour plays out differently in different contexts. So no simple statements can be made about, for example, teaching and learning practices associated with particular disciplines across multiple sites. Other structural factors, such as the prevalence of managerialist discourse and ideology, played out differently in different locales, are significant in conditioning behaviour.   (Trowler, 2013b, p. 1728)

From this point of view, then, disciplines themselves are depicted in quite a different way from the 'essential characteristics' description above. Both elements of disciplines in general (as a concept) and of specific disciplines are seen as proto-practice reservoirs of ways of knowing which, in dynamic combination with other structural phenomena, *can* condition behavioural practices, sets of discourses, ways of thinking, procedures, emotional responses, and motivations; in other words, the moments of TLRs. Together a constellation of factors results in structured dispositions for disciplinary practitioners who, in conjunction with external forces, reshape them in different practice clusters into localized repertoires. While alternative recurrent practices may be in competition within a single discipline, there is common background knowledge about key figures, conflicts, and achievements. Disciplines take organizational form, have internal hierarchies, and bestow power differentially, conferring advantage and disadvantage (Trowler, 2014). The next section elaborates on this.

## Multi-Causality in the Generation of Teaching and Learning Regimes: Some Examples

A moderate essentialist position is consistent with social practice theory in conceptualizing the genesis of teaching and learning regimes. In summary, it is possible to say that such regimes are a product of intersectional forces, both structural and agentic, and always consist of emergent properties which stem from past practices combined with contemporary exigencies. As Marx said:

Men make their own history, but they do not make it as they please; they do not make it under self-selected circumstances, but under circumstances existing already, given and transmitted from the past.   (Marx, 1852)

Disciplinary epistemological differences, and narratives about their determining properties, are significant to a different extent and in different places but represent only one aspect of intersectionality. 'Disciplinary' cultures, therefore, are local, contextually conditioned, and dynamic. However, they usually retain family resemblances to other instantiations of the same discipline, and so are recognizable.

Orr and Shreeve (2018) discuss the case of art and design disciplines. They point out that the knowledge base beyond the university frames what is taught within the university, and that pedagogy in these areas draws on theory from a range of disciplines and is deployed in visual and material ways rather than textual ones. Knowledge and understanding in art and design therefore 'does not lend itself to easily articulated underlying comprehensive and universal theories' (p. 23). Art and design disciplines have a form of abstract knowledge and visual language which is very specific and heavily dependent on historical and cultural background for its particular form and definition. More than this, however, the articulation of knowledge involves engagement with individual identities as practitioners; this is also the case for students, who envisage themselves becoming part of that historical and cultural background. Individuals gradually develop their own identity as an artist or a designer, responding to the subject and making it their own.

For Orr and Shreeve, knowledge is not consistent and stable, reproduced everywhere a particular discipline is enacted. They say that, as with cooking:

> A dish may consist of similar ingredients but may taste very different depending on who has made it, where it is eaten and with whom. Where multiple forms and combinations of knowledge are gained through different experiences, knowing how, knowing why, knowing that, knowing about and where knowledge is apprehended through different senses and accessed through different systems, languages networks and discourses, learning becomes a potentially rich field requiring total engagement of learners and teachers. (Orr and Shreeve, 2018, p. 36)

This is a valuable simile. However, given the significance of 'reservoirs of symbolic structures' (Bernstein, 1999), of assumptions, discourses, and ideologies which *flow into* and condition the family of social practices within a teaching and learning regime, I prefer to modify it to that of a cocktail bar. Different ingredients flow into or are added to the cocktail shaker, guided by the affinities of those present. The performance and experience of the consumption of the cocktail is, as Orr and Shreeve suggest, heavily conditioned by the context of consumption.

The concept of 'embeddedness' (Bager-Elsborg, 2017) neatly sums up this understanding of the genesis of teaching and learning regimes. It sees disciplines as more than knowledge structures, depicting them as a combination of the ways in which they are interpreted and described by lecturers in specific local contexts. The process of meaning construction in operation is conditioned not only by disciplinary characteristics and narratives about them but by contextual conditions. These include local, institutional practice architectures (Kemmis and Mahon, 2017) as well as national policy conditions.

I discussed the nature of institutional practice architectures in the previous chapter. National policy contexts can shape practices in similar ways, structuring discourses, resource-seeking behaviour, power relations, and so on. This was seen in operation in Denmark in an earlier vignette (Krejsler, 2006). An example in the UK is the effect of the National Student Survey, which, in some institutions at least, has a significant influence in shaping practices both at the classroom level and more generally—as discussed in Chapter 2 and illustrated in Figure 2.1. In general, the 'technocratic turn' in government policy on higher education has shaped teaching and learning in the direction of a target-driven approach. Taking this a step further, Michael Barber et al. (2011) talk about 'deliverology', involving a technical apprehension of the nature and goals of higher education. This, combined with notions of the 'value for money' (Office for Students, 2018) of different university courses, conceptualized in terms of students' future earning potential, is another example of discursive shaping and structuring of priorities at the local level. Many of the moments of TLRs, such as discursive repertoires, tacit assumptions, theories of teaching and learning, and conventions of appropriateness, will be impinged upon by policies, discourses, and relations framed in these ways.

However, the generative power of national policy contexts, like that of disciplines and other factors, is variable between places and over time. The wind turbine versus power station simile works here too. This was demonstrated by a comparative study across Scottish and English Education departments in five UK universities sampling forty academic staff (Deem and Lucas, 2007). Their study concludes the following about the influence of the policy context on academic habitus and departmental cultures:

> Between 2003 and 2004 the Scottish policy context (in respect of continuing academic study for trained school teachers and the Applied Education Research Scheme) was indeed significant, whereas the influence of the England-specific policy context...was less evident. It was apparent that in

all five institutions, individuals and departments saw the research/teaching relationship in a variety of ways, from an emphasis on collaborative problem-based learning to more individualised use of personal research in teaching. These perceptions and dispositions were not confined to individual academics but also extended to organisational and departmental cultures and were clearly also utilised by manager-academics in running their departments. Collaboratively oriented departmental research cultures seemed linked to collaborative teaching cultures and also to the initiation of problem-based learning.   (Deem and Lucas, 2007, p. 130)

Moving outside the UK, in comparing the academic departments of law and business administration in a single Danish university, Bager-Elsborg (2018) stresses the importance of meaning construction, mediated by disciplinary dispositions. These two disciplines constructed the 'implied student' (Ulriksen, 2009) very differently, and attached different levels and types of significance to what practitioners in both disciplines perceived as a dominant instrumentalism among their students. This differential attribution of significance was heavily mediated by disciplinary dispositions, both structural (epistemological) and constructed in narratives. Meanwhile, however, the characteristics of the Danish institution in which both disciplines operated, its practice architecture, also had significance in shaping their teaching and learning practices. These included the distribution of teaching tasks, institutional acknowledgement, and other factors. Bager-Elsborg emphasizes the dynamism inherent in these forces, seeing the resultant teaching and learning regime as an on-going accomplishment.

Shay (2003) also provides empirical evidence for the general theoretical points above. She studied assessment practices in two disciplinary groupings, engineering and humanities—different faculties in a high-status South African university. Deploying a social practice lens, she counters the dominant notion that professional judgements of student work offer a degree of robustness, objectivity, and reliability, based on assessment apparatus including assessment criteria, double marking, moderation, and so on. She shows how academics in these two faculties developed what Bourdieu calls a 'feel for the game' of assessment—tacit understandings of appropriateness that are socially developed and disseminated. Novices acquired this feel for the game slowly through a process of socialization rather than explicit transmission. Eventually novices acquire a set of interpretive matrices—frameworks which make the assessment task quite straightforward. While lacking reproducible, objective characteristics, these are far more than personal prejudice or subjective judgement; they are socially created and acquired, shared, and relatively stable frames of reference. Individual markers become socialized into their work-group's 'ways of seeing'.

This induction into a way of seeing takes time. Shay quotes one experienced faculty member who said that it is relatively easy to decide whether a project deserves a first, second, or third-class pass, 'but not the first time' (Shay, 2004, p. 319). Another told her how in his first year his grades were higher than other markers, and in his second year they were lower. This was a common pattern, according to a more experienced staff member: people gradually adjust their marking as they see how it is done. Acquiring a common profes-sional vision can take longer and be more difficult without explicit guidelines or moderation exercises:

> As one faculty member assessing for the first time recalled, 'The impression that we were given as new supervisors is that it's left to academic feeling, that you decide how you want to mark'. (Shay, 2004, p. 319)

Shay is not claiming that epistemological differences generated the contrast-ing approaches she found. Rather, the assessment practices were largely generated locally, specific to the institution, and were dynamic in nature. I recounted in Chapter 1 the situation in which academics moved to the UK from North America having already internalized the US interpretive matri-ces of assessment practices. Despite the fact that they were operating within the same discipline, the interpretive matrices they encountered were very different in the UK context. This example demonstrates that there is no necessary disciplinary commonality in the ways of seeing within the task of assessing students' work. In Shay's study there was no commonality across the disciplines either. The 'feel for the game' was very different in the two faculties she researched; their locally developed interpretive matrices had taken different directions.

So far this account is rather close to Ylijoki's notion of the 'moral order of studying', a dimension of disciplinary culture into which students are social-ized, including notions of quality in their assignments and in assessment:

> The moral order defines the basic beliefs, values, norms and aspirations prevailing in the culture. It forms the background ethos of the group, which determines what is regarded as normal and ordinary, what is regarded as impossible, imaginary and extraordinary, and what is so obvious that it is not even noticed that it is not noticed. (Ylijoki, 2000, p. 341)

However, in Shay's account it is very significant that there were *intra*-faculty differences in the interpretation of quality. Frequently academics would struggle to negotiate and agree a grade, and even explicit conflict between them was observed in some cases. So, a supervisor may disagree with other assessors about their student's work and about prioritizing the criteria upon which it should be assessed. But this conflict was not all that it seemed—as is often the case, 'it was not about what it was about'. Underlying the explicit discussion or argument about assessment priorities were issues of professional identity, status, and power.

Shay's study provides empirical examples of several of the moments of TLRs at work: implicit theories of learning and teaching; conventions of appropriateness; tacit assumptions; subjectivities in interaction and power relations. It also demonstrates the dynamic and contested nature of TLRs. Disciplinary characteristics play their part in shaping those moments in different contexts, but the moments themselves shape narratives about those characteristics. As Boud et al. (2018, p. 1116) say: 'While assessment rules and templates may be generated centrally in universities, they are taken up and sometimes subverted within local groups and departments and made their own.' Surprisingly, given the context of post-apartheid South Africa, issues of context, both institutional and in terms of national policy, are only lightly touched on by Shay. Since 2015 and the development of the #RhodesMustFall, #FeesMustFall, and anti-colonialism movements in that country (particularly in the institution in which Shay conducted her research), these external factors have become foregrounded in very high definition. Some prevalent disciplinary assumptions have been challenged and interpretive matrices for assessment and other social practices have been disrupted (Chikane, 2018; Jansen, 2017b).

## History and the (Re-) Invention of Tradition

History and biography are significant in shaping the present. This is as true for academics and students as it is for departments and universities. In their study of students in an 'elite' Scottish university who had entered it from further education colleges with very different learning experiences, Christie, Tett, Cree, Hounsell, and McCune (2007) show that

> engagement with learning is a subjective experience bound up with other life events and experiences and [we] have drawn attention to its 'social situatedness'. We have also shown the importance of competence to learner

identities and to how a person's activities and choices are both constrained and enabled by their horizons for action.   (p. 24)

As Stuart Hall argued, individual identity is

not an essence but a positioning. Hence there is always a politics of identity, a politics of position...Identity should be seen as a 'production' which is never complete, always in process, and always constituted within, not outside, representation.   (Hall, 1990, pp. 226, 22).

For institutions too, the past weighs upon the present. Physical architecture; the weight of past practices which persist (sometimes inappropriately) in new contexts; the effects of previous decisions, discourses, and traditions—all may be difficult to shift. These are described by Marx as the 'tradition of all dead generations [which weigh] like a nightmare on the brains of the living' (Marx, 1852): the 'social ghosts' of the past.

However, a more agentic process is also occurring: 'elective affinity'. The term is used by Gerth and Mills (1946), who describe Weber's work on religious believers' selective adaptation, preferred selections, and omissions from an original set of ideas over time. The 'election' refers to the nature of these adaptations, selections, and omissions and the way they affect social practices among believers. The 'affinity' in that phrase refers to congruences between parts of the system of ideas and the social contexts and current practices of believers. These affect the choices and subtle adaptations made. Where there are incongruities, these also affect selective forgetting. So there is selective adaptation and interpretation of the parts of the original set of ideas and associated practices that are salient to current contexts, practices, and needs.

The significance of elective affinity at institutional level is that what might seem to be the weight of history can often be the result of these elective processes. Very traditional characteristics and ritualistic social practices such as graduation ceremonies, academic processions, academic titles, and so on are not simply archaic hangovers from the past. These archetypal practices, with their strongly inscribed codes of signification, power relations, and the rest, persist because there is an affinity with current practices and needs: they have valuable roles to play in marketing, status-chasing, institutional reputation, and the value of the academic 'warrant' (Wearden, 2017):

There is evidence...of how degree ceremonies are being increasingly used by institutions for marketing purposes as they are drawn into a global competitive 'reputation race'. In this progressively competitive and fragmented global context the Western model of degree ceremony being perpetuated helps to sustain and project a collective image of higher education. It does so by connecting higher education institutions with the rich heritage of the past, capturing the present, and alluding to future ceremonies to come. In doing so degree ceremonies reinforce the heritage, authority and credentials of higher education as a sector, whilst at the same time provide individual institutions with opportunities and choices about how to build their own distinct institutional reputation.   (Wearden, 2017, p. ii)

## Summary: The Generation of Teaching and Learning Regimes

This chapter and the previous ones lead to the conclusion that the generation of teaching and learning regimes is no simple, uni-causal matter. Instead, we can make the following statements about their formation.

First, multiple factors lead to the current characteristics, not just one, as the proponents of epistemological essentialism would argue. Important among these are the proto-practice reservoirs of ideologies, discourses, dispositions, understandings, and meanings which shape TLR moments directly and indirectly.

Second, history—the TLR backstory—is important in conditioning the nature of the TLR in structural ways which are difficult to shift but are also agentically reconstructed. The past can be selectively reinterpreted and applied for present purposes: it is 'domesticated' through processes directed according to elective affinity.

Third, exigencies such as resource allocation methods, evaluative approaches, and political ideologies shape dominant discourses and priorities, applying change pressures on different TLR moments.

Fourth, TLRs are characterized by internal contest and power plays, resulting in internal dynamics which reshape them in the medium to long term. Personnel changes can be important for these dynamics.

Fifth, socio-material dynamics are also significant. The artefacts available both shape and are shaped by teaching and learning regimes as the social and the material interact. Software, hardware, architectural characteristics, departmental physical layouts, and other aspects of the material world have important effects on TLRs. As Schatzki et al. (2001, p. 3) say: 'understanding specific practices always involves apprehending material configurations.'

Finally, workgroup practices do not exist in a bubble, but rather in a nested and bundled situation, with great permeability. TLRs are open natural systems. Consequently, other sets of practices with which they co-exist horizontally, as well as the nature of vertically embedded practices, have significant effects on them, and these are contextually contingent. Contrasting formations in different institutional practice architectures condition whether the locus of control of TLRs lies externally or internally and where the dominant forces shaping them are situated.

Chapter 5 moves from looking at the genesis of TLRs to changing them. This chapter has been important in understanding the nature, and the limits, of TLR formation. Without that, any attempt to introduce changes is done with no map and no radar.

# 6

# Accomplishing Change in Teaching and Learning Regimes

Scott, Coates, and Anderson (2008, p. vii) rightly say that leaders want 'practical, higher education specific and role specific insights into what would be the best approach in taking "good ideas" and making them work'. Leaders want those insights to be specific, not the very general platitudes that are frequently offered in management textbooks: 'communicate well with your staff'; 'be open to new ideas'; 'sound out opinion before taking action', and the rest. The unhelpfulness of such general insights is immediately exposed by turning them to the negative. If they sound ridiculous in that form, then they are so general as to be completely unhelpful: 'don't tell your staff anything'; 'stick to your own ideas no matter what'; 'just act, don't listen'.

The problem is, however, that the specific insights that leaders desire can only come from themselves. Only they (or deeply embedded management consultants) are aware, or can become aware, of the specifics of their role, their own context, the context of change, and the nature of and rationale for change initiatives:

> One of the basic reasons why planning fails is that planners or decision makers of change are unaware of the situations faced by potential implementers ... they introduce change ... without attempting to understand the values, ideas and experiences of those who are essential for implementing change.   (Fuller, 2007, p. 110)

People outside that context, and especially management textbook writers, are not empowered by such knowledge to be able to offer specific, context-aware insights. What works in one context may be disastrous in another, or at the very least have little traction within the new situation. From a social practice perspective especially, cognition, rationality, priorities and pressures, resources, and the effects of the backstory are all highly situated. This is why developing a grounded understanding of the particulars of context, preferably through a light-touch ethnographic approach, is really important in any

*Accomplishing Change in Teaching and Learning Regimes: Higher Education and the Practice Sensibility.*
Paul Trowler, Oxford University Press (2020). © Paul Trowler. DOI: 10.1093/oso/9780198851714.001.0001

change initiative. Blundering ahead without understanding the particulars of context can often lead to stalled initiatives, resentment, loss of morale, and resistance.

Peter Knight and I uncovered many examples of this lack of transferability of good management ideas in the research that resulted in our book *Departmental Leadership in Higher Education* (Knight and Trowler, 2001). We conducted interviews with and constructed a web-based survey for departmental leaders in Canada and the UK. What they told us confirmed what social practice theory predicts—'what works' is contextually contingent:

> At one university I seemed to have the Midas touch . . . That university was much more informal than the one I presently work in and creativity in administration was admired and encouraged. There were very few of the structures there are here—no annual individual faculty reports (no merit pay neither!) Teaching evaluation was not required—you did it if you wanted to find out how things were going. Thus students were far more charitable— they were not being asked 5 times a semester to fill in reports on teaching. When they were asked they tended to take it seriously. Since I came here I find creative administration is inhibited by structure, frequent lengthy reporting, budgeting, etc. You could say the atmosphere is much more business-like here. It is. But the flair and chaos of real academic creativity is missing . . . I am not as good at leadership here, partly I think because I am not the world's most meticulous administrator, but this system selects and promotes that type of personality for positions such as Chair [head of department]. At the same time, this university has far less dead wood and probably provides a better-structured and thought-out education for students.   (Male, experienced leader, Canada; Knight and Trowler, 2001, p. 41)

This quote illustrates how organizational practice architectures (Kemmis and Mahon, 2017) condition what is possible, acceptable, and preferred. One size does not fit all.

## The Social Practice Approach: Developing a Practice Sensibility

What *can* be done, however, is to offer 'good' ideas in the form of concepts and theory, as set out in earlier chapters of the book. These offer a way of understanding the present situation and how it works to better situate a sense of how change can happen. The central argument of this book is, however, that these ideas only form the substrate for the development of a practice sensibility, a way of seeing the world through the framework of these concepts.

The practice sensibility helps understand processes at work in teaching and learning regimes. It sees the teaching workgroup being configured and reconfigured as its members engage in different social practices: assessing students' work; classroom teaching; having staff meetings about programme provision; engaging with students online and face to face. Some or all of these practices will be touched by any change initiative. What gives the regime its defining characteristics are the currents that flow into it from proto-practice reservoirs: educational ideologies; theories of teaching and learning; frameworks of meaning; background assumptions. They shape the moments of the regime as its members engage in different teaching and learning practices. The previous chapter discussed how specific characteristics of the context—its physical layout, the artefacts in use, the subjectivities at work interacting with each other, the ebb and flow of power relations, and the institutional practice architecture—also shape a regime's characteristics.

The practice sensibility looks beyond quotidian events, conflicts, and issues—beyond the immediate contextual concerns (Archer, 2007). Behind them it discerns the nature of these moments and the flow from proto-practice reservoirs of currents which shape but do not determine the features of daily performances of practices. It also helps in discerning the influence of other forces 'above' and 'beside' the teaching and learning regime, forces flowing into it because of its permeable nature. Change processes are complex, but the practice sensibility can render patterns and regularities more obvious.

Deliberative attempts to enhance practices involve reconfiguration. If the features of a teaching and learning regime represent the outcomes of the continuing accomplishment involved in the interaction of its different moments, then making changes involves altering this dynamic. Doing so successfully requires a carefully developed understanding of the features of the context (preferably achieved by an ethnographic-style method) and an appreciation of the potential outcomes of interventions on the regime's moments.

A practice sensibility which can apprehend the complexity of the moments comprising a specific teaching and learning regime involves different forms of knowing, and consequently is developed through a combinatory process.

First, it requires some propositional knowledge—'knowing that', as Ryle (2009) calls it: in this case about the nature of practices and teaching and learning regimes, including the sensitizing concepts about their moments which were set out earlier in the book.

Second, it involves knowing what to look for, which is best achieved through looking outside one's own context (which has become normalized) with attention directed in deliberative ways. Case studies or vignettes can do this, but simply looking around at other contexts with similar concerns can also be helpful. Distinguishing between the important and the less important becomes easier with experience, and this enhances the ability to 'sort things out', augmenting one's understanding of what is going on back at home.

A third aspect of developing a practice sensibility is having an improved sense of knowing *where* to look. A combination of cumulative examples and developed theory of both stasis and change helps in this. Knowing to look beyond the 'dazzle' of individual personalities and conflicts and instead focusing on the daily constitution and reconstitution of practices, the ongoing achievement of producing assemblages and understanding their effects, is very significant. The section which follows says more about this. As with preparing for a musical performance, however, achieving a practice sensibility also requires repetitive rehearsal involving critical reflection and consequent adjustment, leading to incremental skill development.

Lynch and Greaves talk about learning to become a 'tactical practitioner', a concept close to what I am describing here:

> Tactical practitioners use their knowledge of (the proper) place and tune in to temporal opportunities (knowing the right moment)...[They use] memory-in-action that brings together the 'treasure of past experiences' and an 'inventory of multiple possibilities' (de Certeau, 1984, p. 83). [This] knowledge...facilitates an optimisation of outcomes for the practitioner, but it is an agile undertaking that is not pre-planned or entirely rational, and it is not formalised as a strategy that can be decontextualised and reapplied—it belongs to the moment. Practices emerge in time as active productions of singularities, not as the implementation of some predetermined game plan.
>
> (Lynch and Greaves, 2017, pp. 59–60)

'Smart' approaches to change require an understanding of the present and an anthropological appreciation of current contexts, their histories and trajectories. A practice sensibility gives change agents practical knowledge, a kind of wisdom summed up in the Greek words phronesis and mêtis. If phronesis is 'practical intelligence', mêtis is its application in a strategic, fleet-of-foot, goal-directed (even devious) way. Their combination means knowing the right move at the right moment; it involves flair, wisdom, vigilance, and resourcefulness (Lynch and Greaves, 2017; de Certeau, 1984). It gives a feel for what will work, what won't, and what will lead to disaster. It offers a moment-by-moment sense of what is best to do and say when dealing with people, including difficult people. It offers the ability to make some fuzzy predictions about the near and medium-term future, at least locally.

Bourdieu (1990, pp. 81–2) offers a football analogy: the skilful player reacts to possession of the ball not in terms of what she sees but what she foresees, seeing the situation as it will be beyond the perceived present. She doesn't pass the ball to where her teammate is, but to the spot he will reach a moment later. She chooses which teammate through an instantaneous assessment of the anticipations of both teammates and the opposition, predicting their anticipations. This is all done on the fly, in the heat of the moment. It involves physical skill, instantaneous decision-making, embedded knowledge of the game's rules, and empathetic understanding.

Until the final sentence, this analogy is closer to mêtis than to phronesis. It talks about conscious assessment, anticipation, and strategic decision-making, albeit at speed: 'instantaneous decision-making'. The final sentence moves towards phronesis, which involves unconscious, intuitive insight and gut feeling. Underneath the conscious is the now unconscious knowledge of the game's rules and 'empathetic understanding'. But a feel for the game goes deeper than this, too: it is closer to practical consciousness and intelligence, closer to the way a skilled musician interacts with her instrument, the music, the audience. It is a kind of intelligence that is difficult or even impossible to describe explicitly. It is intuitive, based on intense and prolonged practice as well as formally learned rules and procedures. There is judgement and a set of values involved. As noted in Chapter 4, for Haidt (2012) it is instant gut reactions, unconscious responses, that primarily drive our decision-making, but in daily life these are often based on irrational beliefs which are impenetrable to rational argument and evidence-based falsification.

Haidt refers to these 'flashes' of response that happen on a moment-by-moment basis as 'intuition'. But they are not that: rather, they are micro-judgements at an almost instinctive level, coming from a different place than the rational, cognitive, and explicit. Intuition is important, but that comes from phronesis, from practical wisdom built on experience and knowledge. Intuition is tacit, too, and non-rational; it is a sense about how things will go, and about which decisions are favourable and which dangerous to the goals we have. In Afrikaans, the word *voorgevoel* sums it up: fore-sensing. The 'sensing' is important: it does not refer to forecasting, or foreseeing in an explicit way, but to intuitively sensing possible futures.

A short vignette illustrates the practice sensibility. In my five-year ethno-graphic study of NewU looking at how academics' responses to institutional changes were structured and how they could be explained, I identified four response-types in the data. I characterized these as sinking, swimming, coping, and reconstructing. Academics who found themselves in the *sinking* category had become highly stressed, sometimes depressed, sometimes ill, and always overworked. Those who were *swimming* were comfortable in a volatile envir-onment which was quickly changing towards employment-focused, student-centred curricular structures. Those who were *coping* were highly agentic in dealing with a challenging environment, sometimes breaking rules and con-ventions in order to make life easier for themselves. Those who were engaged in *reconstruction* subtly challenged the changes and found ways to circumvent them and create their own.

The data indicated regularities in the structural forces and personal circumstances which conditioned these responses. Personal backstories were very important, for example. Academics with a background in industry tended to feel at home in this newly volatile, customer-centred environment and could swim in it. Those with a background in academia from the days when student numbers were smaller and recruitment was limited to the more academically able tended to sink. They were stuck in the 'Robbins trap'. This means that they deployed the same practices based on the same assumptions and tacit theories that had worked in that very different context but were no longer workable with few resources, many more students, very different students, and different objectives for higher educa-tion. They were, in short, displaced practices of the kind that Diamond (2013) describes.

Behind these backstories were proto-practice reservoirs of different educa-tional ideologies at work: progressivism; traditionalism; enterprise; social reconstructionism (see Chapter 4, 'Subjectivities in Interaction'). In a sense these ideologies *flowed through* the individuals and the workgroups in which they operated, shaping their behaviours and responses.

For these academics, the responses were not explicit or rationally calcu-lated, although all of them were able to describe and rationalize their responses in an interview situation in exactly the way that Haidt (2012) described. How they thought and what they did flowed from tributaries that they were not aware of: ideologies, presage factors (their backstories), and contextual features. Interview transcripts revealed one story, but the conceptual and theoretical apparatus brought to their analysis offered a more nuanced, less linear one.

## Focusing on what matters

From a social practice perspective, there are three key elements to any change process. First is the context of change. Throughout the book I have stressed the significance of contextual contingencies. Second is the nature of any proposed innovation and the way it reprioritizes, recrafts, or reconstructs practices. Exactly what is being changed is highly salient to the process of making the changes. Third is the relationship between context and innovation: how they relate, how harmonious or sympathetic are they to each other, where the 'sharp' points of disjunction lie.

A practice-focused perspective offers a way of seeing each of these three elements. Considerable attention has already been given to the characteristics of context in practice terms. But innovations of different sorts can also be viewed in such terms. Any innovation touches on the different moments in play, bringing some to the fore, backgrounding some, changing others entirely. For example, the physics head of department quoted and discussed in Case Study 3 later in this chapter introduced workshop teaching in his courses, challenging the highly didactic practices among his colleagues. This innovation had particular significance for addressing and attempting to change implicit theories of teaching and learning, recurrent practices, and tacit assumptions, both on the part of academic teachers and of students. Introducing this innovation into highly embedded, previously unchallenged sets of practices was ambitious. This was because the innovation itself 'carried' new ways of doing and thinking about learning and teaching, a constructivist rather than a transmissive theory of knowledge acquisition, and a student-centred rather than teacher-centred approach to enabling it.

Just as there are three key elements to understanding what matters in a particular change situation—context, innovation, and their relationship—there are three key elements in terms of thinking about the degree of challenge any particular innovation presents in any specific context. These are salience, congruence, and profitability.

*Salience* refers to the significance of a change initiative in relation to the priorities, values, and meanings which currently exist within a regime. The fundamental question about any proposal for change is 'does it matter to us/ them?' Subsequent questions arising from this include: 'How much does it matter?' 'Can it be made to matter?' 'Does it matter to others, and if so why?'

*Congruence* refers to the compatibility between a proposed change initiative and current practices. The fundamental question about any proposal for change is: 'Does it fit with what we/they do, believe and feel?' Subsequent questions arising from this include: 'Is the fit so close as to not involve significant change?' 'How significant is any lack of fit?'

*Profitability* refers to the level of benefit any proposed change has for a regime. The fundamental question about any proposal for change is: 'Why would we/they do it?' Subsequent questions arising from this include: 'How much benefit is there?' 'Is the benefit visible and can it be made so?'

Earlier I discussed the ways in which historical practices which might appear antiquated and irrelevant have persisted and been reshaped in the present. Academic processions, heraldic logos, academic titles and ceremonies, and many other examples illustrate the resilience of (often repurposed) prior practices and the way they both reflect and shape contemporary patterns of salience, congruence, and profitability. These trajectories tell us that sustainable initiatives, ones which can continue without the continued support of additional resources and in the face of the vagaries of changing political and managerial priorities, are most likely the ones which have these three characteristics.

Naturally, these critical characteristics are not in themselves adequate to ensure the 'success' of the change initiative (however that is defined), but their absence would impair its sustainability and effectiveness. A number of underlying necessary preconditions also impact on sustainability, effectiveness, and overall success. These include adequate resources sustained over a period of time, consistency in the priority given to the direction of change, the stability of objectives, the adequacy of the causal theory underlying the reform, and adequate induction into new approaches and technologies (Pressman and Wildavsky, 1984; Hood, 1976; Mazmanian and Sabatier, 1981; Ham and Hill, 1984; Cerych and Sabatier, 1986).

## Maintaining optimism

Sadly, these features are frequently absent in higher education, making it remarkably easy to develop a depressing notion that innovations in higher education hardly ever achieve the aspirations which impelled them. So often there is enthusiasm for a project which has gained funds and promises to change things for the better. Enthusiasts come on board and much work is done. Then the funding source dries up and the enthusiasts start leaving for other jobs before the end of the project. The year before the funding stops, momentum has been lost and achievements start to decay. This 'projectitis' seems endemic in higher education. In times of plenty politicians find large pots of money, but are mostly concerned that whatever it is spent on is 'visible from low of orbit' (Kernohan, 2015) for political reasons, rather than being rationally allocated with a view to creating a real legacy (Trowler, Ashwin, and Saunders, 2014). Meanwhile, universities can easily be portrayed as being 'change averse' (Fullan and Scott, 2009) and it is very easy in most contexts to identify the following characteristics, which appear to be prevalent in them:

- Internal embedded practices operate to erode reform.
- Structural processes are slow and internally contradictory: there is no institutional 'learning architecture' (Dill, 1999; Nelles and Vorley, 2010) and so decision-making is not fully joined up; there is limited follow-through, disunity, and conflicting priorities.
- Review and accountability processes are non-aligned.
- There is patchiness in delivery of core activities.
- Prioritization is missing at different levels, so that goals are multiple, unrealistic, and frequently changing.
- There are unformed, inappropriate, and changing implementation strategies and tactics.
- There is lots of talk but little action; lots of strategic discussion but business as usual.
- There is defence of 'turf' and resistance to change among many.

At a national level there is usually turbulence in the policy environment and, contingent on this turbulence, in institutional priorities and focus as universities respond to shifting demands and resource opportunities.

Fullan and Scott (2009, p. 34) offer a sad portrait of US universities which sums up these characteristics:

inefficiency, poor decision making and lack of focus; disengagement; unresponsiveness; unclear accountability and acknowledgement systems; unaligned structures and processes; unproductive planning and review processes; too little focus on implementation; poor leadership identification, focus and support; underdeveloped quality management systems; and unclear standards.

For leaders of change this can lead to experiences such as the following becoming all too familiar:

- Only the 'usual suspects' are engaged with the reform; others quietly withdraw or actively oppose change.

- There is slow acceleration of change initiatives to a plateau and then entropy sets in.
- Turf wars and squabbling result in stalled initiatives.
- There are difficulties in scaling up and even locally there are serious cases of 'projectitis'.

It is unsurprising, then, that change agents and leaders use analogies like the following about their experiences of enhancement initiatives: 'working with a dysfunctional family'; 'wading through a quagmire of bureaucracy'; 'trying to drive a nail into a wall of blancmange—little resistance but no result'; 'being a one-armed paper-hanger working in a gale' (Fullan and Scott, 2009, pp. 107–8). Interestingly, Fullan and Scott report senior leaders such as provosts and deans as deploying much more positive analogies: 'conducting an orchestra'; 'climbing a mountain together'; 'coaching a successful sports team'. This difference is probably because very senior people are not engaged with the detail to the same extent.

The prospects for change initiatives are not all bleak, however. Although universities appear to be relatively unchanging and change averse, in fact they are very adept at adapting. Their ancient architecture and archaic discourse and rituals mask the fact that they have been adapting and changing for centuries, and this has ensured their survival in turbulent environments:

> Taking as a starting point 1530, when the Lutheran Church was founded, some 66 institutions that existed then still exist today in the Western World in recognizable form: the Catholic Church, the Lutheran Church, the parliaments of Iceland and the Isle of Man, and 62 universities.
>
> (Carnegie Council on Policy Studies in Higher Education, 1980, p. 9)

The perceived conservatism of universities is only partly accurate. Moreover, the inability of social practice theory to explain change, as identified by some critics, is also only partly justified, as I argued in Chapter 2. Warde (2005, p. 141) says:

> practices also contain the seeds of constant change. They are dynamic by virtue of their own internal logic of operation, as people in myriad situations adapt, improvise and experiment...In addition, practices are not hermetically sealed off from other adjacent and parallel practices, from which lessons are learnt, innovations borrowed, procedures copied.

However, the trajectories of practices are inherently unstable because they depend upon the recurrent integration of artefacts, meanings, and forms of competence by groups of practitioners who perform practices. Change agents who understand this precarity have a better chance of being successful.

## Other perspectives are available...

Before moving on to examine some case studies of change processes, it is worth setting out some perspectives on change other than the social practice one. Rather than describing them all, which would require several textbooks (which are available), I want to interrogate here some underpinning assumptions about social changes.

### Incentives and sanctions: resource-dependency theory

One common approach views change projects as best implemented through sanctions and rewards. From this point of view, both organizations and individuals chase rewards and avoid sanctions. Many different authors have discussed and categorized the different implementation tools available to change agents from this perspective. Vedung (1998) talks about *carrots*, *sticks*, and *sermons*, which probably need no explanation. Building on this, Bleiklie (2002) distinguishes between the following: *authority tools* (statements enabling, prohibiting, or requiring actions, backed by the legitimate authority of government); *incentive tools* (which give tangible rewards or sanctions for compliance or non-compliance); *capacity tools* (providing resources for increased capacity among different groups); *symbolic or hortatory tools* (the equivalent of 'sermons', which seek to motivate actions through appeal to values); and *learning tools* (those which facilitate learning by target groups to guide and motivate their future actions).

These are constructed from the mindset of senior managers and are all top-down in nature. Underpinning them is a tacit theory of change which is limited and also top-down. As a result the list is not comprehensive, and perhaps naïve. According to this thinking, people are motivated to chase resources; to avoid sanctions, they attend to 'sermons', and, given the capacity, they do what is required. This is a set of tools which might be used to train dogs, but would be of limited utility even in that case, given that we know that dogs apply their brains in situations where their desires conflict with what they are being trained to do (Hare and Woods, 2013).

Missing from this set of tools is an appreciation of the perceptions, values, and consequent motivations of those being managed. Also missing is a focus on the social nature of worklife—of workgroups and social practices, the contexts they inhabit, and the effects of history and an embedded and nested location (Trowler, 1989; Duckett, 2004). All of these things have been bracketed out.

This approach also fails to appreciate the subtleties of discourse. Discursive differences are often more powerful than sermons, but are more nuanced and less palpable. To give one real example: at a high-status English university there was a deliberate discursive shift emanating from faculty level involving a new discourse of 'double-sized rooms' to describe the offices of academic staff in different departments in that faculty. A year or so later, renovations throughout the faculty buildings involved dividing these offices into two. This was a case involving careful groundwork, using discursive repertoires as the tool.

At the organizational level the sanctions and rewards approach is most clearly articulated in *resource-dependency theory*, which argues that higher education institutions keenly respond to an imperative to survive and are driven to chase resources, battling with other organizations to win them. However, a competing perspective, *new institutional theory*, brings a sociological perspective to bear and takes into account the ways in which organizational behaviour is conditioned by historical norms and traditions, as well as how unique cultural characteristics, social relations, processes of decision-making, and diverse organizational purposes mean that the situation is much more complex than simple resource dependency (Frølich et al., 2013; Johnson, 2014). Again, the criticisms of the sanctions and rewards approach at the individual level apply at the organizational level: the situation is considerably more complex than is depicted by that theory, and its focus is on outcomes rather than on the processes which can explain them.

### Rational–purposive theory

A second very common approach is the technicist rational–purposive one. If a change theory is not made explicit and considered carefully, this tends to be the tacit theory relied upon by inexperienced change agents, the default position. It is also the approach aligned with new public management and neo-managerialist ideologies and practices. It sees change processes as a technical issue, to be addressed algorithmically in a sequence of steps. These move incrementally to a grand purpose, achieving a staged sequence of objectives along the way. Targets are set, and their achievement monitored and rewarded. Its rationalism lies in the grand design, constructed to achieve explicit, unitary, and well-defined purposes. It brackets out the 'non-rational': beliefs, ideologies, emotions, and alternative visions. It sees success as lying in good communication, the recruitment of relevant people to the project, and demonstrating the obvious value of the project. In this it relies on being able to change attitudes, behaviours, and choices quite easily. It is innocent of the power of entrenched practices, their resilience, and the historically emergent nature of them. It tends not to see that there are winners and losers or to recognize that opposition can also be based on rational grounds. It is ambitious and optimistic, failing to appreciate the difficulties and obstacles that change, particularly 'transformational' change, can present.

The UK government's '7 lenses of transformation' approach exemplifies these characteristics in a quintessential way (Government Digital Service, 2018). Billions of pounds are being spent on projects with designs guided by this approach, which involves the following 'lenses': creating a vision of the future; designing the details; making a plan (in achievable chunks); using strong leadership to motivate a network of people; collaborating across stakeholders; making people accountable for outcomes linked to the plan; communicating and engaging with people affected by the transformation. This advice stems from management texts of the 1990s. However, the UK government could do worse than reading Pressman and Wildavsky's 1984 book *Implementation: How Great Expectations in Washington Are Dashed in Oakland*. The commentary on Case Study 5 later in this chapter continues this discussion.

Another version of this approach is 'deliverology', discussed in Chapter 5. This combines the sanctions and rewards approach with a rational–purposive, technocratic understanding of change processes.

Stephen Ball (2008) identifies 'a new architecture of regulation', an organizational framework of service delivery based on the rational–purposive approach and on neo-liberalism's management arm, new public management. It is

a new mode of state control—a controlled decontrol, the use of contracts, targets and performance monitoring to 'steer' from a distance, rather than the use of traditional bureaucracies and administrative systems to deliver or micro-manage policy systems, such as education.   (Ball, 2008, p. 41)

In line with rational–purposive change management practices, this architecture involves policy instruments such as setting targets, identifying performance indicators, then evaluating and publishing comparative results to incentivize improved performance and reprioritization of goals.

But approaches such as these, found in the policy literature generally, are pitched at the national level and at quite a general level of specificity, without real guidance on *how* or *when* to apply them. Founded on the 'rationalist delusion' (Haidt, 2012), they miss the fact that decisions are often taken on the basis of a set of beliefs, ideologies, and assumptions which usually have no evidential underpinning: they are 'irrational' in that sense. Such approaches take no account of the issues to which a social practice approach alerts us, in particular the issue of contextual contingency and consequent differential reception and domestication of initiatives and the strategies used to enact them. They also fail to see the way in which policy and decision-making at the top level, at least in higher education, so often results in compromise, fudge, and language which is used to occlude alternative objectives and disputed issues.

### Nudge theory

Closely related is the 'nudge' approach associated with Richard Thaler. This is founded on a neo-liberal understanding of what drives people: behavioural economics. It sees individual choices as being amenable to 'nudging' in the right direction. Individuals make mistakes, usually because they do not have all the facts at hand, according to this view. They inadvertently operate in ways which are not in their interests, or they operate in their own interests but not for the greater good. Individuals mistakenly make short-term choices, being blind to or not caring about longer-term consequences.

Happily, nudge theorists tell us, by making small (and low-cost) changes in the environment, by altering the 'choice architecture', change agents can shape behaviour through insights and actions to make the 'correct' behaviour the path of least resistance:

> Behavioural insights have been used across public services to generate low cost interventions to improve service outcomes. The approach is based on the idea that interventions aimed at encouraging people to make better choices for themselves and society will be more successful if they are based on insights from behavioural science.

> With very little money upfront, people change their behaviour in order to produce better outcomes for themselves and for our society. This helps manage demand for public services, decreasing the cost of them.
>
> (Local Government Association, 2018)

This sounds attractive, and Thaler and Sunstein's book *Nudge* (2009) has sold remarkably well. Thaler won a Nobel prize for his work. Universities have begun to advertise 'Behavioural Insights Adviser' jobs: King's College advertised such a post in 2018, and has a 'Behavioural Insights Team' (Canning et al., 2018) located in the What Works Department, delivering the *What Works Department Strategy*. The British government's 'nudge unit', the official name of which is also the Behavioural Insights Team, was set up because Prime Minister David Cameron was convinced by these arguments. The team began life inside the Cabinet Office in 2010 (Halpern, 2015). But despite great promises, little change has been evident. One major problem with the approach is that it is too often founded on offering change agents multiple examples of nudging without a unifying theoretical thread with the power to help change agents identify 'nudge' opportunities or how they might approach them. The argument may be convincing, but the principles of application are lacking. Moreover, what little theory exists simply replicates the rational–purposive approach but at an individual level: people are rational beings who follow their own interests, but they make mistakes when they do so. Unfortunately, 'irrational' behaviour is much more often founded on sets of values, meanings, and issues of power and identity than on simple individual error or lack of information. In fact, the very notion of rationality is contextually contingent.

### Individualism

Where explicit theory is absent, another default position is the individualistic approach. Schatzki (2015, p. 467) talks about 'ontological individualism', the view of reality which 'maintain[s] that social phenomena are either constructions out of or constructions of individual people'. Applied to the enhancement of teaching and learning in higher education, the theory runs that if enough academic teachers become trained and qualified as 'good teachers' in an institution, this will lift the quality of teaching and learning not only in their classes, but in their departments and throughout the institution as a whole. This thinking lies behind the predominant approach to educational and academic development, which involves training academics as teachers. In the UK, the Professional Standards Framework (UKPSF) offers a warrant to academic teachers, for example. This theory also underpins rewarding 'excellent' academic teachers through, for example, the National Teaching Fellowship Scheme (NTFS), which originally rewarded national teaching Fellows with £50,000 for a teaching project (now reduced to £5,000).

There *is* a positive relationship between higher levels of UKPSF-recognized staff and institutional scores on the UK engagement survey of 2015 (Zaitseva, 2016). There is also a positive relationship between the number of NTFS holders and the achievement of a gold award by institutions in the TEF, the Teaching Excellence Framework (Rolfe, 2017). However, this is only to be expected: institutions more orientated to learning and teaching than to research, for example, are more likely to encourage staff to undertake both of these schemes, and are more likely to do well in exercises such as the TEF. The higher levels of staff qualification are just as likely to be an effect as a cause: correlation is not causation. In fact, no direct causal relationship between lecturer training and student outcomes has been firmly established.

Moreover, it is unclear what the causal links between lecturer training and their effects are supposed to be, or what precisely those effects are. The literature reveals multiple approaches to both, including 'training can improve teachers' focus'; 'training can improve a number of aspects of teaching as judged by students'; 'training can change teachers such that their students improve their learning' (Trowler and Bamber, 2005). Projected outcomes include improved student performance, improved student engagement, improved student satisfaction, and better ('deeper') quality learning.

These propositions may or may not be true: there is no robust evidence either way. But claims that simply increasing numbers of qualified staff will improve the quality of teaching and learning in an institution rest on the assumption that one can simply 'scale up' from the individual to the institutional level. This ignores the twin factors of, on the one hand, institutional practice architectures, which constrain, shape, and direct practices within an HEI, and on the other, local level factors which may also constrain a newly qualified individual's enactment of the 'improved' teaching techniques and approaches. Gibbs and Coffey (2004, p. 9) say this:

> [higher education teacher training course] trainees reported that in their departments teaching was often not valued and that there was pressure to conform to largely teacher-focused teaching conventions...Change was sometimes frowned upon and taken to imply criticism of more experienced colleagues.

The question whether this was or was not the case led to the development of the concept of TLRs: Alison Cooper and I concluded that the effectiveness of teaching qualification schemes in universities was limited by the constraining power of TLRs in place, within which any new practices were located (Trowler and Cooper, 2002). As noted in Chapter 2, Roxå and Mårtensson (2013) suggested, on the basis of an empirical study, that under some conditions individual educational development can lead to wider effects. But this only happens where TLRs have conversation networks in place, both formal and especially informal, and where implicit theories and discourses are aligned towards teaching and learning development. In such circumstances, they argue, individual training can have effects within *and beyond* the workgroup.

## Case Studies

I now move on to offer and interrogate several case studies. Exemplar cases, when situated within an explicit theory of how the social world operates and how it changes, offer readers food for thought about their own contexts and concerns. Thinking about case studies within a well-developed conceptual and theoretical framework helps provide an illuminated perspective on one's own context, the issues to be addressed there, and the likely outcomes of enhancement initiatives. Building on previous chapters, the following examples offer a step in this direction.

### Case study 1: Theory-driven institutional change at an English university

Jackson (2013) and Baker, Jackson, and Longmore (2014) report the details of a whole-institution change initiative with which they were involved, termed the Strategic Development Programme (SDP). The project, generously funded by the Higher Education Funding Council for England (HEFCE), took place at a university in England between 2009 and 2012, informed by the university's strategic plan for 2008–13. From the beginning, the approach to implementing change was driven by complex adaptive systems theory (CAST), which bears close resemblances to social practice theory in its significance for change agency.

The key objectives of both the SDP (the funded programme) and the strategic plan were: a curriculum that better meets market needs through partnerships with employers and employment trainers; improved student employability; more entrepreneurialism among academic staff; more inclusive and innovative teaching and learning approaches; growth of the university with an improved, expanded university estate; impact-focused research; and contributing to social justice and economic competitiveness for the university's host city and its region (summarizing Jackson, 2013, p. 23).

The institution had been energized by its recently acquired status as a university, and the SDP was viewed as a means of strengthening it by providing a distinctive portfolio of courses and innovative ways of working with employers and non-traditional student communities. During its inception the thinking informing the SDP was influenced by national policy agendas such as widening participation, enhancing student employability, and more flexible forms of programme delivery. Flexible delivery was based on the potential provided by e-learning and by viewing courses as combinable small units of learning rather than as rigid block programmes.

This was no small project: fairly radical organizational change would be needed to successfully bring the university to the place it wanted to be. The leaders of the SDP recognized that significant staff and organizational development would be involved; introducing improved and more appropriate IT systems would also be necessary, as would working hard outside the university to set up partnerships and get employers and others involved.

All these initiatives posed significant challenges for the staff and required changes to organizational cultures and pedagogical approaches. The SDP performed the role of an 'attractor' for people who were naturally innovative, and it was hoped that they could help change the culture through example, through their enthusiasm, and through their innovative ideas and hard work. Two such people are quoted by Jackson (2013, p. 40):

> I always put my hand up for those things because I like doing other things. I mean I love teaching but obviously I like getting involved in other projects.

> I respond to challenges and I am always looking for the next thing, the next idea. I come up with lots of ideas. I like following through with them as much as I can. Obviously there does need to be support for that, so yeah. I have got involved as much as I can.

The danger here, of course, was that the innovation would become siloed, failing to reach beyond these enthusiastic 'usual suspects' and unable to scale up from small projects in isolated places to whole-university change.

One of the leaders of the SDP, schooled in social science, was keen to ensure that this did not happen and instilled in the team the importance of operating with an explicit theory of change. Most appropriate here, she felt, was a 'complex-adaptive' change model which, while setting out broad targets, encouraged university staff to change in ways which suited their circumstances and resonated with their interpretations of how their particular area of work needed to develop. She stressed the importance of understanding the emergent and adaptive nature of change processes. The SDP team were happy to accept the use of this approach, although it puzzled some team members:

> [The SDP Manager] based our approach on something called—complex systems...she kept thrusting things in front of me which I probably should have read more thoroughly. But I sort of got it. I got what she was trying to do and we tried to work in an emergent sort of way. But we didn't know it was a theory called complex adaptive systems.
>
> (SDP Team member, quoted in Jackson, 2013, p. 25)

A top-down, rational–purposive approach was eschewed, as was the idea of a highly detailed, 'high definition' vision to be mechanically implemented in a series of incremental steps in a rational–purposive way. The team's approach, derived from its leader, accepted the uncomfortable truth that the higher education environment is turbulent, complex, and only amenable to fuzzy predictions. The multiple goals and agendas which exist there affect the path of change significantly, and actions can have unintended consequences and outcomes, sometimes in areas apparently unrelated to those in which the action is taken.

What this meant for the SDP team, each member having their own responsibility for an aspect of the project, was that they had to be sensitive to the contexts in which they worked, become comfortable with uncertainty, and be willing to allow time for change to occur. They had to be able to build consensus by adapting plans and approaches to local contingencies, understanding that outcomes will be different in different locales because of different histories and differences in context. The team tried hard to develop this willingness to adapt to context, and to be permissive of adaptation rather than simple adoption of innovations, within the broad scope of the project. They paid great attention to the following watchwords of complex adaptive systems theory: broad involvement; shared purpose; low-resolution initial planning; inclusive decision-making; participant engagement; encouragement of challenges to the status quo; high-quality information; self-organization; acceptance of diversity; delayed movement to consensus.

### Enacting the SDP

Some specific examples follow of how the team went about their work. A series of fora of increasing size for various categories of staff took place: the first involved twenty-five people; the second involved more than sixty; and so on. A series of questions was posed about what the strategic plan and programme could mean in terms of desirability and feasibility in the different parts of the university. The individuals given responsibility for different aspects of the SDP produced reports setting out feasible and desirable change in different parts of the university. In some cases the changes were limited; in others there was transformational change. The team fulfilled a number of important roles, including developing relationships of trust with staff, seeking mutual alignment between the needs and interests of different parts of the university and those of the SDP, raising awareness of the resources available for change and allocating them, monitoring progress, and evaluating funded projects.

Middle managers provided the main channel through which the SDP touched the working lives of staff within the university. It was possible for staff to avoid the SDP altogether because of the relatively small size of the SDP team and the limited number of projects which were being started. However, as the change programme evolved, middle managers assumed greater responsibility for involving more of their colleagues in the new developments. As more staff became involved and reported their experiences to middle managers, so this information was passed on to the SDP team and senior staff in the university. Consequently, changes were not brought about by a one-way transmission of information from top to bottom, but through communication flows which passed up, down, and across the institution with middle managers situated at the centre of these hubs.

Change happened at various rates and to various degrees across the university's faculties, schools, services, individual subjects, and programmes. Some flagship developments were more obvious, while other changes were quite subtle. University partnerships with specialist local industries were set up, with targeted courses and, in one case, a new, highly specialized academy. The latter linked distinctive local businesses and the university provision in a financially significant area of industry. A new school in the field of art and design was created, again linking to local industry. New types of educational programme began to be delivered, including an MSc in a regionally significant employment sector and a foundation degree in health and social care. The syllabi of already existing programmes changed to include employability skills, and new opportunities were created for student engagement with commerce and industry in areas such as fashion design, manufacturing, and marketing. Within the university itself new business systems and processes were introduced. E-learning courses were initiated, offering provision for those who, for employment reasons, were not able to attend the university in person.

## Commentary

The SDP team had worked with the cultural grain, allowing the path to grow as they walked it, enabling the situation to become, as Weick (1995, p. 11) puts it, 'progressively clarified [recognizing that] it is less often the case that an outcome fulfils some prior definition of a situation and more often the case that an outcome develops that prior definition'. They looked for congruence and planned for diversity in the reception and understanding of the initiative and in the ways in which it was put into practice. By using a devolved team and recruiting change agents within departments, they were able to take contextual factors into account: their ethnographic sensibility was achieved by having appropriately knowledgeable people involved. They were ready to accommodate unplanned outcomes in different contexts and were comfortable with allowing the project to mature within the implementation process. In fact, 'implementation' in this context is the wrong word: 'enactment' better summarizes the open nature of the approach to change.

It was important that the theory of change was explicit and was shared among the change agents. Complex adaptive change theory was often a topic of conversation, engagement, and sometimes tension among them. In this the Strategic Development Project differed markedly from Case Study 5, at the Australian university, where (a very different) explicit change theory was deployed but this was only known about by the top team, not being shared or discussed more widely. The SDP team enacted what Michael Fullan (1999) calls 'a change sandwich', walking a line between top-down direction and bottom-up drivers. The low definition vision combined with an appreciation of contextual contingencies helped with this. Similarly, it was important that they had advocates in the university top team while at the same time finding enthusiastic innovators on the ground and working with them. Jackson sums this up:

> The study of strategic change at [this university] demonstrates the value of bottom-up innovation within a comprehensive and sustained strategic change project. While top down initiatives, like the introduction of new business systems and processes are essential to enabling a university to be more effective, responsive and adaptive in its educational work, it is the innovators who provide the key resource to enact and embody the significant educational changes the university is trying to make.    (Jackson, 2013, p. 34)

For Jackson the SDP case study demonstrates how innovators thrive in a situation of encouragement and support from leaders and managers which empowers them. Resources, especially sufficient available time, are particularly important in this. Jackson enumerates some of them:

> Where the institution's systems and procedures enable rather than hinder progress. Where [innovators]...have the respect, emotional support and encouragement of managers and colleagues and where they can find help when they need it. Where they feel their efforts have been valued and have made a positive difference.   (Jackson, 2013, p. 34)

The SDP had the advantage of being very well resourced and internally directed, with a long timescale and relative freedom of action. Reflecting on the characteristics of this example shows how hopelessly broad such concepts as 'innovation', 'implementation', 'intervention', 'enhancement', and 'change processes' really are. In each circumstance the variables in characteristics are multiple, and they all condition the path to and chances of success. They include:

- Whether the initiative comes from outside or is developed internally, by one person or a group, for example.
- Whether it is prompted by technological change, shifts in the market, or other environmental shifts.
- Whether it occurs in an otherwise stable context, or one which is generally turbulent.
- Whether the initiative involves incremental development or transformational change.
- Whether it addresses tangible or intangible issues: for example, a new virtual learning platform versus cultural change.
- Whether the initiative is well resourced or not.
- Whether the change affects a small group, a whole institution, or a country's higher education system.
- Whether there is fit between the change context and the enhancement initiative or not.
- Whether leaders and change agents are competent or not.

These and other factors mean that every enhancement initiative is unique. There is no template to follow and no general advice or management textbook that can relate to all cases. Even the change agents on the ground had to find their way incrementally, making judgements sequentially.

The SDP case was remarkably successful in a number of areas, even taking into account the invisible hinterland of resistance and stasis: the 'hard to reach', 'hard to touch', and 'hard to change', from whom there is also much to learn. Case study literature tends to focus on the engaged, the innovators, and the indicators of success, but many change initiatives in higher education are less successful than the SDP. Bear traps (conflict which stops or diverts progress), dead ends (with progress blocked), and diversions (projects going in unforeseen and undesired directions) very frequently occur. These dangers can result from practical issues such as lack of resourcing, poor project management, lack of a workable theory of change, inappropriate assumptions, political divisions over what counts as 'progress', or simply change leaders taking their eye off the ball as new priorities come into view. They can also result from insufficient attention being paid to regimes in place, their back-stories, and the significance of different moments.

While the SDP was not founded on social practice theory but rather on complex adaptive systems theory, the two share many characteristics, as the case study shows. A more 'precise' understanding of how to conceptualize local contexts may have assisted the team. However, the general approach to the project was in line with the propositions about change processes that are generated from a social practice approach. I summarize these at the end of this chapter.

## Case study 2: Dealing with difficult people

I was once asked to give a talk for senior and middle managers at a university in South Africa. They were very interested in the topic of 'dealing with difficult people' and wanted me to help them improve at this. Digging a little deeper into this issue in preparation for the talk, I found that by 'difficult people' they were referring to individuals in some very specific departments who were resisting a fairly fundamental change initiative that was being introduced right across the university. I imagine what they wanted me to do was to offer techniques for bringing such individuals round to the university top team's way of thinking: strategies for getting them on board with the change initiative, or at least making them more compliant.

From my perspective, viewing the issue through a practice lens, this whole way of seeing was wrong. The 'problem' as it was being conceptualized ('difficult individuals') was the wrong problem. The focus on individuals, difficult or not, was the wrong focus, foregrounding as it did practitioners, not practices. For me the important questions were: What is it about the practices and the history of these departments that creates an issue in relation to the policy and innovation under discussion? Why is it that there is resistance in these locations in particular, but not in others: what are the significant characteristics of the configuration of practices in those different contexts that result in such different responses? If individuals are incapable of doing their jobs, or unwilling to do them, that is a job for the human resources (HR) department, not a consultant. But other issues seemed relevant here.

The talk that I delivered to those managers was not the one they were expecting. What I tried to do was to help them to see the issue from a different standpoint, through a different lens. I don't think I succeeded. The reason for that was not the fact that I only had one hour, nor that the structure of the session had been set up to be a didactic, TED Talk-style encounter. The more significant reason could be uncovered again by practice theory: these managers in this context shared a set of assumptions, an underlying theory, and a discourse which predisposed them to talk and think about the 'problem' in the way they did. They constituted, in short, a well-grounded workgroup with a fairly intractable set of practices which certainly were not going to be changed by a one-hour talk by some foreigner like me—exactly as Haidt (2012) would have predicted.

I was, however, able to offer them some practical steps which did not necessitate a fundamental change in their perspective. I asked them to reflect on where the centres of 'resistance' lay and where they did not, and to reflect on the nature of the practices in the resistant and compliant locations. I also asked them to consider the nature of the innovation, of the new policy itself. What were the likely effects of this in terms of power relations, discourses, approaches to teaching and learning, and so on? What assumptions was it founded on, and what theory of learning? Most crucially, I asked them to look at the 'fit' between the innovation and the two different types of context: the resistant and the compliant. I suggested that the sources of the issue may be found in the areas of congruence and lack of it between context and innovation, and that there may be areas where what the innovation required rubbed up very dramatically against current practices, against subjectivities in place, and against local sagas about 'who we are'.

This is not to say, of course, that there is no such thing within universities as 'difficult people': people who are arrogant, dismissive (even bullying), unable to work with colleagues; who have an attenuated notion of what constitutes 'a full day's work', who cannot see the impact of their comments on others, who lack empathy generally; those who have no real clue how to do their job without irritating almost everyone, or how to do it at all. But dealing with them is a matter of good management training, sharing management experience, and robust HR policies effectively enforced. That is just the daily work of people management.

## Case study 3: Dealing with difficult people (2)

(Based on Roper and Deal, 2010, pp. 28–32, with permission)

While the previous two case studies are pitched at a general level, this one drills down to a lower level of analysis. Roper and Deal tell the story of a young American university lecturer, Matt, who had set up his science classroom as a series of workstations. Here, small groups of students collaborated on tasks set by Matt, using his course materials and online resources as well as whatever technical equipment was necessary. The room buzzed with activity. Matt moved around, working with and helping students as required. The dean, Phil, visited the classroom and found it a refreshing change from the traditional lecture/laboratory approach.

Gone were rows upon rows of benches where students scribbled notes as the lecturer talked, then worked in isolation in a lab. Now, students were talking to one another and to their teacher. It certainly was noisier, but Phil preferred it that way. Everyone was engaged in helping one another and able to get the academic teacher's attention when needed.

The dean's view was that this had happened because the university president sparked a 'sense of urgency' about reforming learning and teaching in the college of science and mathematics. Phil and the president shared a determination to make their university a leader in student-centred learning.

Previously, Phil and a group of reform-minded lecturers had paid a visit to the Renssalaer Polytechnic Institute (RPI) in New York, where studio classrooms were already in place. They toured the facilities, talked to students, met with academic staff members and administrators. They noticed how the architecture, technology, and furniture encouraged collaborative work among students and a guidance-and-support role for the academic teachers.

Following that visit, the same group, plus additional people, flew to Washington DC to explore funding sources. There they had meetings with staff from relevant funding foundations to discuss potential grant support and were successful in raising money for the enhancement of quality of learning and teaching in the sciences at their university.

The dean knew, however, that there were barriers to address and that the majority of lecturers would be against the initiative: any vote on the issue would fall. He saw the situation as a minority—the 'cheerleaders'—versus a majority of more conservative lecturers. Rather than voting on the issue, he set up a staff meeting agenda where the groups who had been to RPI and Washington presented reports on what they had learned and what their views now were. They reported that the students at RPI were 'totally engaged' and that the lecturers there were free to meet each group, checking their understanding and helping them when they got stuck. They also reported that their review of relevant literature confirmed the effectiveness of studio classrooms in terms of student learning.

At the meeting the dean tried to be supportive but not directive, applauding experimentation but declaring himself ready to be proved wrong. Later, more than one million dollars was allocated to remodelling and equipping the studio classrooms. Volunteers agreed to design the curriculum and develop resources, though they worried about finding time, and worried too about whether their promotion prospects would improve as a result. In order to make guarantees to volunteers that they would benefit, the dean had to change the retention, tenure, and promotion criteria of the university in order to make work in studio classrooms 'count', to make it profitable for them.

The dean knew that such a change would be contentious, so he again avoided calling for a vote at a staff meeting. Instead he sent copies of the revised tenure and promotion criteria to all tenured full and associate lecturers in the unit, asking them to review the new criterion: 'Contributing to the reform of instruction through participation in studio classrooms.' Questions or disagreements were to be sent to him within six weeks. In the event he received none, so the changes went ahead. Additionally, the dean provided ongoing support for the instructors in studio classroom instruction, lightening teaching loads to give time for development work and making a small budget available for equipment and assistants.

Looking back on his efforts to support the college's first chemistry studio classroom, Phil surmised that 'protecting' studio classroom instructors from negative faculty members by revising the tenure and promotion criteria was paramount. Next in importance was protecting the 'naysayers' from pressure to abandon their traditional methods. He admonished the 'cheerleaders' to 'tone down' their criticism of sceptical academic staff. He reminded them that most of the negative reaction was coming from older staff members who were solid traditional teachers and hard workers. The dean warned: 'You won't help your cause by belittling your colleagues.'

However, in a staff meeting, one of the cheerleaders declared that the traditional lecture/lab approach was 'bankrupt'. Phil did his best to disagree, in order to defuse a situation which could have quickly become antagonistic. He believed that, with careful management, most of the resisters could eventually be persuaded, but he left hard-core opponents alone. Instead he invited waverers into the studio classrooms and encouraged them to make their own judgements. He also made himself available to staff so that he could explain the rationale for the change and listen to concerns and suggestions.

'Reformers' were able to easily access travel funds for conferences where they gave papers about studio classrooms to professional associations, sometimes co-presenting with students. Visitors were encouraged to come and observe the studio classrooms in action. The university president brought alumni, potential donors, and senior businesspeople from around the state, as well as his own university governors. All were given material explaining and illustrating the development.

After the first year's success in chemistry and math, members of the physics and statistics departments began working on designing studio classrooms for their majors. Phil hosted a ceremony to launch the new studio classrooms and to celebrate the excellent results from the first year. Everyone in the college of science and mathematics received an invitation. Since the food was great, the programme brief, and the president in attendance, staff turnout was well above average.

Phil started the ceremony's programme with testimonials from students. They enthusiastically praised their instructors and the entire college for designing studio classrooms. Involved academic staff members presented charts showing greater learning gains in studio versus traditional classes in the same subject areas. The president offered his blessing:

> Congratulations are in order. The undergraduate education our students receive in the College of Science and Mathematics is one of the best in the United States. Your studio classrooms are becoming a magnet for your colleagues in other institutions. You should be proud of yourselves. I certainly am very proud of you.

Later, the dean noticed that instruction in the 'traditional' classes was beginning to change, too. Although lectures and labs remained central, many lecturers fostered more student interaction, introduced collaborative workgroups, and expanded the technology used in their classes.

## Commentary

Conflict around introduction of student-centred learning is nothing new or unusual, as the case study of the physics lecturer (and head of department) in South Africa (Chapter 4, 'Recurrent Practices') illustrated. In that example and in the Roper and Deal case we see a division between what the dean here referred to as the 'reformers' and the 'resisters'. For Roper and Deal the case study involves heroes (Phil, Matt, and to a lesser extent the university president) deploying great effort and resources to overcome the resistance from a group of individuals for whom studio-based learning is not how you do your work as a lecturer.

Reframing this case in terms of social practices, however, illuminates two things. The first is that the issue at hand concerns alternative practices, different ways of 'doing and saying' (Schatzki, 1996, p. 89), of learning and teaching, in maths and science. The individuals involved are, as Reckwitz (2002, p. 249) says, 'carriers' of these different practices (though this word is somewhat over-deterministic). Seeing the issue in this way means that the temptation to think in terms of 'difficult' or 'resistant' people becomes irrelevant: some have been recruited to a student-centred set of practices, others have not. Secondly, the account brackets out much of the work in universities, focusing on the one issue and ignoring the other sets of practices in which all the actors are involved: research, income generation, and the rest.

This issue of the enmeshed, bundled nature of practices becomes apparent at only two points in this case study. The first relates to Phil's need to change the RTP criteria in order to reward the reformers. The second relates to Matt's concerns about having enough time to devote to the innovation, which were resolved by relieving him of other duties (and other practice sets). In both cases poor meshing was relatively easily changed, both essentially by managerial fiat. But more complex situations of bundled practices, involving practice paradoxes (cases where practices actually interfere with each other), are not addressed in the case study. Also involved here are actions making the changes profitable, not only in the promotion criteria but in terms of the status of those changes internally and nationally.

The dean's careful and thoughtful handling of the situation demonstrates him applying both mêtis and phronesis: he has a 'feel' for bear traps and potentially productive paths. But in this case study he had a lot going for him: a relatively straightforward issue to be addressed; enthusiasts both in the top team above him and on the ground below him; plenty of resources; and the power to make things happen as and when he wanted them. Things are rarely so straightforward. But as an exaggerated case study, it does illustrate some clever moves to bring about changes in a TLR which are in line with social practice theory.

## Case study 4: Beyond communities of practice

A five-yearly review of an online postgraduate programme in a UK university involved gathering data of various sorts:

- programme documentation and its website;
- interviews with all members of the programme team, including academics, an administrator, and a learning support officer;
- a review of the learning design and organization of the online environment;
- a review of the structure of the programme and the role of individual modules;
- data on recruitment, withdrawal, intercalation (time out of the programme), and progress towards completion;
- student feedback information.

The review revealed the need for some structural changes in the programme. It identified drift in module content and assessment practices since the programme had last been reviewed. This had led to various anomalies, overlaps, and lacunae. There were a series of options to deal with this. Some specific issues were raised. For example, there were very different approaches to marking students' work and to what particular percentage grades mean (see Chapter 1), and this led to considerable anxiety and confusion among students as they moved between modules receiving very different levels of marks. There was also a question about the fundamental basis of the programme's aims: was it about covering the right content, or was it about developing research skills among its students? This affected the possible answers to questions such as 'Does the content need to be expanded or updated?' 'Should quantitative methods be taught, even though only a minority of students use them?' 'Does the programme have a unique identity, and should it?'

Underlying these questions of programme content and identity was a potentially more significant issue. Several of the academic staff had been appointed relatively recently and they felt no ownership of their modules or the programme as a whole. They felt that there was an inappropriate legacy, with modules designed by other people for other times and now constraining them, the newer recruits. The better established and more senior members of the team tended to take the view that the staff should just teach 'their' modules without complaint, and were quite critical of the proposals coming forward from the team. Naivety on the part of the newer members, they felt, meant they were not aware that their suggestions were against regulations, were not practicable, or had been tried before and failed.

The review found that the regular programme team meetings, while well run, tended to involve the suppression of the more junior staff's voices (at least in their own perception) and reluctance to engage in discussions about changing the programme. Team meetings could involve conflict and emotional upset but resulted in very little change. A minority of the staff on the programme had been educated in North American contexts, and their attitudes to issues such as academic freedom, the autonomy of lecturers, assessment practices, and even programme management were quite different from those of the other lecturers, and very different from those of the long-established staff. One comment illustrates this different perspective:

> We should teach what we like, including deciding year-by-year what will be in our modules. Our modules should reflect our current academic interests and research projects, and should change accordingly.

In the UK environment, however, universities are required to be very clear to potential students about their 'offer': applicants need to know what they are applying for. The detailed provision of information about programmes and universities had been a key government policy for some years, because of the neo-liberal emphasis on well-informed student choice.

There was a suspicion that discussing the review report in a full team meeting might not be effective in enhancing the programme. On the contrary, past experience had told the more junior members of the team that very little would change—conservatism would prevail. Notwithstanding the value of any changes and the quality or robustness of suggestions coming forward from the team, there certainly were real issues concerning the different perspectives, the lack of ownership, and the perception that some voices were being repressed. Whether or not the programme changed in its detail, these issues needed to be addressed.

The review team therefore considered it necessary for creative ways to be established to address the review report, given the suspicions about the effectiveness of full team meetings. Suggestions included the formation of task groups and delegation of responsibility for particular issues in the report.

The establishment of ground rules for full team meetings, the possible use of a 'mood monitor', and other suggestions for the full team meetings themselves were also made in order to circumvent conservatism and to moderate the power differentials in play.

## Commentary

This case study illustrates what is so often the case in universities: tensions between divided groups of staff within departments centring on different ideological currents, different backstories, alternative world views, and competing priorities. In dealing with this in her own way, the programme director deployed her power to set the agenda in meetings and to control discussions in them. Power was also deployed in relation to suggestions for change, in this case a claim to have greater experience and knowledge of university regulations and procedures and of the practicalities of running the programme, and the claim of a history of success which should not be threatened.

The moments in play within this TLR were in tension. There were different implicit theories of teaching and learning, different conventions of appropriateness, different discursive repertoires, and different assumptions. We can clearly see here subjectivities in interaction and the mobilization of different kinds of resources to deploy power.

This case study depicts workgroups in a way which contrasts sharply with the communities of practice perspective, which emphasizes how workgroups tend to cleave to consensus and shared values. The fact that the theory was originally founded on case studies of craft industries from previous centuries, such as tailoring and blacksmithing, rather than the multiverse of postmodern narratives of the twenty-first century leaves that perspective looking rather dated. Within universities, the kinds of tensions depicted in this case study represent the more prevalent scenario. Making changes in such situations requires an in-depth understanding of them and a sensibility for practices which can indicate where profitable and less profitable leadership choices lie.

## Case study 5: Top-down curriculum reform at an Australian university

Swerissen's DBA thesis (2017) recounts his experience implementing teaching, learning, and organizational reforms in the faculty of health sciences at an Australian university. He was executive dean of that faculty and initiated the reforms, leading their implementation.

The reforms involved introducing new qualifications at undergraduate and postgraduate levels; a common first year across the faculty; more and denser networks with health agencies; an improved academic quality assurance and enhancement process; the replacement of didactic teaching with enquiry and problem-based approaches to teaching; and new interdisciplinary organizational structures. The last two were the catalyst for a number of issues of interest here.

Across the faculty there were different 'patterns of values, assumptions, beliefs and ideologies' (Swerissen, 2017, p. 39), and these became evident as the change process began. The need for these changes was questioned in some parts of the faculty, as was their extent. Elsewhere, the changes were accepted or even welcomed:

> A passionate minority of staff questioned the extent to which organisational and curriculum issues identified in the discussion papers warranted significant change across the faculty. There was little disagreement that the Faculty faced significant external challenges from competition as new courses in allied health and nursing opened or expanded, putting pressure on clinical placements and student demand. However, there was significant divergence of opinion about the extent to which these problems warranted fundamental reorganisation and change.
>
> Some staff considered the move towards more flexible, interdisciplinary, efficient and student-centred enquiry-based learning models to be a major improvement consistent with their reading of trends in other institutions and across their profession. This was particularly true for enquiry-based learning and the establishment of Graduate Entry Masters programmes which had already been adopted in Occupational Therapy and Speech Pathology. Other staff, particularly those in Human Biosciences and Public Health who supported more traditional didactic, discipline based models of teaching and organisation were more sceptical. They were more likely to question the need for the organisational and curriculum changes proposed in the discussion paper. (Swerissen, 2017, pp. 99–100)

Issues of professional identity ('subjectivities') and power were especially significant, particularly in regard to the loss of discipline or professionally focused departments and the fear of disappearing within new large interdisciplinary schools. On these organizational issues, compromises were reached which allowed there to be schools within the faculty, 'to form internal professionally focused departments, although these departments had no resources or formal decision making power' (p. 103). This pattern of leaders making some compromise, but always with the emphasis on retaining the integrity of the reform model, was a common one. Proposals were modified, especially when this was 'critical to recruiting support from key academic leaders' (p. 102).

In terms of challenges to established teaching practices, the proposal to eliminate the lecture–tutorial format and replace it with an enquiry-based learning (EBL) model evoked particular opposition. Again, the solution was to mollify opposition with a compromise which retained lecturing but positioned it as a support for the EBL process. Likewise, tutorials were retained in some areas but incorporated only in the guise of small learning groups within the EBL model. Where this kind of concern was located depended on the back-stories of staff and departments:

> For staff with a history in the College of Advanced Education sector, identities were more closely tied to the teaching and professional (clinical) programme than to research. Consequently, it is likely that changes to the curriculum, teaching and learning process and clinical placements were perceived as reducing their autonomy and threatening their academic identity more than might have been the case if they had been more research active. (Swerissen, 2017, p. 148)

**Commentary**

This was clearly a top-down directed set of innovations. Power differentials were applied in order to see the reform through; allocating or denying resources played a particularly important role in this. Although probably unaware of it, Swerissen was adopting a similar rational–purposive approach to that set out in the UK government's '7 lenses of transformation' (Government Digital Service, 2018), described previously. This kind of approach exemplifies the 'technocratic turn' discussed in Chapter 5. Both the innovations at Swerissen's university and the '7 lenses' were heavily influenced by rational–purposive theories of the management of change from the 1990s, especially Kotter (1995) and Kanter (1991). Swerissen acknowledges his debt to the latter two theorists (2017, p. 96). This, then, was a change project based on very different principles than that in Case Study 1 (the Strategic Development Project).

The '7 lenses' approach portrays transformational change as relatively easy. Grand statements such as 'it is important to create a culture which empowers people to make appropriate decisions' are breathtakingly naïve. So is the assumption that 'having a single view of the future can motivate people to collaborate towards shared outcomes'.

Swerissen's account reveals that things are not so simple as the UK government publication suggests. Those in powerful positions, such as the 'key academic leaders', with a different vision to the grand plan were able to demand compromises and changes. Achieving 'collaboration' in support of the original plan proved not so easy. Workgroups within the faculty had different types of backstories, and these shaped their reception of these changes, in particular the codes of signification evoked by the changes. In schools largely comprising staff with a health profession background rather than an academic/research one, some changes were particularly unwelcome. Within the academy they saw their identity and status as dependent upon their role transmitting their professional knowledge to students. This was particularly so where staff had been incorporated into Swerissen's university from the college sector.

In a sense, it may seem odd that there was opposition in a health faculty to the introduction of enquiry-based learning, as this had become an almost standard approach in parts of the health field since is first introduction in medical education at Hamilton University, Ontario, many years ago. As Elton (2003) notes, there is salience and congruence between EBL (or at least its sibling PBL, problem-based learning) in health education in universities and the daily professional experience of the health professions. In the latter a patient presents with symptoms, which is effectively a problem that needs to be solved. EBL and PBL simply replicate this. However, this case shows that in some areas of health education, while there may be salience and congruence between professional practices and teaching and learning innovation, issues around profitability (related to identity change and loss of power and status) may trump them.

The picture is a varied one, however: workgroups with different characteristics and practices (both past and present) welcomed these pedagogical changes, particularly in disciplinary areas where enquiry-based learning was already well established—for them such changes were congruent, salient, *and* profitable.

This analysis suggests that the tensions and forces of resistance will not have gone away after the change process has been enacted. There will be continuing attempts in some locales to return to previous teaching and learning practices, to gradually shift away from an EBL approach, and to reinstate the significance of lectures and tutorials. As recent global history tells us, leaders' 'mission accomplished' declarations are frequently followed by insurrections. Conversely, of course, misrecognition of what is really happening on the ground and continuing with business as usual can result in sudden, and surprising, revolution. This happened in South Africa with the #RhodesMustFall/#FeesMustFall/Decolonization sequence of uprisings: there was a sudden shift from the left to the right of Figure 2.1.

## Social Practice Theory and Its Corollaries: The Elements of a Practice Sensibility

This section abstracts a number of corollaries for change agents and leaders which stem from the argument and evidence presented up to this point in the book. These are not in the form of advice, guidance, or even 'frameworks for action' (Bamber, Trowler, and Saunders, 2009). As noted throughout the book, their value is limited by the significance of contextual contingencies: context matters when making decisions about changes. Furthermore, the most important issues which leaders face tend to be 'wicked' ones, with no agreement on what the real issue is, no algorithm to follow to address it, and no single or simple solutions (Trowler, 2012).

Instead, I want to do two key things here. First, significant points are reiterated in summary form from the depiction of what social practice theory says about social reality in general and about teaching and learning regimes in particular, and from the case studies presented. These corollaries are in the form of propositional statements, outlining a form of knowing which is rational, 'embrained' (Blackler, 1995). Second, I want to set out the elements of a practice sensibility—what it feels like to see the world through a practice lens. These depictions are perceptual, 'embodied' in nature. As noted earlier in the book, acquiring the latter requires the former: new ways of seeing are built upon knowledge, concepts, and forms of explanation. These are the substrate without which one cannot acquire perceptual change that can offer insights and indicate appropriate ways of acting.

## Propositional statements: Social practices and change processes

### The engrooved nature of social practices
Social practices are 'engrooved', rooted in the past and habitual in nature, and so are resistant to fundamental change (Trowler, Saunders, and Knight, 2002).

They draw on deep proto-practice reservoirs of ideologies, discourses, symbolic structures, theories, and assumptions. The consequence of this is that radical, rapidly imposed change is unlikely to become deeply embedded, but will rather be superficial and involve only reluctant or surface compliance rather than any sense of ownership. In such cases, changes will not be resilient and sustaining them will require continuing effort and resources. The implications for interventions involve trying to work with the grain of current practices but providing resources (including knowledge resources) to demonstrate the potential profitability and salience of changes.

### Domestication of change initiatives

Appropriation (domestication) of an initiative into an already established order almost always occurs; changes are shaped by context and are rarely realized in the way they were initially envisaged. Change agents should expect different outcomes in different locations because of different established practices and contextual contingencies. By presenting initiatives in a 'low resolution' way, space is allowed for this inevitable domestication within the broad parameters of desired changes.

### Incorporation into frameworks of meaning

The reception of innovation is conditioned by frameworks of meaning, symbolic structures, and discourses which partly shape the moments of a TLR. Discourses are part of social practices, describing the world and having a strong influence on it. Discursive repertoires, like dialects, are localized and, in a university context, multiple. This underlines the significance of having an anthropological awareness of practices on the ground, and of associated sets of meaning. Predicting likely outcomes involves knowing the meanings which will inhabit proposed changes and which will condition their reception. Changes presented in a discursively inappropriate way are likely to jar with repertoires on the ground, evoking resistant responses. The implications for interventions involve focusing on the medium as well as the message, on predicting ways of 'reading' messages in different contexts and the potential implications of those alternative readings. Being self-aware in relation to the repertoires upon which one regularly draws is important in this, and is a significant part of developing a practice sensibility.

### Intuitive and emotional responses

Emotional responses, often just brief flashes, are evoked by the ideas and meanings embedded in changes and change initiatives. Proposals for change are laden with codes of signification which are ingrained in practices, and in proposals for new practices. As with discourses, the semiotics of changes are of significance for potential outcomes:

> Emotions are a kind of information processing. Contrasting emotion with cognition is therefore as pointless as contrasting rain with weather, or cars with vehicles...[There are] two different kinds of cognition: intuition and reasoning...Intuition is the best word to describe the dozens or hundreds of rapid, effortless moral judgements and decisions that we all make every day. Only a few of these intuitions come to us embedded in full-blown emotions.
>
> (Haidt, 2012, p. 45)

As noted earlier, Haidt is incorrect, in my view, to call those flashes of small emotions 'intuition', which implies a gut feeling concerning events about to happen. Rather, they are flashes of emotional response to codes of signification which can become agglomerated into more sustained, fuller, emotional responses. These are rationalized post hoc into an argument for or against something (such as a change initiative). For interventions, the implications of this relate to having a sensitivity towards the feelings that will be evoked. These emotional responses—both immediate, fleeting ones and those that are more sustained—are likely to be particularly strong when they relate to other moments of teaching and learning regimes, especially shifting power relationships, engrooved recurrent practices in place, and academic teachers' subjectivities. Proposals for changes in learning and teaching are never just technical; they always touch on the moments of TLRs. Engaging with such issues is more helpful than avoiding them.

### The agentic power of artefacts

The significance of artefacts and their relational role in practices is not fixed; they are on the move. But we know that artefacts, tools, and the physical world shape practices and are at the same time put to work in ways conditioned by local practices. A practice-sensitive focus also considers the physical world and the tools available, together with the potential for the introduction of new tools, artefacts, and physical environments in specific contexts. The physical arrangement of workspaces, meeting rooms, and social spaces, the proformas in use, the hardware and software deployed, the presentation and constructed availability of internet resources: these all shape practices and condition the path of changes.

### The significance of embodied, procedural behaviours

Routinized ways of using the body are involved in enacting recurrent practices. Learned embodied procedures do matter, though they might not receive as much attention in thinking about change as more cognitive forms of learning. Changing approaches to teaching can involve relearning in this physical sense, acquiring new competences and 'retiring' old ones. Sensitivity to the physicality involved in recurrent practices and the implications of change in this sense is important, partly because proposed changes in this domain evoke emotional, intuitive responses and partly because this kind of change presents specific sorts of challenges.

### Rippling outwards, and inwards

The local and particular is heavily conditioned by discourses, power relations, and practices both horizontally and vertically. National policy contexts, sanctions and rewards, discursive repertoires and ways of thinking are not all-powerful, but they shape ways of thinking, doing, being, and speaking at the everyday, local level. Workgroups and departments within universities are open, natural systems and so are framed and shaped by others around them and by their institutional contexts. The influence of practice architectures at different levels cannot be avoided because of the nested and bundled nature of social practices.

Open natural systems are not only shaped by inward forces. Changes and decisions made locally ripple outwards and have implications elsewhere. Often these implications condition, constrain, or facilitate outcomes. It is important, therefore, not only to be aware of the influence of structures on everyday behaviours, responses, and frameworks of meaning, but also to think beyond the local when considering the implications of local decisions and changes.

### Ripples from the past and into the future

The present is rooted in the past, and the future is emergent from today's realities. Current and future practices are contingent upon past ones and, perhaps especially in educational contexts, the past is evident in the practices of today and shapes what is possible for the future. Although often inappropriate, the practices and discourses from decades and even centuries ago are still found in even the most modern contexts; they are incredibly resilient. This is why declarations of 'educational revolutions', usually envisaged as a result of some technological innovation, are rarely realized. Recognizing and being realistic about this that not only helps avoid disappointment but also offers a pathway towards more practical enactments of innovations with greater chances of success.

## Perceptual statements: What a practice sensibility feels like

A practice sensibility involves both rational cognition and intuition based on conceptual sophistication and experience. The latter usually comes first in any situation, including situations faced by managers and change agents. Explicit consideration of alternative courses of action and the details of enactment follows on. Any change process involves multiple decision points. Myriad interpersonal interactions occur, as do multiple forms and points of interaction with many different players and groups of players. At each critical point the practice sensibility, felt at an intuitive level as well as processed cognitively, can indicate appropriate behaviour.

Addressed at an explicit, rational level, one could depict this as a sensitivity to the different moments of teaching and learning regimes. Aware of the significance of the impact on current power relations within a department, with its different groupings, a manager or leader will instinctively feel alarm bells ringing when asked to implement an initiative which will have significant effects on them. Then, she begins to consider ways of mitigating or circumventing such effects, or of implementing the directive in such a way as to cause the least amount of conflict and resistance, as the dean did in Case Study 3.

A proposed physical move of a workgroup or department to another location may seem simply a practical challenge. However, for a leader sensitive to social practices, the significance of the interaction between materiality and recurrent behaviours, of codes of signification, and of the particulars of subjectivities and power relations within her department mean that the crucial challenges of such a geographical move are social, not physical.

An anthropological understanding of workgroup and departmental contexts includes an awareness of the different identities in play, their own definitions of 'self', and associated definitions of the situation. These factors are important in intuitively understanding possible reactions to innovations and change interventions. In some cases there will be valence, a sense of salience and congruence; in other cases opposition may be evoked. Practical intelligence, phronesis, and 'forward feeling' are guided by tacit understandings of such issues.

Everyday behaviours and usually unconsidered personal routines also become invested with much greater significance when seen with a practice sensibility. Even the most mundane decisions or unconscious routines are important: whether to leave one's office door open or closed, or half open; how to arrange the furniture in one's office; where one eats; whether one engages in 'menial' tasks such as washing up. All of these are 'signs' to be read, and which will be read and evaluated because they carry codes of signification. But they are codes which may be read in different ways. Understanding those different ways requires an anthropological awareness of the immediate environment.

*Voorgevoel*, forward feeling, is a very significant aspect of a practice sensibility. A head of department who is discussing potential changes to teaching and learning, a syllabus, or the curriculum with an individual member of staff or in a staff meeting will, in a sense, simultaneously be 'hearing' that forward feeling coming from their intuition and converting it into explicit questions and concerns. Who will be affected by this and who needs to be consulted and involved? Where will the opposition come from? What is the best way to present this? Is the form of this suggestion being presented the best version in order to achieve the goals, and are those the right ones? *Voorgevoel* gives rise to these questions and provokes a sense of which are the better responses and which the worse.

The more strategic, more conscious aspect of phronesis, mêtis, performs a duet with phronesis in such circumstances. The change agent with a practice sensibility knows that reinventing the wheel is important: people like to feel that it *was* invented here, and that this initiative, whatever it is, is *their* initiative. The forward feeling change agent will be sensitized to ways in which this sense of ownership can be accomplished. She also knows that there are no single right answers, and that the (re-)invention might take different forms in different locales, and probably will. Again, an anthropological awareness of social practices in those different locales gives a solidity to that forward feeling.

Wilkinson and Kemmis (2015) rightly warn us that leaders are not all-powerful, and that 'leading' in specific contexts is itself a social practice. Like other practices, there are arrangements in place which both enable and constrain the conditions for leading practices. While it is important for leaders to have knowledge, understanding, and a practice sensibility, these are not enough in themselves:

> Rather, the pre-existing cultural-discursive, material-economic and social-political set-ups or arrangements which prefigure the conditions for leading practice also must be transformed, for 'practices are not shaped solely by the intentional action and practice knowledge of participants but also by

circumstances and conditions that are '"external to them"' (Kemmis et al., 2012, p.34). Practices of leading play a crucial role in the *orchestration* of such transformations.   (Wilkinson and Kemmis, 2015, p. 344)

'Orchestration' is a valuable simile: leaders can, through their actions, play a role in orchestration. But they can also be orchestrated by practice architectures, exactly as others are. A practice sensibility can heighten awareness of this happening and help shift the process of orchestration in the other direction. Like a successful symphony performance, behind successful change processes lies considerable effort, skill, and knowledge deployed in assembling the circumstances of that success. It is a significant accomplishment.

# 7

# The Practice Sensibility and the Challenges of Change

## Key Ideas: The Book's Argument Summarized

Three dimensions of professional life within universities are elaborated in this book. They are, first, the proto-practice reservoirs from which some of the moments of social practices spring; secondly, specific social practices shaped by those moments and others; and thirdly, teaching and learning regimes which consist of a family of social practices performed by workgroups over an extended period of time. The three are intimately connected and together they result in the constitutive accomplishment that is the daily experience of staff and students in higher education institutions. Those institutions play an important part in conditioning the nature of the TLRs within them through their own practice architectures. The book's key argument is that a practice sensibility allows one to apprehend the interrelationships between these key ideas. Together with light-touch ethnographically derived understandings of context, this can improve change agency and lead to appropriate, sustainable outcomes. As the individual acquires a practice sensibility they also begin to see reality differently; they undergo an 'ontological shift', which changes how they see the world and how they see themselves in it. As Cousin says:

> We are what we know. New understandings are assimilated into our biography, becoming part of who we are, how we see and how we feel.
>
> (Cousin, 2006, p. 4)

The concept 'proto-practice reservoirs' refers to sets of symbolic structures, ideologies, conventions, and discourses which Giddens categorizes as comprising rules and resources. In the educational realm, ideologies comprise traditionalism, progressivism, social reconstructionism, and enterprise. In other realms, such as politics, equal opportunities, or approaches to ethnic disadvantage, the reservoirs have different flavours. Ideologies structure dispositions through the way they shape how issues are conceived and how they prioritize goals and values.

*Accomplishing Change in Teaching and Learning Regimes: Higher Education and the Practice Sensibility.*
Paul Trowler, Oxford University Press (2020). © Paul Trowler. DOI: 10.1093/oso/9780198851714.001.0001

The social practices of interest for our purposes concern those related to teaching and learning. Social groups which are engaged on a common project over an extended period perform recurrent, usually unconsidered practices. They occur in classrooms, when meeting students, when assessing students' work, when meeting with colleagues to discuss teaching and learning. The performance is conditioned by streams flowing from the reservoirs described above. The implicit theories of teaching and learning deployed, the understandings of appropriate conventions, the tacit assumptions that are made about students (for example), the discursive repertoires in use, and the meanings and emotional reactions that are attached to ideas all flow from proto-practice reservoirs to constitute practices. However, practices are also formed agentically, not as thoughtless enactment, structurally determined. Practices take the form of local performances, specific repertoires constituted from a unique mix of currents from reservoirs and local 'shaping' of them.

The concept 'teaching and learning regime' describes the family of social practices in a specific higher education context engaged in teaching. It represents a cultural milieu unique to that context. Because TLRs are constituted from practices, they are also connected to proto-practice reservoirs. Structurally derived (but locally reworked) elements, 'moments', can be discerned in them. The book describes eleven moments, five of which flow directly from reservoirs: implicit theories of teaching and learning; conventions of appropriateness; tacit assumptions; codes of signification; discursive repertoires. Taken together, these constitute locally specific meanings and understandings. Five further moments of any TLR result from the characteristics of the local context, the people involved, and the broader practice architecture in which the TLR operates. Indirectly, however, these are shaped by and shape the other moments; the distinctions are only analytical. The moments are: power relations; subjectivities in interaction; materiality in interaction; backstories in process; and regimes in interaction. The last of the eleven moments, recurrent practices, refers to the specific mix of social practices found in any TLR. To repeat: these are analytical distinctions—separating and categorizing the moments is an artificial exercise undertaken for the purposes of illumination. In reality the moments are inseparably intertwined, mutually contingent.

Individual social practices represent a constitutive accomplishment, dynamically achieved at each occurrence. Likewise, teaching and learning regimes are assembled and reassembled dynamically. Elements change, initiatives are introduced, and the turbulence of the higher education environment has its effects. Like practices, TLRs are in motion, but are not always under control.

Looking at the way these three phenomena are related in terms of their generative capacity, one can describe proto-practice reservoirs as first order, social practices as second order, and TLRs as third order. In terms of movement from the concrete and palpable to the abstract and conceptual, the sequence is changed: social practices are first order, TLRs second order, and proto-practice reservoirs third order. For the purposes of the argument here, the first classification is the more significant. Proto-practice reservoirs may only be apparent through indexical data, but they are nonetheless immensely significant.

Despite this complexity, developing an understanding, a way of seeing, based on this depiction of social reality in universities can be beneficial. A practice sensibility exposes and foregrounds the underpinning forces at work in shaping social practices and conditioning the shape of TLRs. This shifts the attention away from individual attitudes, behaviours, and choices and onto ideologies, discourses, alternative sets of meaning, theories, and ideas of appropriateness. This sensibility shifts the perception of timescale from the immediate, obviously present to trajectories which involve past, present, and likely futures. It 'zooms out' from the dazzle of personalities, interpersonal conflicts, and immediate problems to see the significance of environmental factors in shaping and conditioning local circumstances and events. It appreciates how the constitution of daily professional life is being accomplished, and the limits and opportunities of that accomplishment. The following section discusses the importance of this for improving approaches to change processes in universities.

## Traction Control: Enhancing Use Value

The book offers, then, a fully developed theory of the family of practices found in teaching and learning regimes. This provides a theoretical framework which has purchase or traction of different sorts. By 'traction' I mean that the concepts and theory are able to move from the cognitive level of understanding and be applied, to effect, in the world. The effect of interest in the book is the improvement of teaching and learning and so, indirectly, the enhancement of the student experience and augmentation of outcomes of different sorts for students. This traction is fourfold:

1. Illuminative traction. The practice sensibility illuminates processes occurring in higher education, giving a perspective which goes beyond individual personalities, choices, and difficulties. It lights up the structural

reservoirs which underpin practices and appreciates the emergent and contingent nature of the present day and the significance of context, practice architectures, and the operation of power. As I said in the Preface: The Book's Backstory, armed with a practice sensibility, even the most tedious meeting becomes interesting: mapping the flow of proto-practice reservoirs into the 'texts' being produced in the room becomes compulsive, as does watching the application and flow of power relations and subjectivities in interaction. For the insider researcher who is participating and observing with a practice-focused viewpoint, every event—even the most apparently mundane—becomes data.

2. Empirical traction. Improved understanding and theory-informed change processes can result in better choices and the avoidance of pitfalls. Unfurling vague concepts of 'organizational culture' into descriptions of the moments which shape teaching and learning regimes to form the building blocks of the multiple cultural configuration of universities gives a better grip on empirical reality and more fine-grained indications of pathways to enhancement.

3. Impact traction. The approach set out in these pages is designed to make a difference in the world. It contributes to the agenda of social science with meaning, in the sense that it makes an appreciable difference not only in the academic world of research and publication but also in the lives of students and staff in universities. In the phrase used by Alvesson et al. (2017), it has 'something to say'.

4. Research agenda traction. Related to that, the book sets an agenda for researchers who also want to make a difference. It points the way to productive research projects using ethnographic approaches and, at least implicitly, indicates areas for further research. I make some specific suggestions below. But broader questions about this kind of research include: How would the idea of TLRs need to change if applied to areas of practice other than teaching and learning? How best could longitudinal studies examine the way TLRs emerge and change over time, following the trajectory of the different moments as they change and interlock differently? How can the idea of practice architectures be developed to offer more descriptive and explanatory traction? What combinations of theories and of methods are most productive in offering a fuller picture of contexts of practices? In a context where students are partners in change initiatives, how does this affect the significance of TLRs in place and the advantage of *voorgevoel* offered by the practice sensibility?

Both Walker (2013) and Cousin (2006) point out that passing through the portal to understanding concepts involves a transformative journey for the individual making that transition. I have made that claim for someone who acquires a practice sensibility: they are changed in the process. The development of ideas around TLRs since 2002 has also involved a transformative journey for me. It is encapsulated in this book. The ideas have transformed and developed thanks to insights from researchers who have applied them. The earlier version, its critics claimed, lacked theoretical purchase. This book is the product of the transformative journey involved in engaging and grappling with the deficiencies of the earlier model.

## Research and Professional Action: The Practice Sensibility

Using the conceptual framework summarized above, I have demonstrated how research and professional action can be united in a way which differs from the most prevalent understandings of the relationship between them. This approach differs from action research, for example, which depicts research and professional action as being deployed separately in the following sequence: diagnostic research; professional actions; evaluative research; further actions (McNiff et al., 1996; Koshy, 2009; Coghlan and Brannick, 2010). It differs from insider, work-based research in education which presents the 'research project' as parallel to professional practice, organized in such a way as to collect and analyse data about it and then make recommendations. The two systems are implicitly separated from each other, even in insider research:

> The main reason people undertake such projects is to make an impact in their organisation or professional field and receive academic recognition. The strength of your recommendations can secure the former, which should also help to achieve the latter. (Costley et al., 2010, p. 195)

In contrast to these two systems, the approach set out in these pages situates the relationship between action and research in a way that is closer to Marx's idea of *praxis*: the intertwining of theory and practice to bring about change. The argument is that it is both possible and desirable to develop in higher education practitioners a 'way of seeing' professional contexts, a sensibility which, once acquired, is never lost. In this it has the characteristics of a threshold concept:

> A threshold concept can be considered as akin to a portal, opening up a new and previously inaccessible way of thinking about something. It represents a transformed way of understanding, or interpreting, or viewing something...
> As a consequence of comprehending a threshold concept there may thus be a transformed internal view of subject matter, subject landscape, or even world view.   (Meyer and Land, 2003, p. 1)

Like a threshold concept, a practice sensibility involves both a process—the transformative journey referred to above—and a product: a new way of seeing (Walker, 2013). This acquired sensibility informs action intended to amelior-ate and improve processes, experiences, and outcomes. It is achieved by seeing the social world through a lens which comprises a set of interlinked concepts which offer explanatory power, the conceptual substrate underpinning the perspective. But on its own this is not enough. The depth and resilience of a new sensibility is achieved through exposure to different contexts and issues and by reflecting on them using that lens. Repetitive practice applied in different cases, either in real life or through case studies, embeds any new way of seeing, whether it be in medicine, engineering, or higher education.

A practice sensibility reveals itself in different ways and has value in different forms for the researcher/practitioner. It evokes unconscious gut reactions to situations, a kind of intuition about possible outcomes and a feeling for good and less good responses. It also offers conscious understand-ings of the current situation. Contemplating changes or predicting the poten-tial outcomes of proposed changes requires a good understanding of the status quo, of how context *is* currently, and what forces are at work in maintaining it. Projecting into the future requires understanding the present. And because the present is rooted in the past and strongly influenced by it, thinking about the future also requires a feeling for the flow of history, for backstories. This kind of conscious understanding and reflection deploys the set of three interlinked concepts described above in a considered way. For the leader, change agent, or manager who is tasked with managing change (in whatever sense), the stra-tegic power of métis is reinforced by the acquisition of this conceptual and theoretical substrate.

A significant contribution of the deployment of practice theory in this book is its application to higher education contexts. Since the 'practice turn' in social sciences, SPT has become ubiquitous. However, its application has tended to be mainly restricted to a few areas: consumption and sustainability, for example. It strikes me as odd that there has been so little work applying it to higher education when its utility there is very obvious. The application of SPT to higher education, however, requires a process of refining and focusing its general concepts in a way which makes them specifically applicable to higher education issues. I chose to do this with a focus on teaching and learning. The development of the idea of teaching and learning regimes, TLRs, was the result of that process. A further contribution of this book, however, is to draw on the subsequent work by others which applied, critiqued, and refined the notion of TLRs. Its embodiment in these pages incorporates that later work by a body of scholars to whom I am very grateful. The depiction of TLRs here is a fuller, more detailed, and more robust version than that presented previously. It has moved from a loose framework of concepts to a full-blown theory.

## Designing HE Research Projects with a Practice Sensibility: Some Suggestions

The practice sensibility helps the researcher think through issues of interest in a particular way. Brought to bear on different types of research design, it can offer valuable insights.

For example, an 'elite policy study' designed to gather data about policy-makers' understandings of a 'problem' in higher education and their policy-making in addressing it can be lifted beyond individuals' attitudes and choices. Elite groups engage jointly in the construction of the problem and ways of thinking about it, in sensemaking. Even though they may have had experience on the ground of the issue at hand, their ability to access and see the relevance of that experience is limited by the characteristics of the current regime they inhabit: that of policy-making (Reynolds and Saunders, 1987). Such a policy study, therefore, would direct its attention at the proto-practice reservoirs being drawn on by policymakers in the group and the agentic process of configuring them to accomplish the policy-making performance.

Likewise, an 'implementation staircase' study (Saunders and Sin, 2014) would follow the trajectory of a higher education policy as it moved down (and back up) the implementation staircase. It would research the nature of regimes at different points on that staircase: a university's top team; the management and committees at mid-level, faculty locations; departments and workgroups on the ground. An obvious point of interest would be how the policy was 'filtered' through these different regimes and what the end result was. Weber's concept of elective affinity, discussed in Chapter 5, would be of particular significance in such a study.

'Policy reception studies' examine how policies are received and understood on the ground. Their reception obviously has a strong influence on how those policies are subsequently enacted. Understanding and explaining differential reception is facilitated by a practice sensibility. Proto-practice reservoirs shape the value and level of significance put on policies. Discursive currents have effects on the codes of signification attached to both the medium and the message, both the communication mode and the 'text'. The regimes in place and the family of practices which constitute them will condition the level of concordance or discordance with received policies.

'Policy enactment studies', sometimes called 'implementation studies', go a step beyond reception studies to examine how policies are actually realized. The term 'enactment' highlights the fact that what actually happens as a result of policy is not a simple and direct process of implementation, but is more agentic, selective, interpretive. Once again, the notion of elective affinity can be brought to bear on understanding and explaining the processes involved. The domestication of policy, shaped by current practices and regimes, would be of particular interest in such a study.

Naturally, case studies of TLRs themselves are of interest from a practice-focused perspective. As noted in Chapter 2, the initial version of TLRs and their moments was used primarily as a categorizing or descriptive device, and was valuable for that (Roxå and Mårtensson, 2009b). However, TLRs and their moments can be deployed in much more valuable ways now that they have been conceptually enriched and fleshed out in this book. They can diagnose enhancement possibilities; be used to understand student experiences, satisfaction, and outcomes; be deployed to understand and predict potential and actual outcomes of change processes and to consider the interaction between regimes-in-place and the background assumptions that students bring to them. There are many other avenues for valuable and impactful research.

## From a Framework of Concepts to a Fully Developed Theory

My claim for the book is that it has taken the idea of TLRs from the status of a loose framework to a fully developed, comprehensive theory. In writing it I have consciously addressed each of the characteristics of good theory, drawn from literature on that topic and summarized in Trowler (2012b).

Theory should, first, offer system classification, a set of interconnected concepts to classify the components of the system and how they are related. This is achieved via the eleven moments of a teaching and learning regime, related in a highly integrated way in operation, but conceptually separated for analytical reasons. This quality is also found in the roots of those moments, in the proto-practice reservoirs; in the appreciation of the operation of power, of the significance of institutional practice architectures and broader structural forces conditioning practices. It is also found in the conceptualization of practices as nested and bundled and in the attention given to the emergent and contingent nature of TLRs. The practice architectures of institutional locations are significant in shaping these, as is, to a greater or lesser extent, the national ideological and policy framework in which they exist.

Secondly, theory should offer descriptive propositions: a set of systematically and logically related statements that depict a particular aspect of the operation of the world. Chapter 6 did this. Other chapters have described, through examples, the ways in which TLRs are horizontally and vertically embedded, bundled, and nested. Additionally, the significance of temporality has been demonstrated—the ways in which current practices are tied to the past and shape on-going trajectories. The theory set out here describes and illustrates the significance of a practice sensibility involving the ability to identify regularities in behaviour and to see apparently unique phenomena as instances of broad categories, of concepts—local patterns contingent upon structural forces.

Thirdly, the concepts and propositions being presented should provide an explanation for a range of phenomena by illuminating causal connections. Chapter 5 demonstrated the simplistic nature of mono-causal, essentialist explanations such as those provided from an epistemologically essentialist, determinist framework. Instead it argued that causality is multiple, complex, dynamic, and contextually contingent. Throughout the book I have argued for the necessity of applying the concepts and propositions of social practice theory to *particular* contexts in order to better understand and explain what is going on.

Fourthly, good theory should be communicable to as wide an audience as possible. Just as higher education institutional policy-making around teaching and learning addresses an 'implied student', explanations deriving from theory have an audience, sometimes explicit and sometimes implied. In the physical sciences the explicit first audience is other specialists in the field; research results are published first for them, often through specialist social media and, later, journals. A second audience, some years later, is addressed through broadcast media by popular scientific figures (usually very telegenic) who explain scientific progress to an implied audience of interested and reasonably intelligent viewers and listeners.

Social science generally lacks the latter output for its explanations. Its implied audience usually remains other social scientists. There is great cachet in the use of 'sophisticated' language and abstruse concepts, even though the descriptive and explanatory propositions are sometimes quite mundane. Stanislav Andreski (1972) famously complained of *social sciences as sorcery*: the indulgence in 'doctrinairism couched in a mystifying jargon' designed to impress and confuse so as to raise the status of the author and minimize the chances of critique. Alvesson, Gabriel, and Paulsen (2017) take up and elaborate this theme. Some book and article titles are hardly designed to attract readers who happen to chance on them, for example *Quantum Entanglements and Hauntological Relations of Inheritance: Dis/continuities, SpaceTime Enfoldings, and Justice-to-Come*. Neither are such mind-bending, eye-crossing concepts as 'ethico-onto-epistem-ology'.

A feature of this book, at least in intention, is its accessibility to its implied audience. This is constituted by intelligent, erudite, and well-read individuals in different locations in higher education institutions, some of whom have not had a social science training and so do not appreciate assumed understanding and mystifying jargon.

Fifthly, theory should provide corrigible predictions which reduce uncertainty about the outcomes of a specific set of conditions. In social science these are almost always rough probabilistic, short-term predictions which are contextually specific. They are only contextual because of the dynamic nature of the social world and the essential interconnectedness of teaching and learning regimes as open, natural systems. However, broader understandings of the significance of backstories and of the ways in which practices are slowly shaped by both internal and external processes can lend weight to predictive statements. Intuition also involves a form of prediction which, when based on experience and good theory, can be valuable. I have used the Dutch and Afrikaans word *voorgevoel* to talk about this.

Sixthly, theory should locate local social processes in wider social structures, helping to expose particular characteristics, phenomena, and events as instantiating broader concepts and social forces at work. Theory makes the particular significant by locating it in broader trends, issues, and dynamic forces. The 'flavour' of social practice theory offered here is a social realist one, depicting social processes as both locally generated in an agentic way, for example through the deployment of elective affinity, and as conditioned by broader structural forces such as political and educational ideologies. The 'global higher education policy ensemble' underpinned by neo-liberal ideology is one example of such forces.

I have elsewhere talked about going beyond boundaries and edges, the conceptual bubbles found in much writing about the management of change and enhancement processes in higher education and in other locales (Trowler, 2011a). Policymakers and change agents too often see their initiatives in an isolated, hermetically sealed way. They fail to appreciate that for those on the ground their significance is much less; their reception is located among a multitude of other issues, pressures, and forces for change. Social scientists likewise tend to simplify and abstract from the complexity of social reality. There is a tendency to a reductionism that essentializes and foregrounds the object of interest in a decontextualized way.

Naturally, as I argued in Chapter 5, a form of moderate essentialism is necessary, as is a degree of simplification. Max Weber made a compelling argument for this in his discussion and use of 'ideal types', abstracted versions of reality which emphasize significant points of interest to the analyst in an exaggerated way in order to better highlight causality and difference (Trowler, 2015). Many analysts are less sophisticated, however, and the abstraction goes too far. This leads to mistaken conclusions and exaggerated significance for their object of interest. Much of the work on the 'teaching–research nexus' demonstrates these characteristics (Trowler and Wareham, 2007). Such analysts are confusing the model of reality and the reality of the model.

In carefully situating social practices in universities as both nested and bundled, I have tried to avoid these traps. Social practices are depicted here as open, natural systems which both influence and are influenced by their context horizontally and vertically.

Finally, theory should guide research interventions, helping define research problems and indicating appropriate research designs to investigate them. Chapter 3 discussed in detail appropriate research designs for investigating TLRs' enhancement of teaching and learning and social practices generally. The book stresses that research should make a difference, and that research problems should be formulated in relation to local concerns and issues in specific university contexts.

I thus rest my claim to be presenting a fully developed theory on these criteria.

## Social Reconstructionism

There is, however, an important area where the contribution being made is limited. It is deficient in presenting a fundamentally critical, social reconstructionist approach to the status quo as far as its topic—teaching and learning in universities—is concerned. Social science should ask questions such as 'Whose problem?' 'Which problems most deserve research resources?' 'Why is this defined as a problem?' (Ozga, 1999). I touched on this in Case Study 2 in Chapter 6, about dealing with difficult people. In most cases there is division on the ground in universities about what the significant problems are, and there is often cynicism, frequently justified, about 'reform' and 'enhancement'. Politicians and others often use such words as a smokescreen for cost-cutting 'efficiency' measures.

Defining research problems and issues for enhancement using an ethnographic, practice-focused sensibility therefore presents more of a political than an analytical question. Social practice theory itself cannot answer it, though researchers are usually not slow to impose their own critical perspectives, arguing that research and interventions based on it should address the structural inequalities with which they are most concerned.

The social reconstructionist approach requires theory to be creative and emancipatory. Theory should not just describe and explain the world but should assist in changing it in fundamental ways which address highly embedded inequalities. For feminists and others, theory is a valuable ally in realizing ambitions, illuminating structural inequalities and disadvantage, situating the world in a different way, and helping to change attitudes and practices. Theory can shed a strong light on the different aspects of 'the enchantment of being human' (Archer, 2000). From this perspective the relationship between current reality and theory is turned upside down: theory does not just explain the world; the world is reconstituted through theory. Clegg (2007) sums up this position:

> I have defended thinking about theoretical questions because they are an indispensable resource for critique. My work on critical realism is based on a commitment to understanding and explanation, but also involves a commitment to a view of human agency that means that critique is not just intellectual but is also grounded in our human capacities to act. It is, therefore, hopeful in terms of our capacities to change the world at both the micro political level of the institution, but also more broadly in terms of imagining different futures and outcomes.   (p. 11)

Stephen Ball concurs:

> Theory is a vehicle for 'thinking otherwise', it is a platform for 'outrageous hypotheses' and for 'unleashing criticism'. Theory is destructive, disruptive

and violent. It offers a language for challenge, and modes of thought, other than those articulated for us by dominant others. It provides a language of rigour and irony rather than contingency. The purpose of such theory is to de-familiarise present practices and categories, to make them seem less self-evident and necessary, and to open up spaces for the invention of new forms of experience.   (Ball, 1995, pp. 265–6)

This is an area still to be opened up for social practice theory as applied in higher education, and I do not claim to have achieved Clegg and Ball's ambition. There is a realism inherent in social practice theory which acknowledges that change is difficult and usually slow. Where there is apparent revolutionary change, this is often temporary and illusory: social ghosts, the legacy of the past and of previous practices, are not dissolved overnight.

This book, and SPT in general, give a detailed map and provide an accurate compass for the accomplishment of changes in ways which are congruent, salient, and profitable in relation to current practices and understandings, taking account of the significance of the past and helping to shape the future. Such changes are sustainable: they have resilience. But they do not 'unleash criticism'. Nor are they 'destructive, disruptive and violent'.

## The Dancer and the Dance

The practice-focused approach to change in higher education unites research, theory, and professional practice. It argues for research approaches which examine practices locally but are attentive to their bundled and nested character, seeing workgroups as situated within institutional practice architectures and national ideological policy frameworks. It sees the figure, but it also sees the ground. It breaks the bubble of a narrow focus on what appears be the issue at hand and the places where decisions are made, seeing the frameworks which limit and direct those decisions.

I have argued for an approach to making interventions and to the enactment of change in higher education which, in applying a practice sensibility, makes changes that matter, that make a real difference, and that are sustainable. Pickering (1995) talks about the dance of agency. The key point in this is to take the focus off the dancer, off individual agency, and to widen it to the dance itself: to the choreography, to the performance venue, to the genre, to dance partners, to intent, and to audience response. Yeats asks how we can know the dancer from the dance. Perhaps we can't. Perhaps we shouldn't try.

# References

All websites were last accessed on 9 August 2019

Abes, E. S. (2009) Theoretical borderlands: Using multiple theoretical perspectives to challenge inequitable power structures in student development and theory. *Journal of College Student Development*, 50, 2, 141–6.

Abes, E. S. (2012) Constructivist and intersectional interpretations of a lesbian college student's multiple social identities. *The Journal of Higher Education*, 83, 2, 186–216.

Alvesson, M. (2002) *Understanding organizational culture*. London: Sage.

Alvesson, M., Gabriel, Y., and Paulsen, R. (2017) *Return to meaning: A social science with something to say*. Oxford: Oxford University Press.

Anderson, K. (2009) Ethnographic research: A key to strategy. *Harvard Business Review*, March. https://hbr.org/2009/03/ethnographic-research-a-key-to-strategy

Andreski, S. (1972) *Social sciences as sorcery*. London: Andre Deutsch.

Archer, M. (1995) *Realist social theory: The morphogenetic approach*. Cambridge: Cambridge University Press.

Archer, M. (2000) *Being human: The problem of agency*. Cambridge: Cambridge University Press.

Archer, M. (2007) *Making our way through the world*. Cambridge: Cambridge University Press.

Ashwin, P. (2009) *Analysing teaching–learning interactions in higher education: Accounting for structure and agency*. London: Continuum.

Ashwin, P. (2012) How often are theories developed through empirical research in higher education? *Studies in Higher Education*, 37, 8, 941–55.

Bager-Elsborg, A. (2017) Understanding university teaching in disciplinary contexts: A qualitative case study among lecturers in two departments. Aarhus: University of Aarhus, PhD thesis.

Bager-Elsborg, A. (2018) How lecturers' understanding of change is embedded in disciplinary practices: A multiple case study. *Higher Education*, 76, 195–212.

Baker, P., Jackson, N., and Longmore, J. (2014) *Tackling the wicked challenge of strategic change: The story of how university changed itself*. Bloomington: Author House.

Ball, S. (2008) *The education debate*. Bristol: Policy Press.

Ball, S. J. (1995) Intellectuals or technicians? The urgent role of theory in educational studies. *British Journal of Educational Studies*, 43, 255–71.

Bamber, V., Trowler, P., Saunders, M., and Knight, P. (eds) (2009) *Enhancing learning, teaching, assessment and curriculum in higher education: Theories within practices*. London: Open University Press/SRHE.

Barad, K. (2010) Quantum entanglements and hauntological relations of inheritance: Dis/continuities, spacetime enfoldings, and justice-to-come. *Derrida Today*, 3, 2, 240–68.

Barber, M., Kihn, P., and Moffit, A. (2011) *Deliverology: From idea to implementation*. McKinsey. https://www.mckinsey.com/industries/public-sector/our-insights/deliverology-from-idea-to-implementation

Barnes, B. (2001) Practice as collective action. In T. Schatzki, K. Knorr Cetina, and E. Von Savigny (eds) *The practice turn in contemporary theory*. London: Routledge, pp. 25–36.

Barradell, S., Barrie, S., and Peseta, T. (2017) Ways of thinking and practising: Highlighting the complexities of higher education curriculum. *Innovations in Education and Teaching International*, 55, 3, 266–75.

Becher, T. (1989) *Academic tribes and territories: Intellectual enquiry and the culture of disciplines*. Buckingham: Open University Press.

Berger, G. (1970) *Introduction. OECD-CERI indisciplinarity—Problems of teaching and research in universities*. Nice: CERI/French Ministry of Education.

Berger, P. and Luckmann, T. (1967) *The social construction of reality*. Harmondsworth: Penguin.

Bernstein, B. (1990) *The structuring of pedagogic discourse: Volume IV class codes and control*. London: Routledge.

Bernstein, B. (1999) Vertical and horizontal discourse: An essay. *British Journal of Sociology of Education*, 20, 157–73.

Bernstein, B. (2001) From pedagogies to knowledges. In A. Morais, I. Neves, B. Davies, and H. Daniels (eds) *Towards a sociology of pedagogy: The contribution of Basil Bernstein to research*. New York: Peter Lang.

Bhaskar, R. (2014) Foreword. In P. K. Edwards, J. O'Mahoney, and S. Vincent (2014) (eds) *Studying organisations using critical realism: A practical guide*. Oxford: Oxford University Press, pp. v–xv.

Blackler, F. (1995) Knowledge, knowledge work and organizations: An overview and interpretation. *Organization Studies*, 16, 6, 1021–46.

Blake, W. (1863) *Auguries of Innocence*. Available at: https://www.poetryfoundation.org/poems/43650/auguries-of-innocence

Bleiklie, I. (2002) Explaining change in higher education policy. In P. Trowler (ed.) *Higher Education policy and institutional change: Intentions and outcomes in turbulent environments*. Buckingham: SRHE and Open University Press, pp. 24–45.

Bloxham, S., Boyd, P., and Orr, S. (2011) Mark my words: The role of assessment criteria in UK higher education grading practices. *Studies in Higher Education*, 36, 6, 655–70.

Blumer, Herbert (1954) What is wrong with social theory. American Sociological Review, 18, 3–10.

Boag, B. (2010) *The role of the programme team in the implementation of policy at institutional level: A case study in the UHI Millennium Institute*. PhD thesis, University of Stirling.

Bolman, L. G. and Deal, T. E. (1991) *Reframing organisations: Artistry, choice and leadership*. San Francisco: Jossey-Bass.

Bolman, L. G. and Deal, T. E. (2017) *Reframing organisations: Artistry, choice and leadership*. San Francisco: Jossey-Bass. 6th edition.

Boud, D. (2012) Problematising practice-based education. In J. Higgs, R. Barnett, and S. Billett (eds) *Practice-based education: Perspectives and strategies*. Rotterdam: Sense Publishers, pp. 55–70.

Boud, D., Dawson, P., Bearman, M., Bennett, S., Joughin, G., and Molloy, E. (2018) Reframing assessment research: Through a practice perspective. *Studies in Higher Education*, 43, 7, 1107–18.

Boughey, C. (2018) *Going home: An exploration of the impact of home environments on the acquisition of secondary discourses*. Higher Education Close Up 9 conference, Cape Town. November.

Bourdieu, P. (1990) *The logic of practice*. Cambridge: Polity Press.

Bowden, J. and Marton, F. (1998) *The university of learning: Beyond quality and competence in higher education*. London: Kogan Page.

Bowker, G. C. and Star, S. L. (2000) *Sorting things out: Classification and its consequences*. Cambridge, MA: MIT Press.

Brannen, M. Y., Moore, F., and Mughan, T. (2013) *Strategic ethnography and reinvigorating Tesco plc: Leveraging inside/out bicultural bridging in multicultural teams*. Proceedings of the Ethnographic Praxis in Industry Conference. https://anthrosource.onlinelibrary. wiley.com/doi/pdf/10.1111/j.1559%968918.2013.00024.x

Brew, A. (1999) Research and teaching: Changing relationships in a changing context. *Studies in Higher Education*, 24, 3, 291–301.

Brew, A. (2001) *The nature of research: Inquiry in academic contexts*. London: RoutledgeFalmer.

Brew, A. (2002) Book review of Nowotny, H., Scott, P. and Gibbons, M. (2001). Re-thinking science: Knowledge and the public in an age of uncertainty. Cambridge, Polity Press. *Studies in Higher Education*, 27, 3, 353–4.

Brew, A. (2003) Teaching and research: New relationships and their implications for inquiry-based teaching and learning in higher education. *Higher Education Research and Development*, 22, 1, 3–18.

Caldwell, D. (2017) Printed T-shirts in the linguistic landscape: A reading from functional linguistics. *Linguistic Landscape*, 3, 2, 122–48.

Canning, A-M., Hume, S., Maldnson, L., Koponen, M., Hall, K., and Delargy, C. (2018) *KCLxBIT project report: 2015–2017*. London: King's College London. https://www.kcl.ac. uk/study/assets/pdf/widening-participation/kclxbit-report-sept2018.pdf

Carnegie Council on Policy Studies in Higher Education (1980) *Three thousand futures: The next twenty years for higher education*. San Francisco: Jossey Bass.

Cerych, L. and Sabatier, P. (1986) *Great expectations and mixed performance: The implementation of higher education reforms in Europe*. London: Trentham.

Charmaz, K. (2003). Grounded theory: Objectivist and constructivist methods. In N. K. Denzin and Y. S. Lincoln (eds) *Strategies for qualitative inquiry*. Thousand Oaks, CA: Sage, pp. 249–91. 2nd edition.

Chikane, R. (2018) *Breaking a rainbow, building a nation: The politics behind #MustFall movements*. Johannesburg: Pan Macmillan.

Christie, H., Tett, L., Cree, V. E., Hounsell, J., and McCune, V. (2007) 'A real rollercoaster of confidence and emotions': Learning to be a university student. Online papers archived by the Institute of Geography, School of Geosciences, University of Edinburgh. https://www.era.lib.ed.ac.uk/bitstream/handle/1842/1891/hchristie002.pdf?sequence=1& isAllowed=y

Clark, B. R. (1963) Faculty culture. In T. F. Lunsford (ed.) *The study of campus cultures*. Boulder, Colorado: Western Interstate Commission for Higher Education pp. 39–54.

Clark, B. R. (1972) The organisational saga in higher education. *Administrative Science Quarterly*, 17, 178–83.

Clark, B. R. (1973) The making of an organisational saga. In H. Leavitt and L. Pondy (eds) *Readings in managerial psychology*. Chicago: Chicago University Press, pp. 232–62. 2nd edition.

Clark, B. R. (1987) Conclusions. In B.R. Clark (ed.) *The academic profession*. Berkeley: University of California Press, pp. 371–99.

Clark, B. R. (ed.) (1987) *The academic profession*. Berkeley: University of California Press.

Clark, B. R. (1996) Case studies of innovative universities: A progress report. *Tertiary Education and Management*, 2, 1, 53–62.

Clegg, S. (2007) Extending the boundaries of research into higher education. In *Enhancing higher education, theory and scholarship: Proceedings of the 30th HERDSA Annual Conference*. Adelaide, 8–11 July 2007.

Coghlan, D. and Brannick, T. (2010) *Doing action research in your own organization*. London: Sage. 3rd edition.

Costley, C., Elliott, G., and Gibbs, P. (2010) *Doing work based research*. London: Sage.

Cousin, G. (2006) An introduction to threshold concepts. *Planet*, 17, 1, 4–5.

D'Eon, M., Overgaard, V., and Harding, S. R. (2000) Teaching as a social practice: Implications for faculty development. *Advances in Health Sciences Education*, 5, 151–62.

de Certeau, M. (1984) *The practice of everyday life*. Berkeley: University of California Press.

Deem, R. and Lucas, L. (2007) Research and teaching cultures in two contrasting UK policy contexts: Academic life in education departments in five English and Scottish universities. *Higher Education*, 54, 1, 115–33.

Deming, W. E. (1993) *The new economics for industry, government, education*. Cambridge, MA: MIT Centre for Advanced Engineering Studies.

Devault, M. L. (2006) What is institutional ethnography? *Social Problems*, 53, 3, 294–8.

Diamond, J. (2013) *Collapse: How societies choose to fail or survive*. London: Penguin.

Dill, D. (1999) Academic accountability and university adaptation: The architecture of an academic learning organization. *Higher Education*, 38, 2, 127–54.

Donald, J. (1995) Disciplinary differences in knowledge validation. In N. Hativa and M. Marincovich (eds) *Disciplinary differences in teaching and learning: Implications for practice*. San Francisco: Jossey-Bass, pp. 7–17.

Donald, J. (2002) *Learning to think: Disciplinary perspectives*. San Francisco: Jossey-Bass.

Duckett, H. (2004) *Reconstructing leadership: The perspectives of academics at a new university*. Lancaster University: PhD thesis.

Elton, L. (2003) Dissemination of innovations in higher education: A change theory approach. *Tertiary Education and Management*, 9, 199–214.

Fanghanel, J. (2007) Local responses to institutional policy: A discursive approach to positioning. *Studies in Higher Education*, 32, 2, 187–205.

Fanghanel, J. (2009a) Exploring teaching and learning regimes in higher education settings. In C. Kreber (ed.) *The university and its disciplines: Teaching and learning within and beyond disciplinary boundaries*. Abingdon: Routledge, pp. 196–208.

Fanghanel, J. (2009b) The role of ideology in shaping academics' conceptions of their discipline. *Teaching in Higher Education*, 14, 5, 565–77.

Fenwick, T. J. (2004) Discursive work for educational administrators: Tensions in negotiating partnerships. *Discourse: Studies in The Cultural Politics of Education*, 25, 2, 171–87.

Fenwick, T. J., Edwards, R., and Sawchuk, R. (2011) *Emerging approaches to educational research: Tracing the socio-material*. London: Routledge.

Fenwick, T. and Nerland, M. (eds) (2014) *Reconceptualising professional learning: Socio-material knowledges, practices and responsibilities*. Routledge: London.

Foucault (1979) *Discipline and punish: The birth of the prison*. New York: Vintage.

Friedland, R. and Alford, R. (1991) Bringing society back in: Symbols, practices and institutional contradictions. In W. Powell and P. Dimaggio (eds), *The new institutionalism in organizational analysis*. Chicago: University of Chicago Press, pp. 232–63.

Frølich, N., Huisman, J., Slipersæter, S., Stensaker, B., and Bo´tas, P. C. P. (2013) A reinterpretation of institutional transformations in European higher education: Strategising pluralistic organisations in multiplex environments. *Higher Education*, 65, 79–93.

Fuchs, S. (2001) *Against essentialism: A theory of culture and society*. Cambridge, MA: Harvard University Press.

Fullan, M. (ed.) (1999) *Change forces: The sequel*. London: Falmer.

Fullan, M. and Scott, G. (2009) *Turnaround leadership for higher education*. San Francisco: Jossey-Bass.

Fuller, A. (2007) Learning in communities of practice. In J. Hughes, N. Jewson, and L. Unwin (eds) *Communities of practice: Critical perspectives*. London: Routledge, pp. 17–29.

Geels, F. W. (2003) *The dynamics of transitions and system innovations: A transformation route in the transition from horse-and-carriage to automobiles (1860–1930)*. Presentation at the Open Meeting of the Global Environmental Change Research Community, Montreal, Canada, 16–18 October, 2003, IHDP Conference: Taking stock and moving forward. http://filer.sustrans.dk/39/3.%20Geels%202005%20automobile%20transition%20TASM.pdf

Geertz, C. (1983) *Local Knowledge*. New York: Basic Books.

Georgiou, D. and Carspecken, P. F. (2002) Critical ethnography and ecological psychology: Conceptual and empirical explorations of a synthesis. *Qualitative Inquiry*, 8, 6, 688–706.

Gerth, H. H. and Mills, C. W. (trans and eds) (1946) *From Max Weber: Essays in sociology*. New York: Oxford University Press.

Gherardi, S. (2012) *How to conduct a practice based study: Problems and methods*. Cheltenham: Edward Elgar Publishing.

Gherardi, S. (2014) Professional knowing-in-practice: Rethinking materiality and border resources in telemedicine. In T. Fenwick and M. Nerland (eds) *Reconceptualising professional learning: Sociomaterial knowledges, practices and responsibilities*. Routledge: London, pp. 42–68.

Gherardi, S. (2018) Theorizing affective ethnography for organization studies. *Organization*, OnlineFirst. DOI: 10.1177/1350508418805285

Gibbons, M., Limoges, C., Nowotny, H., Schwartzman, S., Scott, P., and Trow, M. (1994) *The new production of knowledge: The dynamics of science and research in contemporary societies*. London: Sage Publications.

Gibbs, G. and Coffey, M. (2004) The impact of training of university teachers on their teaching skills, their approach to teaching and the approach to learning of their students. *Active Learning in Higher Education*, 5, 1, 87–100.

Giddens, A. (1984) *The constitution of society*. Cambridge: Polity Press.

Goffman, E. (1967) *Interaction ritual*. London: Allen Lane.

Goffman, E. (1969) *The presentation of self in everyday life*. London: Allen Lane.

Government Digital Service (2018) *The 7 lenses of transformation*. https://www.gov.uk/government/publications/7-lenses-of-transformation/the-7-lenses-of-transformation

Grootenboer, P., Edwards-Groves, C., and Choy, S. (2017) Practice theory and education: Diversity and contestation. In P. Grootenboer, C. Edwards-Groves, and S. Choy (eds), *Practice theory perspectives on pedagogy and education: Praxis, diversity and contestation*. Singapore: Springer, pp. 1–21.

Haidt, J. (2012) *The righteous mind: Why good people are divided by politics and religion*. London: Penguin.

Hare, B. and Woods, V. (2013) *Genius of dogs: Discovering the unique intelligence of man's best friend*. London: Oneworld.

Hall, S. (1990) Cultural identity and diaspora. In J. Rutherford (ed.) *Community, culture, difference*. London: Lawrence and Wishart, pp. 222–37.

Halpern, D. (2015) *Inside the nudge unit: How small changes can make a big difference*. London: Penguin.

Ham, C. and Hill, M. (1984) *The policy process in the modern capitalist state*. London: Wheatsheaf.

Hammersley, M. (1993) On the teacher as researcher. In M. Hammersley (ed.) *Educational research: Current issues*. Buckingham: Open University Press, pp. 211–32.

Hannon, J., Garraway, J., Peseta, T., and Winberg, C. (2017) Putting theory to work: Comparing theoretical perspectives on academic practices in teaching and learning change. In B. Leibowitz, V. Bozalek, and Peter Kahn (eds) *Theorising learning to teach in higher education*. London: Routledge, pp. 207–23.

Harries, T. and Rettie, R. (2016) Walking as a social practice: Dispersed walking and the organisation of everyday practices. *Sociology of Health and Illness*, 38, 6, 874–83.

Harvey, D. (1996) *Justice, nature and the geography of difference*. London: Blackwell.

Haugaard, M. (2010) Power: A 'family resemblance' concept. *European Journal of Cultural Studies*, 13, 4, 419–38.

Higgs, J., Barnett, R., Billett, S., and Hutchings, M. (2012) *Practice-based education perspectives and strategies*. Rotterdam: Sense Publishers.

Hillyard, S. (2012) What's (still) wrong with ethnography? In S. Hillyard (ed.) *New frontiers in ethnography: Studies in qualitative methodology volume 11*, pp. 1–18. Bingley: Emerald.

Hood, C. C. (1976) *The limits of administration*. London: Wiley.

Jackson, N. (2013) *The wicked challenge of changing a university: A tale of bottom-up innovation supporting strategic change*. http://www.normanjackson.co.uk/uploads/1/0/8/4/10842717/changing_a_university.pdf

Jacobsen, A. J. (2014) Vignettes of interviews to enhance an ethnographic account. *Ethnography and Education*, 9, 35–50.

Jansen, J. (2017a) *Leading for change: Race, intimacy and leadership on divided university campuses*. London: Routledge.

Jansen, J. (2017b) *As by fire: The end of the South African university*. Cape Town: Tafelberg.

Jarvis, S. (2017) *The practice of authority in academic leadership/management*. PhD thesis, Lancaster University.

Johnson, R. (2014) Resources in the management of change in higher education. In P. Trowler (ed.) *Higher education policy and institutional change: Intentions and outcomes in turbulent environments*. Kindle Direct Publishing, pp. 101–31.

Jonas, M., Littig, B., and Wroblewski, A. (eds) (2017) *Methodological reflections on practice oriented theories*. London: Springer.

Kane, R., Sandretto, S., and Heath, C. (2002) Telling half the story: A critical review of research on the teaching beliefs and practices of university academics. *Review of Educational Research*, 72, 2, 177–228.

Kanter, R. (1991) Transcending business boundaries. *Harvard Business Review*, 69, 3, 151–64.

Kemmis, S. (2009) Understanding professional practice: A synoptic framework. In B. Green (ed.) *Understanding and researching professional practice*, pp. 19–38. Rotterdam: Sense.

Kemmis, S., Bristol, L., Edwards-Groves, C., Grootenboer, P., Hardy, I., and Wilkinson, J. (2013) *Changing practices, changing education*. London: Springer.

Kemmis, S., and Mahon, K. (2017) Practice architectures of university education. In P. Grootenboer, C. Edwards-Groves, and S. Choy (eds), *Practice theory perspectives on pedagogy and education: Praxis, diversity and contestation*. Singapore: Springer, pp. 107–41.

Kemmis, S., Wilkinson, J., Edwards-Groves, C., Hardy, I., Bristol, L., and Grootenboer, P. (2012) *Changing education, changing practices: A report prepared for the 'leading and learning: Developing ecologies of educational practices' project*. Dissemination Seminar, 17 October, Canberra, ACT. Unpublished manuscript.

Kernohan, D. (2015) *CETLs and the ghosts of teaching excellence past*. https://wonkhe.com/blogs/cetls-and-the-ghosts-of-teaching-excellence-past/

Knight, P. and Trowler, P. (2001) *Departmental leadership in higher education*. Buckingham: Open University Press/SRHE.

Koshy, V. (2009) *Action research for improving educational practice: A step-by-step guide*. London: Sage. 2nd edition.

Kotter, J. (1995) Leading change: Why transformation efforts fail. *Harvard Business Review*, March–April, 59–67.

Krejsler, J. (2006) Discursive battles about the meaning of university: The case of Danish university reform and its academics. *European Educational Research Journal*, 5, 3 and 4, 210–20.

Krishnan, A. (2009) *What are academic disciplines? Some observations on the disciplinary vs. interdisciplinarity debate*. ESRC National Centre for Research Methods Working Paper 03/09 http://eprints.ncrm.ac.uk/783/

Latour, B. and Woolgar, S. (1979) *Laboratory life: The social construction of scientific facts*. Beverly Hills: Sage.

Lattuca, L. and Stark, J. (1995) Will disciplinary perspectives impede curricular reform? *Journal of Higher Education*, 65, 4, 401–26.

Lave, J. and E. Wenger (1991) *Situated learning: Legitimate peripheral participation*. Cambridge: Cambridge University Press.

Lee, Y. L. B. (2010) *Managing complex change in a Hong Kong Higher Education Institution: A micro-political perspective*. EdD thesis, University of Leicester. https://ethos.bl.uk/OrderDetails.do?did=1&uin=uk.bl.ethos.593651

Lindblom-Ylänne, S., Trigwell, K., Nevgi, A., and Ashwin, P. (2006) How approaches to teaching are affected by discipline and teaching context. *Studies in Higher Education*, 31, 3, 285–98.

Lisewski, B. (2018) *An examination of how tutor-practitioners conceptualise and enact practice-based-knowing in a small higher education fashion school: A social practice theory approach*. PhD thesis, Lancaster University.

Local Government Association (2018) *What are behavioural insights?* https://www.local.gov.uk/our-support/efficiency-and-income-generation/behavioural-insights/what-are-behavioural-insights

Lukes, S. (2005*) Power: A radical view*. London: Palgrave Macmillan (first published 1974, 2nd edition).

Lynch, J. and Greaves, K. (2017) Michel de Certeau: Research writing as an everyday practice. In J. Lynch, J. Rowlands, T. Gale, and A. Skourdoumbis (eds) *Practice theory and education: Diffractive readings in professional practice*. London: Routledge, pp. 55–70.

Macfarlane, B. and Burg, D. (2018) *Women professors as intellectual leaders*. London: Leadership Foundation for Higher Education.

Mahon, K., Francisco, S., and Kemmis, S. (eds) (2016) *Exploring education and professional practice through the lens of practice architectures*. Singapore: Springer.

Marsh, P. Rosser, E., and Harre, R. (2005) *The rules of disorder*. London: Taylor and Francis. First edition 1978.

Martens, L. and Scott, S. (2017) Understanding everyday kitchen life: Looking at performance, into performances and for practices. In M. Jonas, B. Littig, and A. Wroblewski (eds) *Methodological reflections on practice oriented theories*. London: Springer, pp. 177–91.

Mårtensson, K., Roxå, T., and Stensaker, B. (2014) From quality assurance to quality practices: An investigation of strong microcultures in teaching and learning. *Studies in Higher Education*, 39, 4, 534–45.

Marx, K. (1852) *The 18th brumaire of Louis Bonaparte*. https://www.marxists.org/archive/marx/works/1852/18th-brumaire/ch01.htm

Mathebula, M. and Calitz, T. (2018) #FeesMustFall: A media analysis of students' voices on access to universities in South Africa. In P. Ashwin and J. Case (eds) *Higher education pathways: South African undergraduate education and the public good.* Cape Town: African Minds, pp. 177–91.

Mathieson, S. (2012) Disciplinary cultures of teaching and learning as socially situated practice: rethinking the space between social constructivism and epistemological essentialism from the South African experience. *Higher Education*, 63, 549–64.

Maton, K. (2013) *Knowledge and knowers: Towards a realist sociology of education.* London: Routledge.

Mazmanian, D. and Sabatier, P. (1981) *Implementation and public policy.* Chicago: University Press of America.

McCune, V. (2009) Teaching within and beyond the disciplines: The challenge for faculty. In C. Kreber (ed.) *The university and its disciplines: Teaching and learning within and beyond disciplinary boundaries.* London: Routledge, pp. 231–37.

McDermott, R. and Varenne, H. (1995) Culture as disability. *Anthropology and Education Quarterly*, 26, 3, 324–48.

McDonald, K. (2002) L' intervention sociologique after 25 years: Can it translate into English? *Qualitative Sociology*, 25, 2, 247–60.

McNiff, J., Lomax, P., and Whitehead, J. (1996) *You and your action research project.* London: Routledge and Hyde.

Meyer, J. H. F. and Land, R. (2003) Threshold concepts and troublesome knowledge: Linkages to ways of thinking and practising. In C. Rust (ed.) *Improving student learning: Theory and practice ten years on.* Oxford: Oxford Centre for Staff and Learning Development (OCSLD), pp. 412–24.

Miettinen, R., Samra-Fredericks, D., and Yanow, D. (2009) Re-turn to practice: An introductory essay. *Organization Studies*, 30, 12, 1309–27.

Mikkelsen, E. N. and Wåhlin, R. (2019) Dominant, hidden and forbidden sensemaking: The politics of ideology and emotions in diversity management. *Organisation*, Online-First, 1–21. https://journals.sagepub.com/doi/abs/10.1177/1350508419830620

Mills, C. W. (1959) *The sociological imagination.* Harmondsworth: Penguin.

Minick, N. (1996) Teachers' directives: The social construction of 'literal meanings' and 'real worlds' in classroom discourse. In S. Chaiklin and J. Lave (eds) *Understanding practice: Perspectives on activity and context.* Cambridge: Cambridge University Press, pp. 343–73.

Nelles, J. and Vorley, T. (2010) Constructing an entrepreneurial architecture: An emergent framework for studying the contemporary university beyond the entrepreneurial turn. *Innovation in Higher Education*, 35, 161–76.

Neumann, R. (1996) Researching the teaching-research nexus: A critical review. *Australian Journal of Education*, 40, 1, 5–18.

New Management New Identities website http://edu.au.dk/forskning/omraader/epoke/forskningsprojekter/newmanagementnewidentitiesdanishuniversityreforminaninternat/publications/

Nicolini, D. (2009) Articulating practice through interview with the double. *Management Learning*, 40, 2, 195–212.

Nicolini, D. (2012) *Practice theory, work and organization.* Oxford: Oxford University Press.

Nicolini, D. (2017) Practice theory as a package of theory, method and vocabulary: Affordances and limitations. In M. Jonas, B. Littig, and A. Wroblewski (eds) *Methodological reflections on practice oriented theories.* London: Springer, pp. 19–34.

Nowotny, H., Scott, P., and Gibbons, M. (2001) *Re-thinking science: Knowledge and the public in an age of uncertainty*. Cambridge: Polity Press.

Office for Students (2018) *Value for money: The student perspective*. https://studentsunionresearch.files.wordpress.com/2018/03/value-for-money-the-student-perspective-final-final-final.pdf

Orr, S. and Shreeve, A. (2018) *Art and design pedagogy in higher education: Knowledge, values and ambiguity in the creative curriculum*. London: Routledge.

Ozga, J. (1999) *Policy research in educational settings: Contested terrain*. Buckingham: Open University Press.

Parpala, A., Lindblom-Ylänne, S., Komulainen, E., Litmanen, T., and Hirsto, L. (2010) Students' approaches to learning and their experiences of the teaching-learning environment in different disciplines. *British Journal of Educational Psychology*, 80, 2, 269–82.

Penuel, W. R., DiGiacomo, D. K., Van Horne, K., and Kirshner, B. (2016) A social practice theory of learning and becoming across contexts and time. *Frontline Learning Research*, 4, 4, 30–8.

Pettigrew, A. (1985) *The awakening giant: Continuity and change in ICI*. Oxford: Blackwell.

Pickering, A. (1995) *The mangle of practice: Time, agency, and science*. Chicago: University of Chicago Press.

Pollock, N. and Williams, R. (2010) E-infrastructures: How do we know and understand them: strategic ethnography and the biography of artefacts. *Computer Supported Cooperative Work*, 19, 6, 521–56.

Pollock, N. and Williams, R. (2013) From artefacts to infrastructures. *Computer Supported Cooperative Work*, 22, 4, 575–607.

Porter, S. (1993) Critical realist ethnography: The case of racism and professionalism in a medical setting. *Sociology*, 7, 4, 591–609.

Powell, S. (2013) *Innovating the development of work focussed learning in higher education*. PhD thesis, University of Bolton.

Pressman, J. and Wildavsky, A. (1984) *Implementation: How great expectations in Washington are dashed in Oakland*. Berkeley: University of California Press. First edition 1973.

Quality Assurance Agency (QAA) Scotland (2018) *Enhancement themes*. https://www.enhancementthemes.ac.uk/#

Quinlan, K. M. (1999) Commonalities and controversy in context: A study of academic historians' educational beliefs. *Teaching and Teacher Education*, 15, 4, 447–63.

Randall, V., Brooks, R., Montgomery, A. and McNally, L. (2018) Threshold concepts in medical education. MedEdPublish. Online: https://doi.org/10.15694/mep.2018.0000176.1

Reckwitz, A. (2002) Toward a theory of social practices: A development in culturalist theorising. *European Journal of Social Theory*, 5, 2, 243–63.

Reynolds, J. and Saunders, M. (1987) Teacher responses to curriculum policy: Beyond the 'delivery' metaphor. In J. Calderhead (ed.) *Exploring teachers' thinking*. London: Cassell, pp. 195–214.

Robertson, J. and Bond, C. (2001) Experiences of the relation between teaching and research: What do academics value? *Higher Education Research and Development*, 20, 1, 5–19.

Rolfe, V. (2017) Are these jolly good fellows? https://wonkhe.com/blogs/ntfs-and-the-tef/

Roper, S. S. and Deal, T. E. (2010) *Peak performance for deans and chairs: Reframing higher education's middle*. New York: Rowman and Littlefield Education.

Roxå, T. and Mårtensson, K. (2009a) Significant conversations and significant networks: Exploring the backstage of the teaching arena. *Studies in Higher Education* 34, 5, 547–59.

Roxå, T. and Mårtensson, K. (2009b) Teaching and learning regimes from within: Significant networks as a locus for the social construction of teaching and learning. In C. Kreber (ed.) *The university and its disciplines: Teaching and learning within and beyond disciplinary boundaries*, pp. 209–18. London: Routledge.

Roxå, T. and Mårtensson, K. (2013) How effects from teacher-training of academic teachers propagate into the meso level and beyond. In E. Simon and G. Pleschova (eds) *Teacher development in higher education: Existing programs, program impact, and future trends*. London: Routledge, pp. 213–33.

Roxå, T., Mårtensson, K., and Alveteg, M. (2011) Understanding and influencing teaching and learning cultures at university: A network approach. *Higher Education*, 62, 99–111.

Ryle, G. (2009) *The concept of mind: 60th anniversary edition*. Abingdon and New York: Routledge.

Sampson, A. and Komer, K. (2010) When government tail wags the disciplinary dog: Some consequences of national funding policy on doctoral research in New Zealand. *Higher Education Research and Development*, 29, 3, 275–89.

Saunders, M. and Sin, C. (2014) Middle managers' experience of policy implementation and mediation in the context of the Scottish quality enhancement framework. *Assessment and Evaluation in Higher Education*, 40, 1, 135–50.

Sawyer, R. K. (2002) Unresolved tensions in sociocultural theory: Analogies with contemporary sociological debates. *Culture and Psychology*, 8, 3, 293–305.

Sayer, A. (1997) Essentialism, social constructionism, and beyond. *The Sociological Review*, 45, 3, 453–87.

Schatzki, T. (1996) *Social practices: A Wittgensteinian approach to human activity and the social*. Cambridge: Cambridge University Press.

Schatzki, T. R. (2002) *The site of the social: A philosophical account of the constitution of social life and change*. Philadelphia: Pennsylvania State University Press.

Schatzki, T. R. (2003) A new societist social ontology. *Philosophy of the Social Sciences*, 33, 2, 174–202.

Schatzki, T. R. (2005) The sites of organisations. *Organisation Studies*, 26, 3, 465–84.

Schatzki, T. R. (2012) A primer on practices. In J. Higgs, R. Barnett, and S. Billett (eds) *Practice-based education: Perspectives and strategies*. Rotterdam: Sense Publishers, pp. 13–26.

Schatzki, T. R. (2015) Spaces of practices and of large social phenomena. Espacestemps.net. https://www.espacestemps.net/articles/spaces-of-practices-and-of-large-social-phenomena/

Schatzki, T. R., Knorr Cetina, K., and Von Savigny, E. (eds) (2001) *The practice turn in contemporary theory*. London: Routledge.

Scott, G., Coates, H., and Anderson, M. (2008) *Learning leaders in times of change*. Sydney: University of Western Sydney and Australian Council for Educational Research. Available from: https://research.acer.edu.au/cgi/viewcontent.cgi?article=1001&context=higher_education

Schäfer, H. (2017) Relationality and heterogeneity: Transitive methodology in practice theory and actor-network theory. In M. Jonas, B. Littig, and A. Wroblewski (eds) *Methodological reflections on practice oriented theories*. London: Springer, pp. 47–60.

Sedlačko, M. (2017) Conducting ethnography with a sensibility for practice. In M. Jonas, B. Littig, and A. Wroblewski (eds) *Methodological reflections on practice oriented theories*. London: Springer, pp. 35–46.

Shay, S. B. (2003) *The assessment of undergraduate final year projects: A study of academic professional judgement*. Unpublished PhD thesis, University of Cape Town, 2003.

Shay, S. B. (2004) The assessment of complex performance: A socially-situated interpretive act. *Harvard Educational Review,* 74, 3, 307–29.

Shor, I. (1996) *When students have power.* Chicago: University of Chicago Press.

Shove, E., Pantzar, M., and Watson, M. (2012) *The dynamics of social practice: Everyday life and how it changes.* London: Sage.

Sibeon, Roger (2004) *Rethinking Social Theory.* London: Sage.

Silva, E. B. (2014) Haunting in the material of everyday life. In P. Harvey, E. C. Casella, G. Evans, H. Knox, C. McLean, E. B. Silva, N. Thoburn, and K. Woodward (eds) *Objects and materials: A Routledge companion.* London: Routledge, pp. 187–96.

Sims-Schouten, W. and Riley, S. (2014) Employing a form of critical realist discourse analysis for identity research: An example from women's talk of motherhood, childcare, and employment. In P. K. Edwards, J. O'Mahoney, and S. Vincent (2014) (eds) *Studying organisations using critical realism: A practical guide.* Oxford: Oxford University Press, pp. 46–65.

Smeby, J. (1996) Disciplinary differences in university teaching. *Studies in Higher Education,* 21, 1, 69–79.

Smith, D. E. (2005) *Institutional ethnography: A sociology for people.* Lanham, MD: AltaMira.

Smith, D. (2006) *Institutional ethnography as practice.* New York: Rowman & Littlefield.

Smolensky, P., Legendre, G., and Miyata, Y. (1993) Integrating connectionist and symbolic computation for the theory of language. *Current Science,* 64, 381–91.

Spaargaren, G., Weenink, D., and Lamers, M. (2016) *Practice theory and research: Exploring the dynamics of social life.* London: Routledge.

Spaargaren, G., Weenink, D., and Lamers, M. (2016) Introduction: Using practice theory to research social life. In G. Spaargaren, D. Weenink, and M. Lamers (eds) *Practice theory and research: Exploring the dynamics of social life.* London: Routledge, pp. 2–27.

Spalding, N. J., and Phillips, T. (2007) Exploring the use of vignettes: From validity to trustworthiness. *Qualitative Health Research,* 17, 954–62.

Spurling, N., McMeekin, A., Shove, E., Southerton, D., and Welch, D. (2013) *Interventions in practice: Re-framing policy approaches to consumer behaviour.* Lancaster: Sustainable practices research group. http://www.sprg.ac.uk/uploads/executive-summary-sprg–report-sept-2013-.pdf

Struthers, J. (2012) *Analytic auto ethnography: A tool to inform the lecturer's use of self when teaching mental health nursing.* Lancaster University: PhD thesis.

Sustainable Practices Research Group (2012) *Researching Social Practice and Sustainability: Puzzles and Challenges.* Lancaster University. http://www.sprg.ac.uk/uploads/practices-and-methodological-challenges.pdf

Swerissen, H. (2017) *Curriculum reform in the faculty of health sciences at La Trobe University.* University of Bath: PhD thesis. https://ethos.bl.uk/OrderDetails.do?did=1& uin=uk.bl.ethos.725398

Thaler, R. R. and Sunstein, C. R. (2009) *Nudge: Improving decisions about health, wealth, and happiness.* London: Penguin.

Thomas, W. R. and Thomas, D. S. (1928) *The child in America: Behavior problems and programs.* New York: Knopf.

Thornton, P. H., Ocasio, W., and Lounsbury, M. (2012) *The institutional logics perspective: A new approach to culture, structure, and process.* Oxford: Oxford University Press.

Tight, M. (2019) *Documentary research in the social sciences.* London: Sage.

Touraine, A. et al. (1981) *Le pays contre l'etat.* Paris: Seuil.

Trowler, P. (1998) *Academics responding to change: New higher education frameworks and academic cultures.* Buckingham: SRHE/Open University Press.

Trowler, P. (2001) Captured by the discourse? The socially constitutive power of new higher education discourse in the UK. *Organization*, 8, 2, 183–201.

Trowler, P. (2009) Beyond epistemological essentialism: Academic tribes in the 21st century. In C. Kreber (ed.) *The university and its disciplines: Teaching and learning within and beyond disciplinary boundaries*. London: Routledge, pp. 181–95.

Trowler, P. (2010) UK higher education: Captured by new managerialist discourse? In V. L. Meek, L. Goedegebuure, R. Santiago, and T. Carvalho (eds) *The changing dynamics of higher education middle management*. Dordrecht: Springer, pp. 197–211.

Trowler, P. (2011a) *Beyond boundaries and edges in conceptualising disciplines*. HERDSA conference keynote speech, Queensland Gold Coast.

Trowler, P. (2011b) Researching your own institution. *British Educational Research Association*. http://tinyurl.com/lqjvyoc

Trowler, P. (2012a) *Doing insider research in universities: A short guide*. Kindle Direct Publishing.

Trowler, P. (2012b) Wicked issues in situating theory in close up research. *Higher Education Research and Development*, 31, 3, 273–84.

Trowler, P. (2013a) Practice-focused ethnographies of higher education: Method/ological corollaries of a social practice perspective. *European Journal of Higher Education*, 4, 1, 18–29.

Trowler, P. (2013b) Depicting and researching disciplines: Strong and moderate essentialist approaches. *Studies in Higher Education*, 39, 10, 1720–32.

Trowler, P. (2014) Academic tribes and territories: The theoretical trajectory. *Oesterreichische Zeitschrift fur Geschichtswissenschaften* (Austrian Journal of Historical Studies), 25, 3, 17–26.

Trowler, P. (2015) Student engagement, ideological contest and elective affinity: The Zepke thesis reviewed. *Teaching in Higher Education*. 20, 3, 328–39.

Trowler, P. (2019) *Intellectual threads in the cloth of accomplishing change in teaching and learning regimes* https://paul-trowler.weebly.com/intellectual-threads-in-the-oxford-university-press-cloth.html

Trowler, P., Ashwin, P., and Saunders, M. (2014) *The role of HEFCE in teaching and learning enhancement: A review of evaluative evidence*. York: The Higher Education Academy.

Trowler, P. and Bamber, V. (2005) Compulsory higher education teacher education: Joined-up policies; institutional architectures; enhancement cultures. *International Journal for Academic Development*, 10, 2, 79–93.

Trowler, P. and Cooper, A. (2002) Teaching and learning regimes: Implicit theories and recurrent practices in the enhancement of teaching and learning through educational development programmes. *Higher Education Research and Development*, 21, 3, 221–40.

Trowler, P. and Hinett, K. (1994) Implementing the recording of achievement in higher education. *Capability*, 1, 1, 53–61.

Trowler, P., Saunders, M., and Knight, P. (2002) *Change thinking, change practices: A guide to change for heads of department, programme leaders and other change agents in higher education*. York: LTSN Generic Centre. https://www.academia.edu/10275967/Change_Thinking_Change_Practices

Trowler, P. and Wareham, T. (2007) Reconceptualising the teaching-research nexus. In HERDSA *Proceedings of the Annual HERDSA Conference 2007: Enhancing Higher Education Theory and Scholarship*, 8–11 July 2007, Adelaide, Australia.

Trowler, V. with Trowler, P. and Saunders, M. (2018) *Responding to student voice: Insights into international practice.* Edinburgh: Quality Assurance Agency Scotland. http://www.enhancementthemes.ac.uk/docs/ethemes/evidence-for-enhancement/insights-into-international-practice.pdf

Turner, N. (2018) *Learning through and development of teaching and learning practice in higher education: A social practice view of teaching practice as informal learning.* PhD thesis, Lancaster University.

Turner, S. (2001) Throwing out the tacit rulebook: Learning and practices. In T. R. Schatzki, K. Knorr Cetina, and E. Von Savigny (eds) *The Practice Turn in Contemporary Theory.* London: Routledge, pp. 120–30.

Ulriksen, L. (2009) The implied student. *Studies in Higher Education*, 34, 5, 517–32.

van Kampen, S. (2018) An investigation into uncovering and understanding tacit knowledge in a first-year design studio environment. *The International Journal of Art and Design Education*, 37, 3, 1–13.

Vedung, E. (1998) Policy instruments: typologies and theories. In M-L. Bemelmans-Videc, R. C. Rist, and E. Vedung, *Carrots, Sticks, and Sermons.* New Brunswick, NJ and London: Transaction Publishers, pp 21–58.

Vesa, M. and Vaara, E. (2014) Strategic ethnography 2.0: Four methods for advancing strategy process and practice research. *Strategic Organisation*, 12, 4, 288–98.

Virtanen, P. and Nevgi, A. (2010) Disciplinary and gender differences among higher education students in self-regulated learning strategies. *Educational Psychology*, 30, 3, 323–47.

Walker, G. (2013) A cognitive approach to threshold concepts. *Higher Education*, 65, 247–63.

Warde, A. (2005) Consumption and theories of practice. *Journal of Consumer Culture*, 5, 2, 131–53.

Wearden, S. (2017) *The perpetuation of degree ceremonies.* Lancaster University: PhD thesis.

Weber, M. (1992) *The Protestant ethic and the spirit of capitalism.* Trans, S. Kalberg. New York: Oxford University Press. 1st edition 1930.

Weik, K. (1995) *Sensemaking in organisations.* Thousand Oaks: Sage.

Wenger, E. (1998) *Communities of practice: Learning, meaning and identity.* Cambridge: Cambridge University Press.

Wenger-Trayner, E. and Wenger-Trayner, B. (2015) *Introduction to communities of practice: A brief overview of the concept and its uses.* http://wenger-trayner.com/introduction-to-communities-of-practice/.

Whitchurch, C. (2009) The rise of the blended professional in higher education: a comparison between the United Kingdom, Australia and the United States. *Higher Education*, 58, 407–18.

Wilkinson, J. and Kemmis, S. (2015) Practice theory: Viewing leadership as leading. *Educational Philosophy and Theory, Incorporating ACCESS*, 47, 4, 342–58.

Wittgenstein, L. (1953) *Philosophical investigations.* London: Blackwell Publishing.

Yeats, W. B. (1933) Among school children. In R. J. Finneran (ed.) *The Poems of W. B. Yeats: A New Edition.* New York: Macmillan.

Ylijoki, O-H. (2000) Disciplinary cultures and the moral order of studying. *Higher Education*, 39, 339–62.

Ylonen, A., Gillespie, H., and Green, A. (2018) Disciplinary differences and other variations in assessment cultures in higher education: Exploring variability and inconsistencies in one university in England. *Assessment and Evaluation in Higher Education*, 43, 1009–1017.

Young, M. F. D. (2000) Rescuing the sociology of educational knowledge from the extremes of voice discourse: Towards a new theoretical basis for the sociology of the curriculum. *British Journal of Sociology of Education*, 21, 4, 523–36.

Young, M. F. D. (2008) *Bringing knowledge back in: From social constructivism to social realism in the sociology of education.* London: Routledge.

Zaitseva, E. (2016) *The relationship between HEA Fellowship and student engagement.* York: Higher Education Academy. https://www.heacademy.ac.uk/system/files/downloads/ukes_and_hea_fellowship_correlation_march_2016.pdf

# Index of Names

For the benefit of digital users, indexed terms that span two pages (e.g., 52–53) may, on occasion, appear on only one of those pages.

# General Index

*Note*: Tables are indicated by an italic '*t*' following the page number.

For the benefit of digital users, indexed terms that span two pages (e.g., 52–53) may, on occasion, appear on only one of those pages.